La

力量

من

তা

The
Power
of
Language

The Power of Language

HOW THE CODES WE USE
TO THINK, SPEAK, AND LIVE
TRANSFORM OUR MINDS

VIORICA MARIAN

DUTTON

DUTTON

An imprint of Penguin Random House LLC
penguinrandomhouse.com

LIBRARY OF CONGRESS CATALOGING-IN-PUBLICATION DATA

Names: Marian, Viorica, author.
Title: The power of language: how the codes we use to think, speak, and live transform our minds / Viorica Marian.
Description: [New York, NY] : Dutton, [2023] | Includes bibliographical references and index.
Identifiers: LCCN 2022035014 | ISBN 9780593187074 (hardcover) | ISBN 9780593187081 (ebook)
Subjects: LCSH: Psycholinguistics. | Multilingualism.
Classification: LCC P37.M26 2023 | DDC 401/.9—dc23/eng/20220917
LC record available at https://lccn.loc.gov/2022035014

Printed in the United States of America

1st Printing

BOOK DESIGN BY TIFFANY ESTREICHER

To Aimee, Nadia, and Grace, and to lovers of languages everywhere

CONTENTS

1

To have another language is to possess another soul.
—Attributed to Charlemagne,
the first Holy Roman Emperor

The
Power
of
Language

Introduction—or Welcome!

L egend has it that in the ancient city of Babylon stood a tower so tall we might think of it as humanity's first skyscraper. Historical texts confirm the tower's existence in what is now Iraq. Biblical literature pinpoints the origin of the many languages of the world to this exact tower, the Tower of Babel, which people were building to "reach unto heaven." When God came down and saw that humans were trying to reach heaven, in Genesis 11:6, God said, "Behold, the people is one, and they have all one language; and this they begin to do: and now nothing will be restrained from them, which they have imagined to do." To stop people from reaching heaven, God scattered them around the world and created many languages for them to speak so they could not communicate with one another and could not advance in their work.

Language as the key to reaching heaven certainly asserts its power. The story of the Tower of Babel illustrates the way language can be used both to include and to exclude, to communicate and to hinder communication. Other religions, too, recognize that we must look to language to reach heights that are as great as heaven is in religious belief. The Quran 14:4 reveals that only those religious concepts can be conveyed to humanity for which we have the language to do so: "And We never sent a messenger except in the language of his people to make clear for them."

In his essay "A Tranquil Star," Italian writer and Holocaust survivor Primo Levi writes beautifully about the limits of language and how we think about the world, here in translation:

> For a discussion of stars our language is inadequate and seems laughable, as if someone were trying to plow with a feather. It's a language . . . born with us, suitable for describing objects more or less as large and as long-lasting as we are; it has our dimensions, it's human.

He notes that new words were coined over time for sizes smaller and larger than what could be perceived with the naked eye, temperatures hotter than fire, and numbers like millions and billions—concepts we previously did not know existed.

Does language follow along our latest, most improved understanding of the world, or does our understanding of the world follow along our language? For confirmation that language-thought constraints exist, we can turn to modern machine learning research. When neuroscientists at Stanford University used large sets of behavioral data to study how the brain divides the labor associated with performing cognitive tasks (like reading or decision-making), the computational algorithms clustered patterns of neural activity in ways that did not follow expected patterns of classification based on human language. Much like early efforts to "locate" different languages in the brain revealed largely overlapping networks, the boundaries between seemingly distinct mental processes were not reflected in the brain itself. Instead, the classifications made by computational algorithms suggest the existence of constructs for which we do not have labels (yet), a universe of stars that we are trying to plow with a feather. Even our mental constructs for words like *memory* and *perception* were not accurate descriptions of the constructs that emerged from machine learning. Instead, memory and perception overlapped, indicating that the vocabulary we use to refer to them and the way we think about them is still very imprecise. Memory and perception are not categorically distinct from each other in either human or artificial intelligence, despite the labels we use to differentiate them. It may well be that we do not yet have the tools to more precisely study and label both our mental states and the categories that exist in the world. The very notion that there are precise categories that exist outside of our interpretation of reality (whether they are mental states, colors, or types of people) may itself be an illusion perpetuated by language. Regardless of whether there are "real" categories that exist out in the world, the linguistic and mental categories we create matter. They have consequences for areas as distinct as perception, science, and bigotry.

Psycholinguistics is a field that focuses on the relationship between mind and language. When I first started graduate school thirty years ago, I wanted to understand not only how multilinguals like me process language but also human cognitive and neural capacities and limits more generally. This book synthesizes my own and others' original research on language and the mind as seen through the prism of multilingualism. I wrote this book in English, my third language, while also drawing on my knowledge of Romanian and Russian, my native and second languages, as well as on the languages whose speakers I studied in my research, including American Sign Language, Cantonese, Dutch, French, German, Japanese, Korean, Mandarin, Polish, Spanish, Thai, Ukrainian, and many others.

As a child, I would notice curious things about the languages around me, as many people who have studied another language do. Why do Russians refer to bridges as "he" and see them as having masculine gender, whereas Germans refer to bridges as "she" and see them as having feminine gender, while the English refer to bridges as "it" with no gender whatsoever? And then there's Romanian, my native language, with this trippy property: a bridge is masculine if there's only one, but is feminine if there are two or more—what does this do to people's minds and to how they think about bridges, especially if they know multiple languages with contrasting grammatical genders for the same object?

Recent cognitive science experiments show that German speakers are more likely to perceive and describe a bridge as *beautiful, elegant, fragile, peaceful, pretty,* and *slender.* Spanish speakers are more likely to perceive and describe the same bridge as *big, dangerous, long, strong, sturdy,* and *towering.* The difference? *Bridge* has different grammatical gender in German and Spanish. Can you guess which is which from the adjectives used? Yes, *bridge* is masculine in Spanish. The jury is still out about the gender-shifting Romanian bridges. (In Romanian, many nouns that are masculine in singular form become feminine in plural form.) The extent to which grammatical gender of inanimate objects influences how we think about objects bears relevance to modern debates about the use of gender pronouns and gender language more broadly, precisely because gender pronouns are so effective at generating implicit associations that influence people's perception of themselves and others.

The labels we use matter. Something as simple as changing the labels we use to refer to someone—for example, instead of *slaves,* saying *enslaved people* or *people who were enslaved*—makes an immediate difference in how we mentally represent those we are speaking about.

Engaging with a variety of languages gives us crucial abilities that the human race will need to heal burgeoning social discord and to formulate solutions to looming global problems. If you can appreciate firsthand the utility and beauty of another language and worldview, it is not hard to imagine you are less prone to bigotry, to demonizing things or people who are different from you.

Understanding the power of language also makes you more aware when you are being manipulated by others through words, whether those others are politicians, advertisers, lawyers, coworkers, or family members. People are paid a great deal of money to manipulate language in a way that makes one buy specific products, vote a particular way, or render certain verdicts. When you know multiple languages, you are more attuned to how words make you feel, because you already have firsthand experience with subtle linguistic variations.

Failure to account for the differences between languages can lead to devastating results. NASA's Mars Climate Orbiter burned into pieces, and hundreds of millions of dollars, years of work, and months of space travel were lost, all because someone did not convert the measurement units from the English system to the metric system. But an even more tragic mistranslation, or at least misinterpretation, can be found in the United States National Security Agency's unclassified documents.

In 1945, when Allied leaders met in Germany at the end of the Second World War, Truman, Churchill, Stalin, and Chiang Kai-shek sent the Japanese premier, Kantarō Suzuki, a declaration of surrender terms, asking that Japan surrender unconditionally. The declaration also stated that any negative answer would elicit "prompt and utter destruction." When reporters questioned Premier Suzuki about his reaction, he replied with the usual political fallback that he was withholding comment. The Japanese word he used, *mokusatsu*, derived from the word for silence, can be translated in multiple ways, from "remaining in wise inactivity" to "taking no notice" to "treating with silent contempt." In a diplomatic failure of epochal proportions, an ill-chosen translation was interpreted in the West as a hostile response. The National Security Agency writes:

The word has other meanings quite different from that intended by Suzuki. Alas, international news agencies saw fit to tell the world that in the eyes of the Japanese government the ulti-matum was "not worthy of comment." U.S. officials, angered by the tone of Suzuki's statement . . . decided on stern measures. Within ten days the decision was made to drop the atomic bomb, the bomb was dropped, and Hiroshima was leveled.

On a lighter note, when I was a graduate student at Emory University in President Carter's home state of Georgia, he met every year with the international students. To put us at ease, with his signature affability and sense of humor, President Carter shared a story about a speech he gave in Japan. He said that he opened with a joke, and that immediately after the interpreter translated the joke from English to Japanese, every single person in the audience laughed. Later that day, Carter asked the interpreter why the joke elicited such an enthusiastic response. After some coaxing, the interpreter admitted that he was not sure how to translate the joke into Japanese and instead said, "President Carter made a joke. Everyone must laugh."

I wish I could end my own jokes with "Everyone must laugh." Learning another language will not suddenly make you funny, or a genius, or the sexiest person alive. You will not grow a full head of hair or become a billionaire as a result—although there is, in fact, a correlation between multilingualism and income.

Here is a sample of findings from laboratories around the world on consequences of learning another language:

- In older adults, multilingualism delays Alzheimer's and other types of dementia by four to six years and increases cognitive reserve.

- In children, learning a second language means early understanding that the connection between objects and their names is arbitrary—you can call milk *milk* or *leche* or *moloko* or you can use a made-up word. Understanding that reality and the symbolic system used to denote it are not one and the same leads to more developed metalinguistic skills that lay the foundation for even more advanced metacognitive processes and higher-order reasoning.

- Across the life span, speaking more than one language improves performance on executive-function tasks, making it easier to focus on what matters and ignore what is irrelevant.

- Knowing multiple languages enables people to make connections between things in ways that others do not see and results in higher scores on creativity and divergent-thinking tasks.

- Using a non-native language renders people more likely to make decisions that are more logical and of greater social benefit.

The rapidly growing global online community and the increased accessibility of travel mean that most of us will interact with people who speak other languages at some point in our lives. We will fall in love with them, become their friends, welcome them into our families, go to school with them, or work with them in professional settings.

Everyone uses language. But few comprehend its power. It's like owning something incredibly valuable and not even knowing it. Sometimes I feel like an *Antiques Roadshow* appraiser who reveals that the old thing you've had lying around in the attic forever is a priceless treasure.

I became a psycholinguist because I love languages and I love figuring out how language and mind interact. I hope this book helps you understand the incredible capabilities you already have, gives you a glimpse into the inner workings of your mind, and delivers keys to unlocking your potential in new ways.

PART ONE

SELF

The limits of my language mean the limits of my world.
—Ludwig Wittgenstein

CHAPTER ONE

Mind Boggling

We live in a world of codes. Some are as strict as software, some as fluid as the mother tongue. Some expand like math beyond human experience. Some are loaded with bigotry. Some are like poetry. They are all languages. These are the codes of our minds.

While you may not realize it, your mind already uses multiple codes—math, music, spoken languages, sign languages. The human brain is built to accommodate multiple codes of communication, and as we learn them, doors open to new experiences and knowledge. We come to see the world differently, and our brains are transformed as a result.

Many people continue to miss out on the benefits of learning other languages, say Spanish, Mandarin, or Hindi, simply because the consequences of multilingualism are either misunderstood, minimized, or even politicized. But knowing multiple languages can lead to new ways of thinking that are otherwise unattainable. Just as learning math makes it possible to do things that are otherwise unimaginable—like building artificial intelligence, descending to the depths of the ocean, or ascending to other planets—and just as learning musical notation enables us to hear the sound of patterns composed thousands of miles away or centuries before, learning another language opens up another way of coding reality and new ways of thinking.

If you have ever played Boggle, then there is a good chance you have been irritated at another player for turning the grid around while you were writing down words. You may have even been that person yourself, getting yelled at by the other players, all because at some point your brain made a discovery: that turning the grid changed your perspective and made you see the same letters in a different way, extract more words, and raise your score.

Like a turn of the Boggle board, every new language that we know makes us extract and interpret information differently, altering how we think and feel, what we perceive and remember, the decisions we make, the ideas and insights we have, and the actions we take. Viewing the game board from a new orientation activates a distinct set of neurons in your brain, and different neural networks produce new answers to the question "What words do I see?" Similarly, in everyday life, the brain provides different answers depending on how the incoming input is organized by language.

A single word can convey a complex concept—like gravity, or genome, or love—by encoding large chunks of information into small communicable units, optimizing storage and learning. The concept of language as a symbolic system is a foundational cornerstone in the science of language and the mind.

But one symbolic system can only get you so far. The acquisition and use of multiple symbolic systems changes not only how our mind works but also the structure of the brain itself. The effect is more than additive, it is transformative.

It may be a surprise to learn that the majority of the world's population is bilingual or multilingual. More than seven thousand languages are spoken in the world today. The most common languages spoken are English and Mandarin, with over a billion speakers each, and Hindi and Spanish, with over half a billion each, followed by French, Arabic, Bengali, Russian, and Portuguese. Speaking more than one language is the norm rather than the exception for the human species. Consider: Indonesian is the most spoken language in Indonesia, used by over 94 percent of the population, but it is the primary language of only 20 percent of the population. Javanese is the most common primary language there, but it is spoken by only 30 percent of the population. In many countries in Europe, Asia, Africa, and South America, children grow up with two or more languages from birth and then acquire additional languages in school or as adults. The populations of countries like Luxembourg, Norway, and Estonia are more than 90 percent bilingual or multilingual. Approximately two-thirds of the entire population of Europe speak at least two languages (the European Commission estimates that a quarter speak three or more languages), and more than half of the population of Canada is bilingual. The numbers are even higher for those with an education beyond high school—more than 80 percent of those with some tertiary education reported knowing two or more languages in the European Union.

In many countries, multiple official languages are a matter of national policy. Canada, for example, has two official languages. Belgium has three. South Africa has nine. In India, more than twenty languages are recognized as official by the constitution, and multilingualism is the default. Globally, approximately 66 percent of children are being raised bilingual and, in many countries, a foreign language requirement is part of the school curriculum.

Even in the United States, where monolingualism has traditionally been the norm, the segment of the U.S. population that knows more than one language is rapidly growing. Over one-fifth of people in the United States report speaking a language other than English at home (22 percent in 2020)—these numbers have doubled in the past forty years and continue to go up, with the estimate closer to 50 percent in the bigger cities.

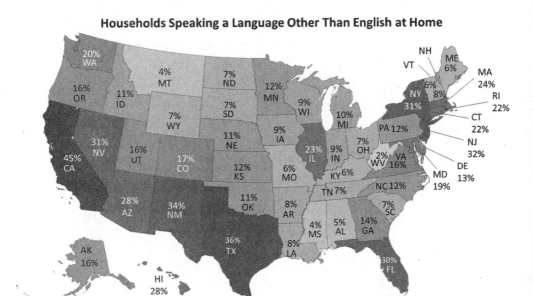

Households Speaking a Language Other Than English at Home

And yet, we are just beginning to understand the multilingual mind. Why? Because science has been playing Boggle without turning the board. Most research has historically focused on monolingual populations, and continues to do so today, which means that our understanding of the brain and of human capacity, viewed only through the lens of single-language speakers, is not only limited and incomplete but in many cases incorrect.

To focus only on monolinguals when studying the human mind is akin to how heart disease and diabetes were studied exclusively in white men under the assumption that the findings applied to everyone. We now know that heart disease manifests differently in women than in men, and that sugar is metabolized differently in the Indigenous populations of North and South America. People who speak more than one language or dialect have different linguistic, cognitive, and neural architectures than people who speak only one language. For too long, these differences have been seen as noise rather than as signal, as problematic rather than as the prototypical complex systems of human nature that they are.

What are the dangers of leaving out linguistic diversity from research? One historical example is the Immigration Act of 1924, which was signed into law by President Calvin Coolidge and dictated the countries from which the United States would accept immigrants (North-Western European nations) and those from which it would restrict immigration (South-Eastern European, Asian, and African nations). This discriminatory policy, aimed at "improving" the genetic pool of the United States, was rationalized as being built on what we now know was faulty psychometric research on the intelligence of various ethnic and racial groups—"eugenic research" that did not take into account linguistic and cultural differences and was based on data collected from people who often did not speak the language they were tested in. Imagine being a farmer, coming fresh off the boat at Ellis Island and suddenly being given an "intelligence" test in a language you did not speak. Is it any wonder that speakers of English or of languages that were similar to English or were also part of the Germanic language group would perform better on these tests and get a leg up on speakers of languages that were less similar to English?

Although the Immigration Act of 1924 was eventually repealed, echoes of biased immigration policies persist. A lack of understanding of people who speak multiple languages continues to result in an incomplete and inaccurate view of human capabilities, more limited personal opportunities, negative attitudes about immigrants and foreign languages, and biased educational and social policies. Including people who speak multiple languages in scientific studies can help accurately answer questions about the human condition.

Until recently, we did not have the tools to study multilingual brains. Advances in science and technology put at our disposal new methods, like functional magnetic resonance imaging (fMRI), which measures blood oxygenation response in the brain; electroencephalography (EEG), which maps electrical activity in the brain; eye tracking, which records pupil movement and dilation; machine learning; and massive international online data sets.

Experiments in my lab use eye-tracking technology to reveal that, as we go about our everyday lives, what we look at, what we pay attention to, and what we remember are influenced by the languages we know and happen to be speaking at any given time.

In these experiments, bilinguals sit at a desk and are asked to move various objects around while their eye movements are recorded. The ingenious part is that the names of some of the objects overlap across languages—like the English word *marker* and the Russian word *marka* (meaning "stamp"), or the English word *glove* and the Russian word *glaz* (meaning "eye"), or the English word *shark* and the Russian word *sharik* (meaning "balloon"). While doing my dissertation research, I used to scour shops for items that could serve as experimental stimuli; now these experiments can be run online with personal webcams. Analyses of eye movements reveal that when bilinguals hear words in one language (like *marker* or *glove* or *shark* in English), they make eye movements to objects whose names overlap in the other language (like *marka*/stamp, *glaz*/eye, and *sharik*/balloon in Russian).

When compared to monolingual English speakers, both bilinguals and monolinguals look at objects with names overlapping in English (like *marker* and *marbles*, or *spear* and *speaker*), but only the Russian–English bilinguals look at objects whose names overlap across the two languages (like *marker* and *marka*/stamp, or *spear* and *spichki*/matches). English monolinguals do not look at the objects with overlapping

Russian names any more than they look at other objects in the displays. This difference between bilinguals and monolinguals tested with exactly the same stimuli suggests that eye movements to a cross-linguistic competitor are due to the parallel activation of the other language in the bilingual mind.

In another simple and ingenious task called the Stroop task, people are asked to name the color of the ink in which names of colors are printed, like the words **BLACK** or **GREEN** printed in either black or green ink. When asked to name the color of the ink and ignore the content of the word, people are usually faster to say that the color of the ink is black when it spells the word **BLACK** than when it spells the word **GREEN**. Multilinguals typically perform better on the Stroop task. Their ability to pay attention to the ink color (relevant information) and ignore the word content (irrelevant information) is a by-product of multilinguals' experience constantly paying attention to one language and controlling competition from other known languages. Over time, controlling competition across multiple languages makes the brain better able to focus on relevant parameters and disregard irrelevant information, a hallmark of executive function.

The impact of multilingualism is not limited to executive function, but extends to memory, emotion, perception, and just about any other aspect of the human experience. In one study, we found that when Mandarin–English bilinguals were asked to name a statue of someone standing with one arm raised while looking into the distance, they were more likely to say *Statue of Liberty* when speaking English and *Chairman Mao* when speaking Mandarin. When asked where and when Japan launched the initial attack during World War II, they were more likely to say *Pearl Harbor, 1941,* when speaking English, and *Lugouqiao, 1937,* when speaking Mandarin (the former referring to the attack on the United States and the latter referring to the attack on China four years earlier). When asked to name a woman who succeeded despite severe physical handicap, they were more likely to say

Helen Keller when speaking English and *Zhang Haidi* when speaking Mandarin. These bilinguals knew both answers, but the speed and likelihood with which one of the two answers came to mind changed depending on the language spoken at any given time. Because language and culture are tightly intertwined, language functions as a vehicle for culture, and changing languages also switches cultural frameworks.

Even personal memories about our lives—our childhoods, relationships, experiences—vary across languages in multilinguals. People are more likely to recall events that happened in a certain language when that same language is used at the time of recall. In another study, bilinguals were more likely to remember events from childhood (before immigration to the United States) when speaking their native language and more likely to remember events from later in life (after immigration to the United States) when speaking English.

A student in one of my seminars sent me this message about deciding to experiment on herself: "I wanted to try this on myself, so when I FaceTimed my mom, I asked her to ask me a question about a memory in Chinese at the beginning of the call, then to ask me the same question again later in English at the end of the call. (It was clearly not the best objective science experiment, but it was still fun to try!) The question she asked was 'What is your earliest memory of being on a playground?' When she asked me that in Cantonese, the first thought that came to mind was playing on the playground with my parents in our old apartment, but when she asked me that in English, the first thought that came to mind was playing 'Princess' at my kindergarten's playground. Though it was strange at first to me how my initial response to the same question was of two different scenarios, the more I thought about it, the more it made sense. When I played on the playground with my parents as a kid I used Cantonese, while my kindergarten was taught in English."

The finding that the accessibility of memories varies across languages—the Language-Dependent Memory phenomenon—has implications for interviewing bilingual witnesses in legal cases, accessing traumatic memories of events, and providing psychotherapy to bilingual clients.

The memories that come to the forefront, in turn, shape how we think about ourselves and the frameworks we use. Languages can even affect how one experiences love and hate. "I love you" feels different in a native versus a non-native language. A native language packs more emotional punch. Which is also why some multilinguals prefer the use of a non-native language when they feel they need some emotional distance. Using another language does not create *Star Trek* Vulcans devoid of emotion, but it can provide more emotional detachment from the intense associations of the native language. As Nelson Mandela famously said, "If you talk to a man in a language he understands, that goes to his head. If you talk to him in his own language, that goes to his heart."

Though it may seem extreme, a multilingual can quite literally feel differently about people, events, or things when using one language versus another. The likelihood of being rattled by curse words or taboo words changes across native and second languages. Speakers of multiple languages not only report feeling different, but their bodies have different physiological reactions (like galvanic skin responses that measure arousal, or event-related potentials and fMRI that measure brain activity) and their minds make different emotionally driven decisions across languages. The exact relationship between positive and negative emotions and language varies across people. For some, the second language carries more positive connotations because it is associated with freedom, opportunity, financial well-being, and escape from persecution, whereas the native language is associated with poverty, persecution, and hardship. For others, the opposite is true—the second language is associated with post-immigration challenges, discrimination, and lack of close relationships, whereas the native language is associated with family, friends, and parental love. And many are somewhere in between, having a mix of positive and negative experiences associated with each language.

There is now a sizable body of research under the umbrella of the Foreign Language Effect suggesting that people make more logical and rational decisions in a non-native language in a variety of spheres ranging from moral judgments to financial allocations. For instance, in one version of the classic trolley dilemma used to study morality and ethics, a trolley is speeding toward five workmen who cannot see it. You are standing on a bridge above a train track next to a large person with a heavy backpack. If you push this man off the bridge onto the tracks below, he will die, but this will stop the trolley, saving the five workmen. Is it permissible to kill one person to save the lives of five people?

When responding in a native language, 20 percent of bilinguals said that pushing one person off the bridge to save five people was permissible. When responding in a foreign language, 33 percent of bilinguals said that pushing one person off the bridge to save five people was permissible. This increase in utilitarian decision-making resulted simply from shifting to the second language.

In another experiment, this time on cheating, bilinguals were asked to privately roll a die (only the roller could see what number they obtained) and then report the outcome for a reward directly proportional to the number they got (the higher the number, the higher the reward). If everyone were honest, one would expect the distribution of outcomes to be a probability value equally divided across the number of possible answers (1 out of 6 for the six sides of the rolled die). Instead, people were more likely to report that they rolled a high number (5 or 6) instead of a low number (1 or 2) when they were asked in a native language than when they were asked in a non-native language. Language, it turns out, influences our likelihood to cheat, how utilitarian we are, and our decision-making more generally. We could even say that honesty speaks louder in a second language.

In essence, language makes *people* different, bringing to the forefront different aspects of themselves, "turning on" different identities. Although not quite to the extent of Jckyll and Hyde, a different language can release a new aspect of your identity that lies dormant in your native language.

Beyond your identity, your memories, and your relationships, learning another language gives you new ways of structuring the universe. As an English speaker, you typically think of the rainbow as containing seven colors. But the rainbow consists of an infinite number of colors, a multitude of hues within the color spectrum, one color changing into another seamlessly and without borders. How we see and think about rainbows is influenced by the color words we have at our disposal, and speakers of other languages, with different color words, see and talk about rainbows differently.

The demarcations we place on our perception of the colors of the rainbow, and on our perception of the universe more generally, as a result of the words through which we filter the world are not limited to visual perception but also apply to smell, taste, touch, our perception of time, and countless other human experiences. A wine or scotch connoisseur, for example, has a much richer vocabulary at their disposal to describe the fullness, finish, flavors, and aroma of the drink, which in turn improves their ability to recognize and remember subtle differences to which a non-expert may be oblivious. Similarly, a chef or perfumer has at their disposal labels for flavors and smells that allow them to perceive, differentiate among, prepare, and remember subtle variations. The labels that we have at our disposal, be they in one language or many, influence how we see the world around us. Regardless of where you place the limits of linguistic effects on cognition, there is evidence that at least some of the things that we perceive and remember differ depending on what labels we use. Learning another language makes it possible to process the environment around us without the constraints imposed by the limits of a single language.

Our perception of reality is tied not only to the words we know but also to the patterns of activation in our brains, and these patterns vary across people based on individual experiences. What we perceive as reality is essentially brain activity. Because our perceptions and thoughts are bound by patterns of neural activation, and because different languages activate different neural networks, those who speak multiple languages can cross these mental boundaries in ways that are nothing short of awe-inspiring. What we see or hear is influenced by which neurons are most likely to fire, and which neurons are most likely to fire depends on which prior neurons were activated by recent experiences. When bilinguals switch languages, their networks of neural activation change as well, and with them, so do their perception and interpretation of reality, allowing them to move across multiple planes of neural co-activation—and hence, arguably, across multiple planes of existence.

CHAPTER TWO

The Parallel-Processing Super-Organism

Growing up during the Cold War on the other side of the Iron Curtain, I read my share of spy novels. The Soviet equivalent of the West's James Bond is Max Otto von Stierlitz, the protagonist of countless movies, books, TV series, jokes, and parodies. You would be hard-pressed to find anyone from the old Soviet states or from modern Russia who has not heard of Stierlitz. Where 007 movies are action-oriented and packed with sex and pop culture, Stierlitz's stories were about a battle of wits in a shadowy intelligence world. A common component of both stories, however, and of the story arcs of most spy movies and novels, is each side trying to identify the undercover moles. The plots of spy movies and mystery novels, and the activities of real-life intelligence agencies, often revolve around figuring out who knows what information.

It may sound incredible, but psycholinguistic experiments, like the ones carried out with bilinguals, can be used to catch spies and provide answers in the world of espionage. Many of these experiments use eye movements and brain imaging to figure out how the mind processes information.

Eye tracking, as the name implies, uses equipment to record someone's eye movements, either remotely or using small cameras mounted on headbands, caps, or glasses. Eye movements happen in fractions of a second, and while some of them are voluntarily controlled and executed at will (like directing your gaze toward something you want to look at), others are involuntary and automatic and happen without a person's conscious awareness. It is by recording these unconscious eye movements that one can gain insight into a person's mind.

Psycholinguistics research reveals that what someone knows (like the languages they speak) changes mental processes (indexed by eye movements). Flipping around the flow of information in that sentence, you can see that if you study how someone's eyes move, you can find out what information they know by looking at what involuntarily captures their attention. The same techniques can be capitalized upon to figure out if someone knows something they may not want you to know.

In theory, this means that a Russian spy could be exposed with clever recording of saccadic eye movements or brain activity, because saccadic eye movements are involuntary, as is the firing of synapses in the brain. Simply recording someone's eye movements could tell us what languages they speak and what information they know. Eye tracking is ideally suited for identifying the features of the environment that capture attention. By observing what people attend to, it is possible to make inferences regarding their mental processes. (Brain-imaging technology, as we will see later in the book, is steadily moving in the direction of being able to provide revealing information about a person's thoughts.)

For a long time, the scientific community thought that the bilingual brain switched between languages, turning one language off

Example of a computer display in which participants were asked to click on the speaker. The display also included matches; the Russian word for *matches* is *speachkey*. When asked in English to "click on the speaker," Russian–English bilinguals looked at the matches more often than at other distracter objects in the display and more often than English monolinguals did.

when not in use, turning the other language on, and alternating between the two. The unexpected discovery that when speakers of multiple languages hear words in one language, they make eye movements toward items with names that sound similar in the other languages has been—dare I pun it—eye-opening. It became clear that even when not overtly used, the other language remains constantly active and is automatically processed by the bilingual brain. What does this tell us about the mind and about language? That question sent me on a decades-long quest.

Keeping all languages co-activated and processing them in parallel is especially surprising because at first glance such a system doesn't seem efficient. Why not just shut one off so you don't have to do double the work? Wouldn't it be more efficient to just search through one language for the meaning of a word instead? It turns out that the answer is no.

This is because a serial processing system, where you hear a word and then try to map it onto meaning, one word at a time, would not be very efficient at all.

When someone asks you to pick up a speaker, if you tried to match the word *speaker* to every item in your environment one by one until you reach the correct one—*Is this a speaker? No, it's a cup. Is this a speaker? No, it's a phone. Is this a speaker? No, it's a pencil*—it would take forever. Instead, as the word unfolds, your brain co-activates all possible items in your mental registry that start with *s* (*soap, spray, spear* . . .) and then, as more and more of the word is recognized— *s-p-e-* . . . —the auditory input is integrated with the visual input from your environment so that only one final meaning remains, in a winner-takes-all fashion.

In multilinguals, this parallel activation cascades across all the languages they know, so that in addition to the English words *soap, spray, spear,* and so on, the incoming sounds also co-activate words in the other language (in this case, the Russian words *slon*/elephant, *speert*/alcohol, *speachkey*/matches, and others), resulting in many more co-activated words. This allows the brain to remain open to all possible mappings of sound to meaning, regardless of language, so that it is always ready for any language input, even in unpredictable circumstances, and can understand and respond faster than if it had to reboot a turned-off language.

Since those first experiments with Russian–English bilinguals, numerous eye-tracking studies around the world have replicated the findings of parallel activation during language comprehension, spanning a diverse set of language pairs, including Spanish and English, Japanese and English, Dutch and English, German and Dutch, German and English, French and German, Hindi and English, and many others.

Parallel processing refers to the brain's ability to simultaneously execute multiple tasks and deal with multiple stimuli and sources of

Within-Language Competition

Between-Language Competition

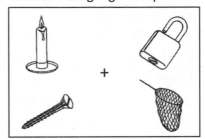

Control (No Competition)

Filler

Visual search displays in experiments with Spanish–English bilinguals. Competition trials (top row) feature either within-language competition (*candle-candy*) or between-language competition (*candle-candado*/lock). Competition trials were compared to control trials without phonological overlap (*candle-wing*), while filler trials were used to mask the experimental manipulation.

input at the same time. The brain does not duplicate effort; instead, it changes how it processes information. In multilinguals, it expands its parallel-processing capacity and, in turn, changes higher-order cognitive processing necessary to control this parallel activation across languages. The brain is, in essence, a parallel-processing super-organism, and even more so in multilinguals.

In addition to this "overt" co-activation, where both languages are activated when words sound similar across languages, we also found evidence of co-activation when words do not sound similar across languages but their translations do. Evidence for such "covert co-activation" comes from a study with Spanish–English bilinguals who heard words like *duck* in English and had to click on the target among a set of four items. The Spanish translation of duck, *pato*, overlapped phonologically with the Spanish name for another object in the display, shovel (Spanish *pala*). When Spanish–English bilinguals were asked to click on a picture of a duck in English, they were more likely to look at a picture of a shovel than at other distracter images in the display.

Not only do the words we hear activate other similar-sounding words, and not only do we look at objects whose names share sounds or letters across languages, but the translations of those words in other languages become activated as well in speakers of more than one language. Bilinguals access both of their languages, even in the absence of overlapping input.

Beyond words, there is evidence of parallel activation for syntax and grammar as well. One way to assess syntactic co-activation using eye tracking is to present participants with sentences that lead to different interpretations depending on the syntax of each language. For example, the sentence "Which cow is the goat pushing?" unambiguously identifies the goat as the pusher according to English syntactic rules, yet activation of German syntax could lead to the conclusion that the cow is the pusher. When the syntax of two languages leads to conflicting interpretations, German–English bilinguals look more often at a picture depicting the scene that aligns with the syntax of the non-target language compared to when there is no conflict.

The spreading activation in the multilingual language system is like a multidimensional ripple effect. When you throw a pebble in the water, it sends ripples in all directions, and as they spread farther and farther out, the height of the ripples becomes lower, but the circles become bigger. Similarly, when you hear or read a word, other words that are connected to that word become activated; the more connected they are to the initial word, the stronger the activation, and the further the activation spreads, the greater the number of words affected.

For instance, the English word POT, which is pronounced /pot/, can refer to a cooking container, a sum of bets in a hand of poker, an herb, or the action of planting something like a flower, among other meanings. When an English speaker reads the word POT, all meanings of the word become activated to some extent in their subconscious, with the strength of the activation varying across people depending on their recent experiences (like how often they cook or play poker).

A Russian–English bilingual, when reading the English word POT, activates not only all the meanings of the English word POT but also all the meanings of the English word ROT, because *p* is pronounced *r* in Russian and the letters P-O-T are mapped onto the sounds R-O-T in Russian. In Russian, the word ROT means "mouth," and as a result, all the meanings associated with the word *mouth* become activated (including nouns like *nose* and *teeth,* verbs like *close* and *kissing,* adjectives like *big* and *pouty,* and so on). And because the sound POT (with a *p* and not an *r*) means "sweat" in Russian, all the associations of the word *sweat* are activated as well. *Hearing* a word in one language activates the spoken and written forms in both the first and second languages. Similarly, *reading* a word in one language activates the written and spoken forms of both languages as well. This is true even if the two languages differ in letter-to-sound mappings.

If that seems like a lot already, consider that not only do visual and auditory inputs (like reading or hearing a word) activate word meanings in both languages, but all the translations of those meanings in both languages become activated as well. Because the letters P-O-T activate the word *mouth* in Russian and the sound P-O-T activates the word *sweat* in Russian, those words are now activated in English as well, and the Russian translations of the many other words associated with the English words *mouth* and *sweat* also become activated.

Further, the words that share some meaning or form in either language with any of those words and translations become activated in the mind as well. This activation of mental representations spreads in

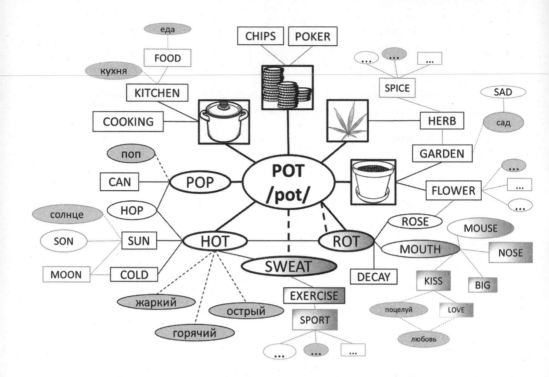

a ripple effect to words that are related to all the interpretations of the original English word POT in either meaning (like *kitchen, poker, lighter, gardening . . .*) or form (like *pop, hot, pit . . .*), to words that are related to the Russian word ROT/mouth in either meaning (like *kiss, big, teeth . . .*) or form (like *rose, role, rope . . .*), and to words that are related to the Russian word POT/sweat in either meaning (like *exercise, heart, anxiety . . .*) or form (like *post, pole/field . . .*).

This is just a small example of a massive process that illustrates the parallel co-activation across both languages in bilinguals. If one three-letter word can generate so much spreading activation, imagine the spreading activation across a language system that encompasses tens of thousands of words in multiple languages.

Additional languages lead to exponential growth. As an English-Russian-Romanian trilingual, for me the word POT also activates its

Romanian meaning (to be able to do something, as in "I can" or "they can") and all the associations that follow from that in both form and meaning, plus the translation of that meaning into English and Russian, plus all the overlapping and associated words across all three languages. All of this happens "on the fly" as a conversation unfolds, in fractions of milliseconds, with the brain continuously processing information.

To what extent the two languages are activated depends on a constellation of factors—the structure and form of each language, at what age the languages were acquired and in what order, the proficiency and experience with each language, recency of use, and how similar or different the two languages are. Languages that have not been used recently are co-activated less, which is why when someone first arrives in a country that speaks a language they have not used in a while, it may take them some hours or days to regain their fluency before they feel like it all "came back." Similarly, languages that are more similar are more likely to interfere with each other, with a word from Italian more likely to pop up when you are trying to speak French than when you are trying to speak Korean. As recency of use, similarity, and proficiency change, the thresholds of activation for these languages change as well.

Eye-tracking studies have implications for applied settings ranging from consumer behavior (what goods we look at in a store) to the military (searching in complex visual fields for the enemy) to art (what our eyes are drawn to) and show that the languages you know influence how you see the world quite literally, down to the mechanics of your eye movements. Understanding that people's eye movements and attention may be drawn to different parts of an image may change how you decide to approach a task that relies on visual input, whether you are an artist who paints or an advertiser who pitches for a living.

Co-activation is even found across different modalities, as is the case of a sign language and a spoken language in American Sign

Language (ASL)–English bilinguals. The experiments with sign language are particularly notable because in ASL–English bilinguals, not only is there no overlap in input (like in the marker-*marka* experiments), but there is not even overlap in modality (auditory versus visual), which speaks to the mind's capacity for language co-activation. We found that the ASL–English bimodal bilinguals make eye movements to words that overlap in sign components in ASL, whereas English monolinguals do not.

While for an English monolingual, the words *potato* and *church* do not sound similar, in American Sign Language the signs for *potato* and *church* share three of the four sign components (location, motion, and orientation), but differ in handshape. When ASL–English bilinguals hear the word *potato*, they make eye movements to *church* more

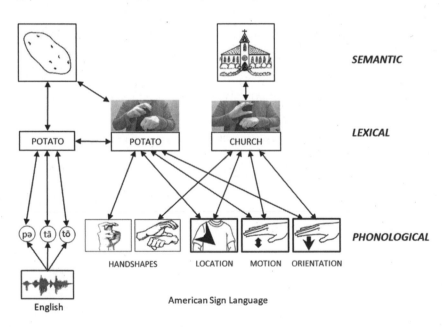

An illustration of the ASL experiment showing that English sounds activate the word (*potato*) and its meaning, which then activates its translation equivalent in the non-target language (the ASL sign for *potato*), spreading to other words in ASL that are signed similarly (the ASL sign for *church*, which resembles the sign for *potato*).

than to other distracter objects in the display, and more than monolinguals.

Most stunning, speakers of different languages differ in their patterns of eye movements *even when no words are used at all!* In a simple
visual search task in which people had to find a previously seen object
among other objects, their eyes moved differently depending on the
languages they knew.

For example, when looking for a fly, English speakers also looked
at a flag. Spanish speakers, on the other hand, when looking for the
same fly, looked at a windmill, because the Spanish names for fly
and windmill—*mosca* and *molino*—overlap. Remarkably, bilingual
Spanish–English speakers looking for a fly looked at both a flag and a
windmill. In other words, for bilinguals, an image activates both languages even when no linguistic labels are used. In follow-up studies,
we found this to be true even when a mental load was added to the task
that prevented participants from sub-vocally labeling or rehearsing
the target name.

The changes to eye movements in the absence of language input tell
us that multilingualism affects not only the language system but other

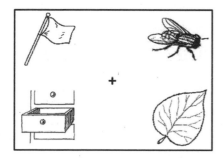 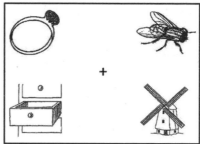

When looking for a previously seen fly, with no language input, English monolinguals were likely to make eye movements to a flag, Spanish monolinguals
were likely to make eye movements to a windmill (because *mosca* and *molino*
overlap in Spanish), and Spanish–English bilinguals were likely to make eye
movements to either a fly or a windmill or both.

systems, too, and that parallel activation has repercussions for perception, attention, memory, and other cognitive functions. These are not independent modules, and our minds are not modular. In academic terms, domain-specific experience with language translates to domain-general changes to cognition.

The best way to think about multilingualism is not as a fixed construct but as a mental state in perpetual flux. This mental state is constantly changing based on the information the brain receives continuously from the auditory, visual, tactile, olfactory, gustatory, vestibular, and proprioceptive inputs.

Because there is more co-activation in the system with two or more languages, more cognitive control is needed to manage the competition across languages, especially when speaking and producing language. Once we understand the parallel co-activation across the highly interconnected and dynamic multilingual language network, we understand what drives the consequences of multilingualism.

This highly interconnected cognitive architecture has remarkable real-world consequences.

CHAPTER THREE

On Creativity, Perception, and Thought

Creativity is a curious thing. Difficult to define, impossible to quantify, hard to will into existence, yet widely sought after and aspired to. Spending time writing this book in isolation at a lake house, when one has children and a full-time job, makes me think of the Odesa joke about the guy who tells his wife he is with his mistress and his mistress he is with his wife, only to hide alone with his books and read. Creativity, it turns out, takes time, discipline, and either sacrifices or resources or both.

Writing in my third language provides distance from the intimacy and vulnerability of my formative years, from the raw emotions of a native language. I can record feelings and thoughts with more detachment, almost like an outside observer.

But the differences are even more marked. I am quite certain that writing this book in any language other than English would be impossible for me, not only because I do not have the academic and scientific vocabulary to talk about cognitive science and neuroscience in

Romanian or Russian but also because those languages are associated in my mind with more sexist cultures and roles. Writing in English frees me from the constraints imposed by the gender roles tied to my native language and culture, allowing me to be the thinker, writer, and scientist that women in many languages do not have the opportunity to be. To borrow Obama's words from the 2004 Democratic National Convention, "in no other country on Earth is my story even possible": in no other language is my writing this book possible.

What, then, is the relationship between multilingualism and creativity? Other than freeing us from the constraints and rules tied to our native language and culture, does knowing multiple languages alter our creative thinking in any substantial ways?

Research on creative cognition shows that people who have close relationships with someone from another country become more creative and score higher on creativity tests. Close friendships and romantic relationships with someone from another country boost creativity, workplace innovation, and entrepreneurship. In a longitudinal study across a ten-month period, intercultural dating improved performance on standard creativity measures, including coming up with multiple possible solutions and bringing together different ideas to arrive at a single solution. The longer the duration of past intercultural romantic relationships, the higher the ability of current employees to generate creative names for marketing products. The higher the frequency of contact with foreign friends, the higher the performance on creative outcomes like entrepreneurship and workplace innovation. Even the creativity of the fashion lines at major fashion houses is related to the amount of time fashion designers spend immersed in a different culture.

But mere exposure to diverse languages, cultures, ideas, and views doesn't tell the whole story. A powerful link between multilingualism and creative thinking originates in the way in which knowing another language changes our cognitive architecture and facilitates the impressive parallel processing and co-activation described in the previous chapter.

Historically, most research on creativity has been done with monolinguals. But recent studies on the architecture of the multilingual mind show that knowing more than one language increases performance on many creativity tasks. Because the brain keeps all languages co-activated and processes them in parallel, multilinguals see relationships among items and draw connections between seemingly unrelated things—a cornerstone of creativity.

As we saw in the previous chapter, some words share form across languages, be it in letters, sounds, characters in non-alphabetic languages, or tones in tonal languages. As a result of the overlap in form, those words are co-activated together repeatedly in the multilingual mind, resulting in co-occurring neural firings. And because neurons that fire together wire together, these co-activations of form result in co-activation of the meaning of these words as well. When we think of a bike, such features as wheels or handlebars may also come to mind.

The semantic features for the word *bike* may be more likely to include exercising and a gym for English speakers in the United States, and transportation and a basket for Dutch speakers in the Netherlands. Some of the features will overlap across all languages spoken, some will be unique to one language, and some will overlap across some languages but not others. The French translation of the word *bike* may include overlapping features across all languages (like wheels), overlapping features between Dutch and French (like a basket), and unique features specific to French (like a baguette, for one is likely to find a fresh loaf in the bike's basket).

When researchers analyzed the semantic features of 1,010 word meanings across 41 languages, they found that the meanings differed quite a bit, in ways that reflected the culture, history, and geography of their users. And we are not talking just about abstract words here, like *beauty*, or other words that are known to be culture-dependent, like *family.* Words that we may assume to be the same across cultures, like body parts (what a *back* is) differ across languages as well.

As the co-activation of two words impacts connectivity in the brain, the features of those co-activated objects across multiple languages become more connected too. Speakers of multiple languages are likely to see relationships between items that single-language speakers do not see (such as between wheels and baguettes) and to experience insights triggered by features and items that do not generate such associations or insights in monolinguals.

It is not surprising, then, that people who speak more than one language often score higher on creativity and divergent-thinking tasks. The constant co-activation of multiple languages strengthens the links between the sounds, letters, and words in a bilingual's mind, which results in denser networks and stronger connections at the levels of concepts and meaning. In a series of recent experiments using behavioral and brain measures, we found that people who speak more than one language give higher relatedness ratings to items that speakers of only one language do not see as related. In other words, knowing multiple languages enables people to make connections between things that others do not see. These links are crucial for generating ideas, solving problems, and experiencing insights.

In addition to connections among semantic features, speakers of multiple languages perceive things as more related in meaning if words overlap in form across languages. For example, Hebrew–English bilinguals rate the words *dish* and *tool* as more similar—both translate onto the same word, *kli*, in Hebrew.

A Mandarin–English bilingual graduate student told me that when she was having trouble falling asleep, she would sometimes count goats instead of sheep. In Mandarin, *sheep* and *goat* share the same character when referred to with one character, and share one of the two characters when referred to with two characters.

This ability to see relationships among items and draw connections

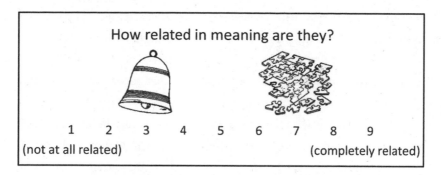

In a series of experiments, English monolinguals, Spanish–English bilinguals, and Mandarin–English bilinguals were asked to rate how related in meaning two objects were. Bilingual participants rated pairs of objects (even apparently unrelated ones such as a bell and a jigsaw puzzle) as more related than monolingual participants, seemingly connecting items together in ways that monolinguals did not. The electrical activity of their brains measured using EEG confirmed that the brains of bilingual participants processed items as more related than those of monolinguals.

between seemingly unrelated things is a skill that is difficult to train and teach. Indeed, this ability is viewed by many as an innate skill, one that is a hallmark of insight and innovation.

In his poem "Persimmons," the poet Li-Young Lee describes how his mind perceived sound and meaning relationships between words when he was still learning English as an elementary-school boy. He would confuse the words *persimmon* and *precision* because of how they sound, while at the same time linking their meaning because choosing the perfect persimmon required precision. "Other words that got me into trouble," Lee writes, "were fight and fright, wren and yarn."

> *Fight was what I did when I was frightened,*
> *Fright was what I felt when I was fighting.*
> *Wrens are small, plain birds,*
> *yarn is what one knits with.*
> *Wrens are soft as yarn.*
> *My mother made birds out of yarn.*

Lee's multilingual mind sees patterns of connection where others may see delineation of separateness. His relational representations are what gives his poetry its unique feel.

Bilingual adults and children have been found to perform differently on various creativity and divergent-thinking tasks than monolingual counterparts. For example, in an ambiguous-figure task, where the same picture can be interpreted as two different images (Seal/ Horse, Lady/Man, Faces/Apple, Rat/Man, Sax/Lady, Squirrel/Swan, Body/Face), young adults who were bilingual identified the second image faster than monolinguals.

In similar experiments with younger children, differences were found in bilingual and monolingual children as young as three years old. Bilingual children required fewer clues to see the second image. Though the effect sizes are small, they are consistent, and statistically significant (meaning unlikely to happen by chance). These results come from the general population, and it is possible that the differences would be greater in individuals who are at the higher end of the creative spectrum.

Another task that has been used to measure creativity was developed by my late colleague, psychologist Annette Karmiloff-Smith, and involves drawing nonexistent objects. In a study with four- and five-year-olds, bilingual English–Hebrew and Arabic–Hebrew children were asked to draw a flower and a house that do not exist, and their drawings were compared to those of a monolingual sample. The drawings of monolingual children were more likely to contain element deletions (missing leaves, one petal, no stalk, no roots) or size and shape differences (flower shaped as a heart). The drawings of bilingual children were more likely to contain cross-category insertions (giraffe flower, flower with a tail, camel flower, "lion flower with lots of hair, a lot of tails and shoes," flower with arms and legs, flower with teeth, tree flower, flower with a door, butterfly flower, kite flower, robot house, chair house, ball house). In general, when performing this task, younger

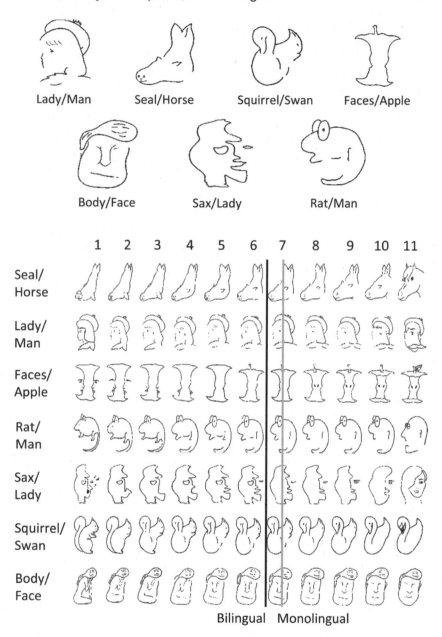

After seeing the first image, participants are given one card at a time until they can identify a new image. On average, bilinguals required fewer cards than monolinguals before switching perspectives to seeing another image (for example from seal to horse).

children tend to make size or shape changes or to delete elements, whereas older children tend to change the position of elements, add extra elements from the same category, or synthesize additions across different categories. Bilingual children's drawing, then, tends to resemble the patterns that monolingual children develop at a later age.

Creativity in childhood is also predictive of creative accomplishments later in life. In longitudinal research, children tested in the 1950s with the Torrance Test of Creative Thinking were evaluated again fifty years later. Childhood scores predicted personal achievement in one's adult life, and some of the indicators predicted public achievement as well. (Interpreting the public versus private achievement results should be done with caution. For example, the study also reported that men were higher in public achievement than women, but there was no gender difference in personal achievement. I would venture to guess that whether one realized their creative potential in the public sphere during that period was influenced by sociocultural variables of their time, including differences in gender roles and expectations for women and men.)

Some of the most influential minds of our time speak or were exposed to multiple languages. Sergey Brin, co-founder of Google; Steve Chen, YouTube co-founder; designer Carolina Herrera; *Huffington Post* founder Arianna Huffington; Hamdi Ulukaya, the founder of Chobani yogurt; and countless other entrepreneurs, creative titans, political leaders, inventors, and influential thinkers throughout history knew or were exposed to multiple languages. We often invoke immigrant roots and extraordinary work ethic to explain their achievements, but leave out the impact that knowing multiple languages has on the ability to connect ideas in ways that others don't see.

A review of the literature on creativity and bilingualism found that twenty out of twenty-four studies on this topic reported that bilinguals performed better than monolinguals on various creativity tasks (one study found no difference and three found worse performance in bilinguals; this level of variability is not surprising for mental pro-cesses). A widely used task for measuring creativity is the Alternate Uses Task. In this task, divergent thinking is assessed by presenting people with a common object and asking them to think of as many creative uses for it as possible within a short time. When asked for al-ternate uses of paper, frequent answers may include paper airplane or paper hat or toilet paper, original answers may include lampshade or filter or game of cards, and very original answers may include sound amplifier, pinwheel, or artificial snow for decoration. Performance on the Alternate Uses Task correlates with achievement in the arts and sciences. Notably, performance is improved when bilinguals are asked to switch languages during testing compared to when they are asked to stay with the same language.

There have been proposals to assess creativity automatically using a computational platform that relies on natural language processing and quantifies the semantic distance between words in texts to generate a score of verbal creativity. But this approach takes a very narrow view of creativity and illustrates the challenges inherent in measuring it.

Who decides what defines creativity? While tests that measure cre-ativity exist, an exact measure remains elusive. Who is more creative: Someone who comes up with many small discoveries or one big, paradigm-shifting discovery? Someone whose innovation has practical or financial implications, or someone whose innovation has artistic or emotional implications? There are no obvious answers. It is not yet pos-sible to compute a unified Creativity Quotient or a unified Bilingual-ism Quotient.

A creative inclination does not necessarily mean achieving fame in a creative endeavor; for most people, it can manifest in everyday life as being better at problem-solving, being good at telling stories, or being open to new experiences and ideas. Openness to experiences is one trait that correlates highly with both creativity and multilingualism. And while learning another language will not take your creativity from zero to a hundred, it can help increase it from none to some, from some to more, and can give you the extra edge you need if you are already in a creative profession.

When it comes to creativity, language itself is a creative and generative process. One of the most unique aspects of language is that it allows us to combine a finite number of words to express an infinite number of thoughts, feelings, and actions. The number of possible combinations grows exponentially with multilingualism, especially when combinations are possible not only within a language but also across languages.

———————

What's in a name? That which we call a rose
By any other name would smell as sweet

SHAKESPEARE has his character Juliet, in the throes of her love for Romeo, proclaim that the name of something does not change how our senses perceive it—naming a rose anything else does not change how it smells.

Using words interchangeably without changing the meanings and seeing language as a game is more or less the German philosopher Ludwig Wittgenstein's theory of *Sprachspiel,* or *language-game,* the idea that words have meaning only because we all agree to follow the "rules" of the "game" being played.

But are Shakespeare and Wittgenstein right? Would a rose by any other name smell as sweet? Nearly a century ago, linguists Edward Sapir and Benjamin Whorf proposed that language shapes thought and our perception of reality in what became known as the Sapir–Whorf hypothesis:

We dissect nature along lines laid down by our native languages. The categories and types that we isolate from the world of phenomena we do not find there because they stare every observer in the face; on the contrary, the world is presented in a kaleidoscopic flux of impressions which has to be organized by our minds—and this means largely by the linguistic systems in our minds. We cut nature up, organize it into concepts, and ascribe significances as we do, largely because we are parties to . . . an agreement that holds throughout our speech community and is codified in the patterns of our language.

The Sapir–Whorf hypothesis puts forward two main arguments: linguistic determinism and linguistic relativity. Linguistic determinism proposes that language determines thought, and linguistic relativity proposes that thought is relative to language and that speakers of different languages think differently. Hotly debated ever since it was introduced in 1929, at its extreme, the Sapir–Whorf hypothesis suggests that the absence of certain words precludes thinking about the things those words refer to, with much of the debate centering on how one defines and measures thought and language.

The best-known example used to support Whorf's theory focused on the number of words the Inuit people have for snow (more than fifty). Because snow is a crucial part of the Inuit way of life and because Inuit people use snow in many ways—the argument goes—their perception of snow differs from that of someone who has less experience with snow. Whorf described the Hopi as not having any linguistic markers for past, present, and future tenses and argued that the Hopi language points to a different way of perceiving time by its speakers.

Since then, it has been pointed out that speakers of other languages are just as able to distinguish between types of snow linguistically. The only difference is that instead of a single word, they may use multiple words or phrases—falling snow, snow on the ground, packed snow, icy snow, slushy snow, wet snow, and so on. Although the Hopi language does not mark tense in the same way as English or many other languages, speakers of Hopi are able to communicate about past, present, and future phenomena by referencing natural markers of time (the ascent and descent of celestial bodies like the sun and the moon, the seasons of the year, the level of water in the rivers, the crops, and so on).

The pushback on linguistic determinism is largely justified. Determinism takes an absolute view of language equaling thought, does not recognize the limits of linguistic influences, and often produces inconsistent research results. Concepts in one language are for the most part translatable, even if not always to a high degree of exactitude, and even if they may require explanation using multiple words. Why then does the Sapir–Whorf hypothesis continue to garner so much interest and fascination? Psychologist John Carroll writes, "Perhaps it is the suggestion that all one's life one has been tricked, all unaware, by the structure of language into a certain way of perceiving reality, with the implication that awareness of this trickery will enable one to see the world with fresh insight." One of my students even wondered whether learning a foreign language may help them think outside the racial schemas and prejudices imposed through the use of their Standard American English and African American English dialects.

Philosopher Friedrich Nietzsche went so far as to call language a "prisonhouse" when referring to the limitations it places on the mind, long before Sapir and Whorf described linguistic determinism and linguistic relativity, or before the scientific community started to test these ideas empirically.

Does multilingualism hold the keys to the prisonhouse? If language is a colander that strains the input around us to interpret reality, then new languages poke more holes, or poke bigger holes, to allow us to see and learn more about the universe.

I don't believe all thoughts, memories, emotions, or learning are necessarily linguistic. Linguistic determinism comes up short in accounting for know-it-when-you-see-it phenomena that are difficult to put into words, like love, or honor. Riding a bike or swimming are just some of the many examples of learning that do not necessarily require language. Classical conditioning, like the famous Pavlovian experiments where one learns to associate the sound of a bell with food and begins to salivate when hearing the bell, is another example of non-linguistic learning.

In memory research, a famous pinprick experiment more than a century ago demonstrated the brain's ability to learn and remember without language. Swiss neurologist Édouard Claparède was treating a woman with anterograde amnesia (anterograde amnesia refers to the inability to form new memories and remember new information). Claparède's patient remembered childhood events and older memories, but could not create any new memories. If Claparède left the room for an hour, she promptly forgot who he was or ever having met him despite interacting with him and being tested by him daily. One day, Claparède hid a pin in the palm of his hand and, when reaching to shake the patient's hand upon greeting her, pricked her with the pin. The next day, even though she had no conscious recollection of ever meeting Claparède before, let alone of having been pricked by him, the patient refused to shake Claparède's hand, despite having done so every day before and without being able to explain why she no longer wanted to shake his hand. Even though she was not consciously aware of what happened, the memory was there. Fans of Christopher Nolan's movie *Memento* may recall that an insurance agent used a similar tactic to determine whether a patient was faking a memory disorder.

It is clear that language and thought are not one and the same. Although language does not fully *determine* thought, it is one of the key factors that meaningfully *contribute to* and *influence* how we think and who we are. Like the ability to talk about snow or time by using phrases or sentences rather than single words, the influence of language on thought appears to be less about *what* you can represent mentally than *how* you represent it.

For instance, on Twitter and Reddit, multilinguals point out that, in Spanish, attention is something that you "lend," because you kind of want it back. In French, you "make" it, because it is not there if you don't. In English, you "pay" it, because it's valuable. And in German, you "gift" it, because it is really a present. Linguistic insights like these are supported by empirical research. Color perception, time, spatial relations, and frames of reference are just some of the domains influenced by language. When it comes to color, the languages of the world vary greatly in the number of basic color words they use. The World Color Survey estimates that at least twenty world languages have only three or four basic color words (one word for white or light, one word for red-yellow hues, and one word for black-green-blue hues). Because language is a guide to features in our input that are culturally important to us, and because each language only lexicalizes a subset of the possible options, speakers of different languages perceive and remember color differently.

English has one word for "blue," whereas Russian has different words for light blue (*goluboy*) and dark blue (*siniy*). (There are of course ways to describe various shades of blue in English using word combinations or phrases, but these are less common and not typically the primary colors that kids learn growing up.) When speakers of English and Russian were tested on a color-discrimination task, Russian speakers were faster to discriminate two colors when they fell into different linguistic categories. A similar result was found in a study with Greek speakers and English speakers when the electrical activity of the brain was measured using EEG. Greek, too, has two different words to distinguish between light blue (*galazio*) and dark blue (*ble*). EEG responses showed that Greek speakers were more sensitive to light versus dark changes for the color blue than for green, but English speakers showed no such difference.

Of course, speakers of languages that do not have different words for light blue and dark blue can still distinguish between different shades of blue when they look at them. Not having different labels for different shades of blue, just like not having different labels for different kinds of snow, does not prevent us from being able to perceive and experience variation in our environment. It does, however, seem to affect how fast we respond and how we encode the environment into memory. It is easier to remember the distinct colors of two people's eyes or items of clothing if you use a completely different label to describe each (blue and green) than if you use one label (blue) or a modified label (light blue and dark blue)—and certainly easier to describe to a friend. As I write this sentence, I realize that I visualize my children's eyes as being a slightly darker shade of blue when I am speaking in English (and use the word *blue*) than when I am speaking in Russian (and use the word *golubyye*), because the prototypical shades of the two colors differ and shift my mental representations.

Another domain that has been studied extensively is the concept of time. In the sci-fi movie *Arrival* (spoiler alert!), a linguist played by Amy Adams is able to travel through time after learning an alien language that encoded temporal dimensions and time shifting. And while we do not (yet) know of any language that allows for time travel, speakers of different languages do indeed seem to think about time differently, with language playing a notable role in shaping mental representations of time. (Undoubtedly, future attempts to communicate with an alien consciousness will need to include psycholinguistics experts familiar with different codes of communication.)

Some people think of time as progressing horizontally, others think of it as moving vertically, and yet others perceive time circularly. English speakers are more likely to use language that represents time in a horizontal line, by referring to things that happened before or after something—they "look forward" to events, or "think back" to their childhoods. Mandarin speakers, on the other hand, represent time both vertically and horizontally. They talk about events that happened earlier as up (*shang*) and events that happened later as down (*xia*). Research on how language shapes the representation of time shows that when asked if March comes before May, English speakers respond faster after just seeing horizontal arrays, whereas Mandarin speakers respond faster after just seeing vertical arrays. (But English speakers are also able to learn to think of time in vertical terms: one can learn new ways of talking and thinking.) Of course, in reality, time is not a line at all, though physicists do believe that time does not exist without space.

Speakers of different languages also vary on whether they think of time primarily as quantity or as distance. English speakers use both distance and quantity metaphors when talking about time, with distance metaphors more frequent (*let's move the meeting forward*; *a short intermission*; and so on) than quantity metaphors (*lots of time*; *saving time*; and so on). That is not the case for other languages.

In two experiments on how time metaphors affect time estimation, native speakers of English, Indonesian, Spanish, and Greek were asked to estimate the time it took for lines to grow to full length and for cups to fill with water. Speakers of languages with more *distance* metaphors for time (like English and Indonesian) were influenced more by the *length of the line*. Speakers of languages with more *quantity* metaphors for time (like Greek and Spanish) were influenced more by the *amount of water*.

Language has also been found to influence our sense of direction. English allows cardinal directions like north, east, south, and west, as well as egocentric coordinates that are body-relative like left, right, front, and back. Some languages do not have both options. In languages in which only cardinal directions are an option, the speakers must know at all times where north, south, east, and west are so that they may use them to describe locations, directions, and even the orientation of their own body and limbs (like holding an apple in their south hand).

Not all studies find differences in time representation or color perception. For some phenomena that fall under the Sapir–Whorf hypothesis, there remains a need to identify the conditions in which language effects are present. The variability in findings within research on linguistic determinism is partly a result of the definitions and measures used for each construct. Even who qualifies as a bilingual, or trilingual, or multilingual, is a matter of definition. At what point does a learner of a second (or third or fourth . . .) language pass the threshold to become a bona fide denizen of that language? Who considers themselves bilingual or multilingual varies not only across individuals but also across studies.

We have yet to understand exactly which cognitive functions are and are not malleable by language (as well as when and why and how). It is increasingly clear, however, that while language does not determine thought, it helps shape it in powerful ways. In the words of Edward Sapir, "It is quite an illusion to imagine . . . language is merely an incidental means of solving specific problems of communication and reflection. The fact of the matter is that the 'real world' is to a large extent unconsciously built up on the language habits of the group."

OCCASIONALLY, illusions are precisely what give us a glimpse into how subjective the brain's interpretation of reality is. Illusions violate our intuition that perception is direct, that we perceive unfiltered versions of the external environment, and that we all share perceptions of the same reality. Senses, after all, shouldn't be a matter of opinion. Which is why we are so surprised when someone insists that the gold dress we see is blue, or that what we clearly hear as "Yanny" sounds to them like "Laurel." These are just two of the perceptual illusions widely shared online in recent years.

In the Yanny/Laurel auditory illusion, the same sound is perceived by some listeners as "Yanny," while others hear it as "Laurel." In the blue-gold dress visual illusion, the exact same dress is perceived by some viewers as blue and black and by others as white and gold (both await you at the other end of a Google search). Perceptual illusions like these demonstrate that what you hear or see is influenced by which neurons are most likely to fire in your brain, and which neurons are most likely to fire in your brain depends on which prior neurons were activated by recent experiences. People hear different words (for example, "brainstorm" or "green needle") when listening to the exact same sound, depending on what word they read prior to hearing it.

Moment by moment, experiences continually rewire our neural networks so the neurons that fire are never exactly the same for the exact same stimulus. The same person can see the dress as one color one day and a different color another day, or hear Yanny in the morning and Laurel in the afternoon. Many times the differences in the networks that fire are not strong enough to produce noticeably different experiences, but sometimes they cross a threshold that results in distinct sensory perceptions of the same input. We are used to accepting that the same environmental input can elicit different *emotions* across people, but find it more difficult to accept that the same environmental input can elicit different *sensory experiences*.

The truth is that both, emotions and senses, are subjective. Sensory perception can be nudged, distorted, and transformed by anything from the surrounding visual context to the languages we speak.

When bilinguals switch languages, their networks of neural activation change, and so do their perception and interpretation of reality. In the classic double-flash illusion, hearing two tones transforms a single flash of light into what appears to be two flashes. For multilinguals, the auditory and visual stimuli need to be timed more closely than for monolinguals, otherwise they will not fall for the illusion. In other words, in the absence of a natural correspondence between cross-modal inputs, bilingual experience may enhance sensitivity to features such as timing. It has been proposed that this is due to more efficient top-down control while determining when sights and sounds should be combined (based on spatial, temporal, and semantic characteristics).

In addition to affecting the *perception* of sensory information, language experience also changes the *integration* of inputs across perceptual modalities. The most dramatic illustration of multisensory integration is synesthesia—the experience of one sensory experience being tied to another sensory experience, for example sounds being tied to colors or physiological sensations. Painter Wassily Kandinsky heard music when looking at paintings, physicist Richard Feynman saw colors when looking at equations, and artist Pharrell Williams sees colors when listening to music. While most of us do not experience this extreme level of cross-modal integration, we, too, are subject to cross-modal influences. For instance, listening to smooth music enhances the perceived creaminess of chocolate. All of us engage in combining information from different modalities, including when processing language, as we perceive auditory and visual input simultaneously.

While multilinguals are more attuned to timing when processing nonlinguistic stimuli like tones and flashes that do not inherently go together in the double-flash illusion, they appear to be more likely to integrate visual and auditory input when processing language. When integrating speech input, multilinguals are more likely to fuse the auditory sounds and visual lip movements of the speaker.

The McGurk effect refers to the phenomenon that if your eyes see someone's lips make one sound (like "ga-ga") while at the same time your ears hear a different sound (like "ba-ba"), what your brain perceives is neither, but a brand-new sound altogether ("da-da"). Multisensory integration is inherent during speech comprehension from the earliest stages of language development. In people who can hear and see, the brain learns to pair certain visual inputs with specific sounds, and these links are solidified over time. When an unexpected mismatch takes place, the brain attempts to reconcile it in a way that produces the McGurk effect.

Our research shows that bilinguals are more likely to experience the McGurk effect than monolinguals, suggesting that multilingual experience alters multisensory integration. This may be because bilinguals need (at least initially) to rely more on visual information to make sense of speech when they are still learning another language. Language learners often report paying more attention to the mouth of someone speaking the new language to improve their speech perception. The flip side to that is greater difficulty understanding a new language over the phone than in person because the visual information is absent. Indeed, babies growing up in multilingual households attend to the mouths of speakers to a greater degree than monolingual infants do. These early differences in how bilinguals and monolinguals attend to speech-relevant inputs continue to shape sensory processing throughout their lives.

Visual and auditory perception are not the only senses that are affected by language, although studies of other modalities are rare. Languages vary in the ways they code perception. Not only does the number of words available for various senses differ across languages; the consistency with which speakers of the same language describe senses also varies. Smell, for example, is almost universally more poorly coded than other senses across languages. Research on imagining tasting and smelling and touching different things found that multilinguals reported less vivid mental imagery of sensory experiences in their foreign languages than in their native tongue for touch, kinesthetics, hearing, and vision, which suggests that the original experiences of life are tied to the native language.

Language can even influence our perception of pain. Using swearwords makes it possible for people to hold their hand in ice water for a longer duration of time, likely due to a change in pain thresholds and the physiological release of stress through language. Consider this experimentally backed evidence an excuse you can use next time you stub your toe or step on your kid's LEGOs (let it fly, you'll feel better!).

Language is one of the most powerful tools at our disposal for processing and organizing the information from the world around us. Our perception of reality is filtered through our linguistic systems, and learning another language makes it possible to perceive the environment around us without the constraints imposed by the limit of a single language. Multilinguals are able to perceive more of the universe around them because they are able to transcend the scalar gradients imposed by a single language. Who needs mind-altering drugs when we have language(s)?

CHAPTER FOUR

The Word Made Flesh

In the beginning was the Word. . . .
And the Word became flesh.
—John 1:1–14

first started to study multilingual brains in the '90s. I would travel five hours from Ithaca to New York City, where the Memorial Sloan Kettering Cancer Center is located, to scan bilingual brains at a time when functional magnetic resonance imaging of cognitive processing in the human brain was just getting started. I would pore over brain images late into the night with neuroscientist Joy Hirsch, who taught me how to use fMRI. Functional magnetic resonance imaging refers to using an MRI machine like the ones you may be familiar with from getting body scans at the doctor, only it measures the function (as opposed to the structure) of the brain with technology that keeps track of the blood flow and oxygenation levels of various brain regions.

Initially, MRI was used to locate tumors and visualize brain anatomy. It then became part of surgical planning to assist the surgeon in preserving critical brain regions needed for essential life functions. But as the identification of brain structures and functions

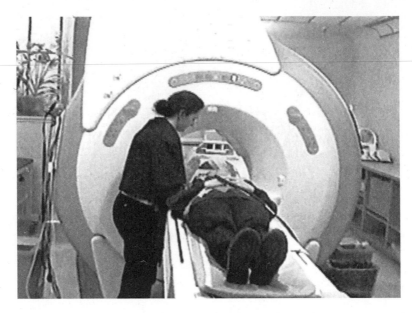

Photograph of author preparing to test a bilingual in an fMRI scanner at the Memorial Sloan Kettering Cancer Center in New York City, 1998.

evolved, new approaches were developed to examine how the brain functions during cognitive tasks.

The blood oxygenation level dependent contrast began to be used for functional imaging of the human brain in action. When an area of the brain is involved in a cognitive task, there is a localized increase in neural activity associated with performing that task. The increased neural activity leads to dilation of the blood vessels and to an increased metabolic rate in that area. The blood volume and blood flow in that location increase. The increased blood flow changes the oxygenation ratio in that area of the brain. fMRI scanners can then detect the changes in oxygenation levels of various brain regions. Simply put, when we perform a mental task, blood flow in the brain area where that task is performed increases, and a powerful magnet can measure changes in the oxygenation of those areas to identify where the task is performed by the brain.

Initially, studies of the multilingual brain attempted to pinpoint the location of the native and non-native languages in the brain. Those early erroneous efforts stemmed from clinical studies of how the brain recovers from injury.

Aphasia is losing the ability to understand or express language after brain damage. A trilingual who has suffered a stroke may lose the ability to understand two of the three languages they knew prior to the stroke and later recover one of the two languages lost. A curious case of multilingual aphasia is that of a nun who was born in Casablanca to a French-speaking family and started learning Arabic at the age of ten. She was fluent in both languages and had worked for twenty-four years as a pediatric nurse in a hospital where she spoke primarily Arabic with patients and relatives and French with the medical personnel of the hospital. At the age of forty-eight she was in a car accident that resulted in brain trauma and loss of consciousness. When she recovered, she was unable to speak, with global aphasia in both languages. Four days later, she was able to speak a few words in Arabic only. No other neuropsychological problems were detected, she was lucid, and her intelligence was preserved. Over the course of the next fourteen months, her language recovery would alternate; on some days her Arabic would be stronger and her French would be weaker, and on others the reverse would be true. Even after she recovered both languages, she was still unable to say the Hail Mary and the Lord's Prayer in Latin, in spite of having known these by heart and having said them thousands of times in the past. Such unusual cases of aphasia, called alternate antagonism aphasia, are not as rare as one may think.

One of the earliest systematic studies of multilingual aphasia was published in 1895. Neurologist Albert Pitres wanted to describe the patterns of loss and recovery of various languages in multilingual aphasia, but the task proved impossible because of the variability across individuals. The patterns of selective language loss and recovery depend on many factors: which processes in the brain have been disrupted, how recently the languages were learned, how they were learned, how well they were learned, and how recently they were used.

In neurolinguistics, multilingual aphasia has been studied in speakers of as few as two languages and as many as fifty-four languages. These cases span first-language loss and recovery; second-language loss and recovery; paradoxical recovery of a dead language (classical Greek and Latin); selective aphasia (losing only one language out of many); differential aphasia (inability to comprehend one language and inability to speak another language); alternating aphasia (loss of one language at some times and another language at other times); and pathological mixing (mixing two languages without the ability to control which language is being used when).

Initially, the finding that multilinguals can lose the ability to speak one language but not another was interpreted as a sign that the languages were processed in different brain areas. Selective language loss and recovery in multilinguals with aphasia sent early research down the wrong path of searching for distinct and localized regions in the brain. At the end of the nineteenth century, surgeons began using direct electrical stimulation to identify areas of the brain that were involved in language in an attempt to spare them during surgery when removing tumors or alleviating seizures. Early research on multilingual brains used cortical stimulation in sedated or awake speakers of multiple languages to localize the different languages in the brain, continuing down the rabbit hole of trying to find a specific location for each language.

Selective disruption of some but not other languages in multilinguals through cortical stimulation has fueled research into the shared and separate locations of languages in the brain. We now know that a multilingual's languages rely on largely overlapping networks of the brain, with some variability depending on the properties of the language and its mastery, and that selective impairments to one language but not others can have multiple causes.

Asking whether a multilingual's languages are processed in the same or different brain areas turned out to be misguided. The brain does not process each language in one specific area. Instead, a broad and highly interconnected and distributed neural network is used both within and across languages.

In recent years, the field of neuroscience has made giant leaps in measuring how the brain works, how language is processed neurally, and how learning new languages rewires the brain. Multiple studies now convincingly show that language spans a broad array of interacting regions, including the frontal, temporal, parietal, and occipital lobes, as well as the brain stem.

The extensive parallel processing of language in the cognitive system is of course not unique to multilinguals. Recent studies suggest that sensory and lexico-semantic information is processed in parallel in the language system in general, including in monolinguals. It turns out that areas of the brain that were previously thought to come online later during language processing actually come into play right away when sound is present. Scientists used to think that speech processing followed a serial path, where simple acoustic information like sound frequency was processed first by the primary auditory cortex, and only later was the sound transformed into meaningful words in the superior temporal gyrus. New methodologies make it possible to place small electrodes covering the entire auditory cortex to simultaneously collect neural signals for language mapping. These new neuroscience experiments reveal that rather than transforming low-level representation of sounds into high-level representation of words in a serial manner, the brain processes them in parallel.

The parallel activation in multilingual language processing also provides another way to shine a light on the non-modularity of the human mind. The seeds of the debate about the modularity of mind lie in the pseudoscience of phrenology dating to the 1700s and 1800s. Phrenologists such as Franz Joseph Gall (1758–1828) claimed that a person's mental faculties could be located to specific physical areas of the brain. When you see images of the brain that show a specific area dedicated to X, another area dedicated to Y, and a third area dedicated to Z, that's a form of phrenology.

In the twentieth century, the work of philosopher Jerry Fodor breathed new life into the idea of mind modularity. Although his book *Modularity of Mind* removed the notion that mental faculties have precise physical locations in the brain, it provocatively argued that the functions themselves are modular. That is, that the mind consists of distinct, established, and evolutionarily developed modules that do not interact or influence one another—a separate module for language, a separate module for perception, a separate module for memory, and so on.

New methodologies now provide data that Fodor did not have access to decades ago and show that the brain is in fact not modular. A brain's overall function and the intelligence it generates cannot be understood by studying modules independently. The massive parallel co-activation of multiple languages and its impact on other cognitive functions is yet another nail in the coffin of the modularity of mind.

The modern understanding of neurolinguistics is ultimately less spatial. Think of the neural networks of your brain as any other complex system explained by emergence theory. Complex systems have two key properties: (1) the whole is greater than the sum of its parts, and (2) they are highly interconnected and dynamic.

Our capacity for language (all languages) can be considered an emergent property of the whole brain working in concert. Extending the concert analogy, speaking English versus French is less like playing the tuba versus the violin and more like the entire orchestra playing Beethoven's Fifth versus Tchaikovsky's Sixth. A multilingual person may selectively lose one language but not another despite their reliance on largely overlapping neural networks; even if two symphonies are played by the same orchestra, losing the violinists could be more detrimental for one piece than the other.

The way that language abilities can change over time is explained by the second property: the brain is a self-organizing organism that learns and adapts based on input and experience. Neural networks emerge and change, connections strengthen as a result of use, and synaptic pruning occurs with disuse. The principle behind emergence was described mathematically by Alan Turing to demonstrate that a complex organism could assemble itself without a master planner.

Self-organizing systems are present in both nature (like slime-mold behavior and ant colonies) and the industrial world (like the layouts of cities), and humans are now creating increasingly complex self-organizing networks using artificial intelligence. AI can learn autonomously by trying to solve a problem again and again, countless times, in an endless game of trial and error. Over time the system figures out what works best and can even beat grand masters at chess, something once considered impossible. This automatic self-organization and self-replication of artificial neural networks has parallels to human intelligence emerging as a result of the interaction among multiple components of the brain.

While each individual neuron has a limited capacity, when many neurons connect and interact with one another, the sum becomes greater than its parts and can self-organize in ways that enable complex cognitive function. In multilinguals with their many languages, the complexity of this self-organizing system is even greater. When two neurons respond to a stimulus (such as a spoken word), they begin to form chemical and physical pathways to each other, which are strengthened or weakened depending on how often they are co-activated together. For instance, the words *sleep* and *tired* are more likely to occur together than the words *sleep* and *green*. Over time, changes to how the neurocognitive system functions can alter the physical structure of the brain.

Neural firing is the basis for learning and is reflected in the formation of gray matter and white matter in the brain. Learning another language doesn't just give you different words or more words. It rewires your brain and transforms it, creating a denser tapestry of connectivity. Yes, language allows us to transmit information externally, makes communication possible, and connects us to other people. But it also builds connections internally, among firing neurons, forging new neural pathways and strengthening existing ones to make more efficient use of brain structures and to maximize learning and optimize function.

Just as exercise can change our bodies, so can mental activity, such as learning and using another language, shape the physical structures of our brains. Bilinguals have been found to have increased gray-matter density in frontal regions. Gray matter is where the brain houses neural cell bodies and serves to process information; white matter is made up of myelinated axons and transmits signals from one gray-matter region to another through nerve impulses. A simplified analogy is to think of cities connected by highways. In this analogy, the gray matter is where the processing happens (the cities) and the white matter is what provides the communication (the highways) between gray-matter areas. A study in the journal *Nature* reported that bilinguals with higher second-language proficiency and earlier age of second-language acquisition had higher gray-matter density in several cortical areas.

Multilinguals also have increased white matter in the tracts connecting frontal control areas to posterior and subcortical sensory and motor regions. This difference may allow them to offload some of the work that is typically done by frontal areas that perform cognitive tasks to areas that handle more procedural activities.

Although gray-matter volume and white-matter integrity both decline with age, knowing multiple languages can help slow that decline. Through experiences, our brains have the remarkable ability to reorganize and form new connections between neurons. Multilingual experience not only changes brain structures involved in language processing but also alters the connectivity among brain areas and structures that are not specific to language, and changes performance even when no language is involved.

THE newest research on multilingual brains is even more surprising than the findings that multilingual experience changes the gray- and white-matter regions of the brain.

In addition to the structure, organization, and function of the brain, using multiple languages directly changes the chemical and metabolic concentrations of cells. Because neural processes in the brain are energy demanding, metabolite concentrations vary with both neural degeneration and experience-driven brain plasticity. Changes in metabolic and neurochemical activity in the brain are associated with cognitive deficits in Alzheimer's disease, multiple sclerosis, Parkinson's and Huntington's diseases, and primary progressive aphasia. Changes in metabolite levels are also present in cognitive aging. In healthy individuals, metabolite concentrations are influenced by cognitive function such as memory, executive control, and reading. Measuring metabolite concentrations is especially useful because it provides a more sensitive measure of the neurochemical state of the brain than can be observed with relatively coarse behavioral measures.

Magnetic resonance spectroscopy studies of metabolic correlates of the bilingual brain revealed differences in metabolite levels between the brains of bilinguals and monolinguals. The bilingual brains showed increased concentrations of myo-inositol and decreased concentrations of N-acetyl-aspartate, two metabolites that have been linked to experience-based brain restructuring. Both concentrations correlated with the amount of bilingual engagement. It seems that using multiple languages provides just the kind of demanding cognitive experience that alters the metabolite concentrations in the brain.

In addition to changing the biochemical metabolites in brain cells, other cellular differences that are likely to be associated with multilingualism may take place epigenetically. Epigenetics refers to the study of changes in organisms caused by modification of gene expression rather than by alteration of the actual genetic code. The word *epigenetics* comes from the Greek prefix *epi-* meaning "on top of" or "in addition"—like inheritance that is on top of genetics. Epigenetic changes alter whether and which proteins are made and are due to behavior and environment.

Epigenetic changes, such as DNA methylation, can turn genes "on" and "off." These changes are both reversible and heritable, depending on the life experiences of an individual or their ancestors. We see epigenetic changes reversing when an individual smokes and then quits. Smokers' DNA has lower methylation levels than that of nonsmokers. Methylation typically turns genes "off" and demethylation turns genes "on," so demethylation is more likely to result in turning "on" genes that are associated with certain diseases. After quitting smoking, with time, levels of DNA methylation can reach levels similar to those of nonsmokers.

My favorite example of heritability due to epigenetics comes from water fleas. Some water fleas have spiny helmets; others do not. The DNA of the fleas with bare heads and those with helmets are identical. What determines whether a flea will have a helmet is the mother's life experience. If mama flea encountered a predator, her baby flea will be born with a helmet. If mama flea did not encounter a predator during her life, her baby flea will be born bareheaded. The mama fleas and the baby fleas have the same genetic material, but the experience of the mother influences which genes will be expressed in the offspring through epigenetic changes, determining if the baby flea will have a helmet.

Among those who study epigenetics, such phenomena are known as "bite the mother, fight the daughter" and are not unique to water fleas. Even offspring of wild radishes are changed by whether the parent plant was attacked by butterfly larvae. Epigenetic changes were passed down for two generations when a mouse received an electric shock as it smelled a cherry blossom scent, with the offspring of the shocked mouse and the offspring's offspring demonstrating a similar fear of cherry blossoms. Note that epigenetics is qualitatively different from Charles Darwin's conception of evolution, which proposes that variation is inherited and traits are selected across a longer timeframe through multiple generations, as opposed to after the direct experience of a parent.

It has even been proposed that epigenetic markers responsible for extensive information exchanges within cells serve as the "language of the cell." What exactly turns some genes "on" and others "off" and to what extent epigenetic changes contribute to how these genes are expressed is still not well understood. This is in part because the entire field of epigenetics was highly controversial and even considered discredited for more than two hundred years. Even now some scientists remain skeptical.

It seems that negative experiences are not the only ones that produce epigenetic changes. Epigenetic changes also occur as a result of positive and enriching experiences. Rat studies show that stimulating environments preconceptionally in fathers and prenatally in mothers change offspring epigenome, brain, and behavior. When male sires are placed in enriched environments prior to mating and female rats are placed in enriched environments prior to conception and during pregnancy, their offspring have decreased methylation levels in the hippocampus and frontal cortex. For rats, an enriched stimulating environment means larger cages, multiple levels for exploration, an abundance of stimulating toys, and cage mates for social interaction.

The study of how enriching experiences change the epigenetic traits inherited by humans is still in its infancy. Environmental factors such as drugs, alcohol, tobacco, toxins, food, famine, temperature, and light can all influence gene expression. Recent studies report epigenetic changes in children of Holocaust survivors and children of trauma survivors following the World Trade Center 9/11 collapse. Epigenetic influences play a role in early child development, including brain development, learning, and language acquisition and disorders. Epigenetic processes have also been implicated in cognitive and language disorders in humans.

Whether multilingualism produces epigenetic changes remains an open question. We know that both linguistic giftedness (at one end of the language ability continuum) and language disorders (at the other end) have a heritability component. That is not to say one specific gene determines whether a person will have a talent for learning languages, as linguistic ability is associated with multiple genes and their expression.

Brain cells can use DNA double-strand breaks to quickly express genes related to learning and memory. Knowing that enriching environments produce epigenetic changes in rats and that gene expression changes learning and memory in humans, it is reasonable to propose that enriching linguistic and social environments such as those associated with multilingualism can change gene expression in humans. Multilingualism, with its sounds, sights, and experiences of multiple languages and cultures, may similarly drive epigenetic changes. For now, this is a theoretical hypothesis that will require resources to be tested empirically. But the idea that multilingualism is associated with epigenetic changes is consistent with epigenetic theory.

The findings that multilingualism changes the structure and function of the brain, that it changes the chemistry at the cellular level, and the idea that it may even be tied to epigenetic changes, are all the more striking when we realize that something intangible, like language and words, changes something tangible, like the brain and its physical matter. From changes in eye movements described earlier in the book to changes in vibrations of the hair cells in your inner ear described later in the book, learning another language changes your physical body.

It may remind you of that line from the Bible, "the Word became flesh." The Gospel according to John doesn't just mention it somewhere in passing, it's in the opening chapter. Language changing matter is an idea found in many religions, spiritual practices, mythologies, and cultures around the world. Prayers and chants are built on language. Even those who believe in spells do so because they believe that words and codes can make people feel or behave a certain way. But isn't that what language does in the first place? It is magic we can all use.

The Japanese word *kotodama*, or "word spirit," refers to the idea that words have the power to alter physical reality. It is reflected in Japan's tradition of naming eras, like the current era of Reiwa, or "harmony," ushered in by Emperor Naruhito when he ascended the Chrysanthemum Throne. What was once the domain of mythology is now becoming a topic of scientific investigation. We see that language can indeed affect the physical world, including altering the physiology of our bodies.

CHAPTER FIVE

Childhood, Aging, and In-Between

The search for a Holy Grail—an elixir of eternal youth—is at least as old as the Bible. Today, we study the "blue zones," places on Earth where people have longer life spans and higher concentrations of centenarians, in an attempt to learn how to prolong the span and quality of life in our later years. And while a Holy Grail has yet to be found, several variables have been identified as contributing to healthy aging, most notably exercise, nutrition, and education. Bilingualism is another factor that has been shown to provide protection against the cognitive declines that are sometimes associated with aging and that are characteristic of dementia.

Imagine taking a certain road home every day after work for many years until one day the road that takes you home collapses, and that route is no longer available for you to take. If you live in an area where many roads have been built over time, the collapse of one road will not prevent you from reaching your destination, because you can take an alternative route to reach your home. But if that is the only way that exists to your home, or the only way you know, then you have a problem. In the same way, if one pathway in the brain has decayed and is no longer available for accessing memories or information, a multilingual has other pathways that have been built over time as a result of the links between words, memories, and experiences accumulated in the other languages or across two or more languages.

My octogenarian Dutch mother-in-law, Wilhelmina, is fluent in five languages; her mind remains sharp as a tack. She is just one of many older adults whose experiences agree with emerging research: knowing multiple languages is beneficial for brain health.

One of the most striking recent discoveries in the neuroscience of multilingualism is that knowing more than one language delays Alzheimer's and other types of dementia by four to six years on average. The benefits of knowing more than one language for brain health as we age are especially astounding when you consider that, other than exercise and diet, we know of nothing else that can provide benefits of this magnitude. A delay of several years in developing dementia means more time enjoying life and living independently, and may mean the difference between playing with your grandchildren and seeing them grow, or never recognizing them.

The constant juggling of two or more languages creates a more interconnected neural network that compensates functionally for anatomical deterioration. It is not that the brain does not undergo decay in bilinguals with dementia, it is that the more interconnected networks make it possible to operate better with what remains. In other words, it is not that a multilingual will not develop dementia, it is that the everyday symptoms of their dementia will be less severe than those of a monolingual with the same level of anatomical decay. They will be able to cope with it better behaviorally. If you compared a monolingual brain and a bilingual brain with the same level of severity of anatomical deterioration, the bilingual person would show on average less severe memory loss, less cognitive decline, and better performance on standardized cognitive tests like the MMSE (or mini-mental state examination) than the monolingual person.

This delay in dementia onset in speakers of more than one language is attributed to what has been dubbed "cognitive reserve." This is the difference between the physical state of the brain and its level of cognitive function. The availability of alternative cognitive resources (in reserve) is particularly helpful under duress, be it brain disease, stress, or other challenges. Think of it as resilience against damage to the brain. A person with high cognitive reserve will perform better on cognitive tasks than a person with low cognitive reserve, despite similar levels of brain deterioration due to disease, aging, stress, or temporary health setbacks.

In the movie *Still Alice*, inspired by a true story, Julianne Moore plays a linguistics professor who develops dementia. Her character uses external memory aids like notes, journals, and reminders to help maintain her ability to function in the everyday world. Knowing the research and having the smarts to come up with external mnemonic devices to help her remember made it possible for Alice to cope with dementia more successfully early on and continue living her life for a longer time before the inevitable heartbreaking conclusion. Research on dementia and cognitive decline suggests that education level and knowing another language are two variables that can help slow down disease progression. Both of these lifestyle factors, along with exercise, stress management, and a lifetime of curiosity help keep the brain's agility longer.

Of course, knowing another language is not the only type of experience that is enriching and beneficial to brain health. Music is a form of rich auditory experience that benefits sensory processing as well. Simply reading is a form of cognitive experience that forges connections between words and meanings. Even playing video games has a positive impact on mental functions such as cognitive control. Actively engaging in new pursuits, be they travel or doing crossword or jigsaw puzzles, helps maintain our brain health into older age.

Education, especially, seems to make a difference. Authors of a recent study suggest that the memory abilities of an eighty-year-old woman with a bachelor's degree would be on average as good as those of a sixty-year-old woman with a high school education and interpreted the four extra years of education as making up for the memory losses associated with twenty years of aging.

Where multilingualism stands out is that its impact is broader and combines all the benefits of the other activities listed above. The benefits of multilingualism include the auditory enrichment that we see with musical training, the richer connections between words and meanings that we see with reading, the enhanced cognitive control that we see with playing video games, the brain health that we see with engaging in stimulating activities, the improved learning that we see with education, and the delayed dementia that we see with physical exercise. Meta-analyses (meaning analyses of multiple studies) find that the effect of bilingualism on cognitive outcomes is about the same as the effect of exercise on cognitive outcomes.

Another thing that is unique to multilingualism is that, once you already know another language, you do not have to take time from your day to engage in it to continuously reap the benefits. With other activities that stimulate your brain, like taking college classes, or completing crossword or Sudoku puzzles, or exercising, or reading, you need to specifically dedicate time and sometimes money to benefit from them. When you are multilingual, you simply go about your life using one language or another as circumstances require while your brain constantly engages in the cognitive exercise of managing multiple languages. Language selection, inhibition, facilitation, and control are automatized in those who know multiple languages. The brain gymnastics needed to maneuver the languages you know changes your brain and increases your chances of staying sharper longer.

Neuroscientists now make a distinction between cognitive reserve and neural reserve. Cognitive reserve is becoming increasingly used to refer to the building up of compensatory cognitive ability in the presence of neural degeneration. Neural reserve is more selectively used to refer to the progressive "reinforcement" of the brain with changes such as increasing gray-matter volume, white-matter integrity, and structural and functional connectivity. Both types of reserve appear to be improved by bilingualism and become more prominent when bilingual proficiency and exposure are kept high throughout life.

In research with older adults (with an average age of eighty-one), we found that bilingual speakers of English and another language remembered pictures of scenes they had seen earlier better than their monolingual peers, despite the two groups being matched on nonverbal intelligence, number of years of education, and English vocabulary. Within the bilingual group, earlier second-language learning and more years speaking two languages were associated with better memory. Others found that older multilingual adults who practiced more than two languages were at a lower risk of cognitive impairment, and the findings held after controlling for age and education level.

Although comparisons between bilinguals and speakers of more than two languages are infrequent, it seems that trilinguals show even larger advantages than bilinguals in some aspects of cognitive function. A population health study reports that the incidence of Alzheimer's is lower in multilingual countries. Countries in which the mean number of languages spoken was one had a higher incidence of Alzheimer's than countries in which two or more languages were spoken. The incidence of Alzheimer's continued to decrease with each additional language, and there was a direct relationship between the number of languages spoken in a country and the incidence of Alzheimer's disease.

When you learn another language, an entire new world opens up to you in how you connect with people who speak that language and how you travel and experience the world. The effects of learning another language emerge early—they can already be observed in infants—and persist across the life span into old age.

DURING a visit to the pediatrician, a nurse heard me speak with a foreign accent and told me to use only English with my child. Speaking another language would "confuse" my daughter and hurt her long-term, she said.

She was wrong.

Despite persistent myths, there is no evidence that speaking more than one language or dialect will have negative outcomes and will cause the child to develop communicative disorders. Nor does bilingualism or bidialectalism lead to increased incidence of cognitive disability. Children raised with multiple languages or dialects do not stutter more, they are not at an increased risk of developing a hearing impairment, and they will not be "confused." Of course, many children who grow up with two or more languages may develop communicative or learning disorders, but the incidence of such disorders in multilinguals is not higher than in monolinguals; these children would have likely developed disorders regardless of how many languages they grew up with.

Some new parents trust ill-informed nurses, doctors, teachers, school administrators, family members, and even cabdrivers, following the mistaken advice to speak only one language to their children. In the process, they deprive their children not only of exposure to another language and culture that would enrich their lives but also of the cognitive, neural, social, and economic advantages.

Common myths that bilingualism has negative consequences have not only been dispelled in recent years, they have been replaced with evidence that bilingualism is associated with lifelong benefits for children who grow up with two or more languages. In children, these include better performance on a number of perceptual and classification tasks, as well as increased cognitive flexibility and metacognitive skills.

Metacognition means thinking about thinking. It refers to processes and awareness used to plan, monitor, and assess one's understanding, learning, and performance. Metalinguistic ability, in simple terms, refers to the ability to reflect on the nature of language. Bilingual children understand at an earlier age than monolingual children that objects and their names are not one and the same, that one object can have more than one name, and that the connections between the objects around them and the names of those objects are arbitrary. This understanding that language is a symbolic reference system is an important milestone in cognitive development.

In one study, we used a repeated word association task to examine how words are organized in the minds of Mandarin–English bilingual children and English monolingual children. Their ages ranged between five and eight, and bilinguals and monolinguals were matched on performance IQ. The children produced three associations to word prompts in both languages (in response to *dog*, a child may produce *cat*, *bark*, and *leash*). Syntagmatic responses (such as dog–bark) appear at an earlier age and reflect a less developed conceptual system than paradigmatic responses (such as dog–cat). At age five, most children respond to words with syntagmatic responses; by age nine, most children respond to words with paradigmatic responses. Although the responses of the bilingual and monolingual children tested in our study were similar in many ways, bilingual children had more paradigmatic responses for verbs and for their first association response. This suggests that bilingualism changes how we organize information from an early age and enhances our ability to think in terms of categories.

Another cognitive advantage in children who grow up with two or more languages is being better at switching between tasks. An example is the Dimensional Change Card Sort, in which children are asked to switch between categorizing objects (like boats and bunnies that are blue or red) either by color (red bunnies and red boats go together and blue bunnies and blue boats go together) or by shape (red boats and blue boats go together and red bunnies and blue bunnies go together). When sorting by shape, children need to ignore color; when sorting by color, children need to ignore shape. Some find it difficult to switch and change to a new way of sorting after learning the first rule and getting used to performing the task a certain way. Bilingual children tend to perform better on various versions of this task that requires one to flexibly change what dimensions they are paying attention to.

Bilingual children are also better at focusing on what's important and ignoring what is not important. For instance, in a version of the Flanker task, participants need to identify the direction of the fish swimming to the left and ignore the irrelevant distracting fish swimming to the right. It takes only a second or two, but bilingual children tend to perform faster on tasks like this than monolingual children.

There is even evidence suggesting that bilingual children understand at an earlier age that others can hold different beliefs and knowledge than they do, based on performance on theory-of-mind and false-belief tasks. Theory of mind refers to the ability to attribute mental states to ourselves and others and the understanding that other people's mental states or intentions can differ from our own. An example of a false-belief task is having the child observe two puppets playing with a toy. One puppet then puts the toy in a box and leaves. While the first puppet is away, the other puppet moves the toy to a different location. When the first puppet comes back, the child is asked where the puppet will look for the toy. Children around the age of four

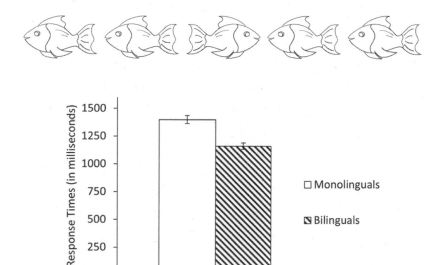

or older will typically answer correctly that the puppet who had left the room will look for the toy in the box where it was originally placed before the first puppet left the room. However, younger children and many children on the autism spectrum tend to respond by saying that the puppet will look for the toy in the new location, which is a response that reflects their own knowledge and does not show understanding of false belief in others. Several studies have now found that bilingual children as young as three are successful on the false-belief task. It seems that because bilingual children must learn to pay extra attention to the language of the person they are interacting with, they develop sociolinguistic sensitivity earlier. Bilingualism benefits the development of social cognition, either because it improves appreciation of another person's perspective or because it helps inhibit one's own conflicting perspective. (Interestingly, bilingual adults are also less susceptible to having an egocentric bias on false-belief tasks than monolingual adults. When the eye movements of young adults performing a typical false-belief task were tracked, despite answering the question correctly, monolingual adults were more likely to momentarily consider the incorrect, egocentric response before correcting that tendency and providing the perspective of the puppet.)

Perhaps most surprising, some of the cognitive advantages associated with being raised with two languages appear even before children can speak. In experiments with prelinguistic babies as young as seven months old, infants learned to direct anticipatory looks to one side of a screen where a reward was about to appear, but only babies who were being raised with two languages learned to redirect anticipatory looks to a new location when the cue began signaling the reward on the opposite side, and to suppress looks to the earlier location.

Fascinating research has also been done on how babies learn language. When we are born, we're able to hear and learn to produce the sounds of all languages—but as we learn the sounds of the language around us, our brain and articulatory system become tuned to the sounds of our native language and we lose the ability to recognize many of the sounds of other languages, usually by the time we enter our second year of life. In a process known as perceptual narrowing, neural pathways corresponding to native phonemes are strengthened, while those corresponding to foreign sounds are pruned. We go from being "citizens of the world" who can differentiate between the sounds of all languages to being "citizens of one country" who only differentiate between the sounds of our native language. For multilinguals, this window of "universal" sound processing stays open longer.

A rich body of research suggests that our brains, both in infancy and throughout life, implicitly extract statistical regularities from the continuous input around us to learn the probabilities of different sounds occurring together. For instance, English speakers learn that a word starting with an /r/ sound is more likely to be followed by a vowel than a consonant. In remarkable research on infant cognition and statistical learning, psychologist Jenny Saffran and colleagues show that babies are able to extract and learn probabilities from the surrounding linguistic environment, suggesting that from a very early age our minds keep track of the likelihood of co-occurring inputs. For multilinguals, each language has its own distinct probabilities of sounds co-occurring. Yet infants immersed in multilingual linguistic environments can keep track of and learn multiple distinct sets of statistical probabilities simultaneously.

In addition to implicit learning via immersion, oftentimes new languages are learned through explicit instruction, such as when a parent points at an object and says its name or when a textbook provides a foreign-language translation of a familiar word. In a study in which we compared Spanish–English bilinguals, Mandarin–English bilinguals, and English monolinguals on their ability to learn a new language, both bilingual groups performed better than the monolingual group on learning phonologically unfamiliar words. Multiple studies have now demonstrated that multilinguals acquire a new language easier than monolinguals.

Similarities have also been found between multilingualism and musicality. Broadly speaking, both multilingualism and music are forms of enriched auditory input and are the kind of experiences that influence brain plasticity. They engage processes that enable one to detect variations in pitch, rhythm, and tone. Studies have found that musicians are often better language learners and many multilinguals perform better on certain music-related tasks (although this is true on average, it is not true for every musician or multilingual). Even nine-month-old bilingual babies were better able to discriminate between two violin notes than their monolingual counterparts, suggesting that early experience detecting and distinguishing subtle differences between two languages may transfer to non-speech sound perception, like music.

Learning to speak a second language and learning to play a musical instrument have also both been found to increase executive function through experience-dependent plasticity. However, the combined effects of bilingualism and musicianship on executive control are un-known. In our lab, we found that both bilinguals and musicians per-formed better than monolingual non-musicians on an executive-function task. To determine whether bilingualism, musicianship, and combined bilingualism and musicianship improve executive control, we tested young adults on a nonlinguistic, non-musical, visual-spatial task called the Simon task that measures the ability to ignore an irrelevant and mis-informative spatial cue. Results revealed that bilinguals, musicians, and bilingual musicians showed an enhanced ability to ignore a distracting cue relative to monolingual non-musicians, with mostly similar levels of performance among bilinguals, musicians, and bilingual musicians.

There is also reason to think that using another language on a regular basis supports mathematical abilities in children, in part due to a link between executive function and math achievement. Two large-scale data sets found that bilingualism was a significant predictor on stan-dardized tests of mathematical reasoning and problem-solving in pre-kindergarteners aged four and five.

In one study, we compared academic performance on standard-ized assessments of math and reading in elementary school children in grades 3, 4, and 5 who were enrolled in one of three programs of instruction—a mainstream English-only classroom, a bilingual two-way immersion (TWI) program that combined the majority lan-guage (English) and the minority language (Spanish), or a transitional English-as-a-second-language (ESL) program. We found that bilin-gual TWI programs benefited the academic performance of both minority-language and majority-language students. Minority-language students in TWI programs outperformed their peers in transitional programs of instruction, while majority-language students in TWI outperformed their peers in mainstream monolingual classrooms. It appears that bilingual TWI programs may enhance reading and math skills in both minority-language and majority-language elementary school children. Other benefits of two-way immersion include positive attitudes toward others who are culturally and linguistically different and executive-function advantages.

Many believe bilingual children in early childhood have smaller vocabularies. This is in part because bilingual children are often tested in one language only and in part because even when tested in both languages, their vocabulary size is often assessed as the number of concepts for which a child has a label, and not the total number of labels a child knows across languages. In other words, if a child has a label in one language and another label for the same item in a second language, their vocabulary is assessed by the number of concepts and not the number of labels (in the case of translation equivalents, only one is counted). A monolingual English child who knows the words *milk*, *house*, and *dog* will be assessed as having a larger vocabulary than a Spanish–English bilingual child who knows the words *milk*, *leche*, *house*, and *casa*. Even though the bilingual child knows four words, the labels map onto two conceptual representations, compared with the three conceptual representations of the monolingual child. This assessment approach frequently places bilingual children at a disadvantage.

When counted across both languages, bilingual children know a comparable combined number of words as their monolingual counterparts. By the time they reach high school, bilingual children no longer differ from monolingual children in vocabulary size in one language. At that point, one if not both of their languages will have a similar vocabulary size to that of a monolingual speaker, but now they have the repertoire of two languages to draw from.

THE control system used to manage the different languages of a multilingual is part of a higher-level cognitive skill set known as executive function. I've mentioned it a few times, but let's dig into it a little deeper. Executive function refers to a set of cognitive processes that includes attention, inhibition, facilitation, working memory, and cognitive flexibility. These functions develop over one's lifetime. They can deteriorate as a result of diseases such as dementia or injuries to the brain, extreme stress, or just plain old aging. The executive-function network enables us to initiate or discontinue a response, monitor our environment and behaviors, and plan future behaviors when faced with novel tasks. Historically, such functions were believed to be regulated by the frontal lobes, but more recent findings suggest that other brain regions are involved in executive function as well, most likely in a whole-brain pattern.

In demonstrations of the famous Stroop effect (described in chapter 1), when asked to name the color of the ink in which a word is written, people take longer to name the ink color if the word they see spells the name of a color that is different from the ink color used (if the word **RED** is written in black ink, for instance). When the word and the ink color match (the word **BLACK** is written in black ink), people name the ink color faster. Why? When the word (**RED**) and the ink color (black) are different, the brain must ignore the irrelevant word and focus only on the relevant color. The ability to decide between relevant and irrelevant information and to choose which to act upon is one of the brain's executive functions known as cognitive control. Cognitive control includes both inhibition, or the suppression of irrelevant information (in the case of the Stroop task, inhibiting the word), and facilitation, or giving preference to relevant information (in the case of the Stroop task, facilitating the color).

When we drive, we need to be able to focus on the road and ignore distractions. When we are in a classroom, we need to pay attention to what is being taught and ignore irrelevant information. Whether you are a surgeon performing an operation, a sniper scoping a target, or a farmer tending to your crops, you need to be able to pay attention to what is relevant and ignore what is irrelevant to complete the task at hand. In other words, inhibitory control is something that all of us use all the time; you are using it now to focus on what you are reading and ignore distracting thoughts like what you are going to eat later. Numerous laboratory experiments have shown that people who know more than one language perform better at many aspects of executive function.

This ability to switch between tasks, to change what to ignore and what to pay attention to, is one that is honed in the multilingual mind by the repeated need to switch between words and rules of different languages and to ignore competition from the irrelevant language. Like a highway with more lanes, the parallel processing across multiple languages optimizes the brain.

As the brain continuously collects and processes data, it filters incoming information through the prisms of previous experiences, including linguistic experiences. The bottom-up input that comes from hearing different languages changes the top-down processing of information by the executive functions of the brain. Because bilinguals are routinely switching between languages or having to ignore irrelevant and competing linguistic information, this form of mental exercise enables them to develop a more efficient control system.

The need to control competition from co-activated languages places unique demands, to the point where the brain regions recruited to resolve linguistic competition become more efficient in bilinguals. In an experiment using fMRI, we found that the bilingual brain exerts less effort than the monolingual brain when resolving linguistic competition, like finding a target object (such as a *can*dy) among an array of objects that include within-language competitors (such as a *can*dle).

The brain's need to continuously manage multiple languages is profoundly transformative. And while it is possible to transmit information from speakers of one language to speakers of another through translation, relying on translated information does not accomplish the same neural changes to the brain that come from direct experience with two or more languages.

A recent MIT study used fMRI to look at the brains of polyglots and hyperpolyglots. Definitions vary across researchers, but in this study, polyglots were people who knew more than three languages and hyperpolyglots were people who knew ten to fifty-five languages. Compared to matched controls, the polyglots and hyperpolyglots used fewer neural resources to process language. The decreased activity within the language network in these speakers of more than three languages is consistent with neuroimaging findings that bilingual brains show less activation when resolving competition from linguistic competitors, and confirms that multilingual brains may be making more efficient use of neural resources for language processing.

Just as having stronger muscles allows you to lift weights with less effort, bilinguals' increased gray matter in classic executive-control regions of the brain makes it easier to manage competition between relevant and irrelevant information (stemming from the experience of constantly managing languages that are relevant or irrelevant at any given time). Think of it this way: both a fit person who regularly does strength training and someone who never exercises can lift a twenty-pound weight, but the task is much easier for the fit person, who can hold the weight longer and do more reps with it. In the same way, a multilingual brain does not have to work as hard to perform a language competition task as a monolingual brain.

It is not possible to know whether the differences observed in these neuroimaging studies are a result of knowing multiple languages or a precursor to it (genetic and longitudinal studies could answer that question). Research on brain plasticity and on changes to the brain as a result of language learning suggests that both of these explanations play a role.

The brains of multilinguals reveal that the effects of language experience may reflect a qualitative difference between monolingual and multilingual processing rather than a cumulative effect of increased linguistic knowledge. Because the same neural machinery can be used for both language and non-language tasks, the benefits gained from experiences in the domain of language can translate to domain-general changes and affect other processes, such as a person's perception and attention.

Bilingual people show greater brain-matter density and volume in regions associated with sensory processing, such as the primary auditory cortex, as well as in regions associated with executive function, such as the prefrontal cortex. The behavioral correlates of these physical changes can be significant, as greater gray matter in the Heschl's gyrus of the primary auditory cortex predicts better speech perception, while increased gray matter in the prefrontal cortex is associated with enhanced cognitive control.

In addition to cortical functions, *subcortical* functions are also influenced by knowing multiple languages. It is especially striking to see changes to subcortical areas of the brain, which are not usually considered to be involved in cognitive function but are brain areas we share with our oldest common ancestors. In a study in the *Proceedings of the National Academy of Sciences,* we found that when adolescents listened to speech syllables, the brain stem of bilinguals encoded the stimulus more robustly than age-matched monolinguals. This enhancement was also associated with executive-function advantages. It appears that with bilingual experience, the auditory system becomes highly efficient at processing sound. This study provides evidence for neural plasticity due to bilingual auditory expertise and for a tight coupling of sensory and cognitive functions. To see changes in the brain stem as a result of bilingualism suggests that the transformation is system-wide, broadly affecting the brain networks at large, and is not limited to language.

Paying attention to what matters and ignoring what does not is important not only for linguistic processing but also for thought in general, including memory, decision-making, and interpersonal relationships. The effect of knowing more than one language on executive function, while not necessarily large, is statistically significant in the majority of studies on this topic. If the brain is an engine, bilingualism appears to improve its mileage, allowing it to go further on the same amount of fuel.

The implications of these changes for real-world cognitive function are not yet fully understood. Obtaining a more nuanced view should help us understand *which* aspects of bilingualism change *which* aspects of executive function under *which* circumstances. It should also help explain why some studies do not find substantial differences between bilinguals and monolinguals. (In studies in which multilinguals do not perform better than monolinguals on executive-function tasks, they perform similarly but not worse.) Like many other things in nature, executive-function differences between groups are not consistently stable over time. But every individual's lifetime can be an ongoing learning adventure.

CHAPTER SIX

Another Language, Another Soul

To learn a language is to have one more window from which to look at the world," says a Chinese proverb. Multilinguals often become somewhat different versions of themselves when they speak another language. In English, the scientist and professor aspects of my identity are more likely to come forward. In Romanian, the daughter and relative aspects of my identity are more likely to come forward. There are also aspects of my identity that are universal across languages—most notably, my identity as a learner is core to who I am. I also noticed that I have different tolerance levels for various behaviors across languages. In English, I find unfounded confidence and arrogance more off-putting than in Romanian, probably because Romanian was my primary language during childhood when I was still ill-equipped to evaluate competence and whether someone's confidence was founded or unfounded, especially in adults. (This may be a good place to share a quote attributed to Moldovan writer Ion Creangă: "I know I am not smart, but when I look around, I gain courage.")

When more than a thousand bilinguals were asked if they feel like a different person when they use their different languages, two-thirds said yes. It's as if multiple mental states and versions of one's self co-exist internally.

In psychology, a well-established taxonomy of personality traits proposes Extraversion, Agreeableness, Openness, Conscientiousness, and Neuroticism as the "Big Five" (the acronyms OCEAN or CANOE provide a mnemonic for remembering them). Bilinguals frequently score differently on these personality traits in their native versus their second languages. In a series of studies with Spanish–English bilinguals, young adults scored higher on Extraversion, Agreeableness, and Conscientiousness when tested in English than when tested in Spanish. In another study, Persian–English bilinguals scored higher on Extraversion, Agreeableness, Openness, and Neuroticism when tested in Persian compared to English. Similarly, Chinese–English bilinguals in Hong Kong scored higher on Extraversion, Openness, and Assertiveness when tested in English than when tested in Chinese. Just as H_2O can be a solid, a liquid, or a gas depending on temperature, a person can be a different version of themselves depending on which language they are using.

In a study with Chinese–English bilinguals, participants exhibited more group-oriented self-descriptions and lower levels of self-esteem when responding in Chinese. Using a foreign language can reduce adherence to social norms and superstitious beliefs, as well as decrease the perceived negativity of aversive stimuli and the perceived risk of potential hazards. These differences in personality when tested in different languages are typically attributed to "cultural frame switching." Such switching refers to modifying one's behavior to different cultural norms. Because language and culture are so tightly intertwined, when multilinguals change languages, they access different cultural frameworks and mental perspectives of the world.

These cross-linguistic differences in multilinguals' self-identification, attitudes, and attributions can already be observed during childhood. Even parenting and parent-child interactions can vary across languages in bilingual families. In an ongoing large-scale research project with Thai–English bilinguals, we are finding that both mothers and children interact with each other differently depending on which language they are speaking in tasks ranging from toy play to book sharing to reminiscing about recent events. These variations in behavior reflect cultural differences between the American child-centered and story-builder, story co-constructor approach and the Thai adult-centered and storyteller, story-audience approach, and align with individualistic versus collectivist cultural norms associated with American and Thai cultures. Switching languages changes the patterns in which a person behaves with their family.

When I was taking French in college, my professor, a Frenchwoman from Bretagne full of flair, charm, and generosity, had us keep a diary in French. Leafing through it recently, I was amused at the way the diary entries channeled what I imagined the French culture and lifestyle to be (referencing sitting at an outside café and smoking a cigarette—thanks, Camus!), giving a very different vibe from my entries in Romanian about feeling homesick or in English about school and work.

My first formal research project on bilingualism was an undergraduate honors thesis at the University of Alaska. In it, I compared how bilinguals gesture when using one language versus the other. I asked Russian–English bilinguals to tell the story of Little Red Riding Hood either in English or in Russian (because the fairy tale is very similar in the two languages). I then transcribed the videotapes of the narratives, classified the gestures into different types according to a system that researchers of nonverbal communication use, and compared them across languages. The results showed that bilinguals used similar *iconic* gestures across their two languages, but different *metaphoric* gestures in English versus Russian. Iconic gestures refers to gestures that physically resemble the meaning of the word they stand for, such as holding the thumb and pointer finger closely together to show that something is small or holding a finger gun when talking about shooting (like when the hunters shot the wolf). Metaphoric gestures refer to representations of more abstract concepts and ideas, like those that may accompany statements like "the next day" or descriptions of happiness or fright. Thirty years later, we are replicating the finding that bilinguals gesture differently across languages in a study of Thai–English and English–Thai bilingual mothers and children. It seems that bilinguals not only use different spoken codes when switching languages but also change their nonverbal communication and body language.

Several mechanisms may drive the influence of language on psychological processes.

Perhaps the most unexpected one is tied to differences in language structure. Economic behavior, including saving rates and retirement assets, as well as health behaviors such as smoking less or practicing safer sex, have been tied to the syntactic structure of a nation's language. Analyses of large national data sets from multiple countries on a range of economic and health-related behaviors revealed that speakers of languages that make obligatory grammatical distinctions between present tense and future tense are less likely to engage in future-oriented behaviors (like healthier eating habits) than speakers of languages that do not make obligatory future-time distinctions in their syntax. Languages that distinguish grammatically between present versus future tenses are known as strong–Future Time Reference languages and include French, Greek, Italian, Spanish, and English, whereas languages that do not distinguish grammatically between present versus future tenses are known as weak–Future Time Reference languages and include Mandarin, Estonian, and Finnish. Speakers of languages that do not distinguish the future from the present in their grammar are more likely to engage in behaviors that benefit their future selves.

Such syntactic distinctions seem to lead speakers to behaviors less likely to account for their future selves in decisions as personal as condom use and as social as national saving rates. Similar effects have been found for visual perception. People are more likely to save money after seeing an age-progression image of their face. Several financial companies are now using facial aging software on their websites in hopes that users will invest more. When our future seems less distant, our behavior changes.

Of course, it is possible that the linguistic structure is not a cause of but a reflection of differences between the speakers of such languages. In other words, it is possible that both the linguistic structure of the language and the future-oriented behaviors are outcomes of other differences between groups, like culture. Even when bilinguals who grew up in one country show cross-linguistic differences, it is still not possible to attribute them to language only, as cultural differences often exist within a country and within speakers of the same language (just look at California and Florida).

A third potential explanation of language-mediated psychological processes comes from what Nobel Prize–winning psychologist Daniel Kahneman labeled "The Framing Effect." Kahneman argued that preferences are constructed and that what we construct is influenced by what comes to mind. What comes to mind is influenced by language. Linguistic components can direct attention and highlight distinct features that subsequently influence experience. In addition to directing attention and highlighting certain features over others, switching languages can also act as a prime. A language primes information associated with it over information associated with other languages. Priming bilinguals with linguistic cues can elicit thoughts and behaviors consistent with knowledge, scripts, and schemas of the associated language and culture, including social judgments and consumer decisions.

A BILINGUAL writer describes pondering major life decisions like marriage and career in two languages in her autobiography:

> *Should you marry him? the question comes in English.*
>   *Yes.*
> *Should you marry him? the question echoes in Polish.*
>   *No.*
>
>   . . .
>
> *Should you become a pianist? the question comes in English.*
>   *No, you mustn't. You can't.*
> *Should you become a pianist? the question echoes in Polish.*
>   *Yes, you must. At all costs.*

Though this scene may seem extreme, it is not uncommon for a person to shift how they feel across languages.

Emotional responses can vary depending on whether a native or second language is used. The native language generally elicits stronger emotional responses, likely because it is more often acquired in emotionally rich contexts. Most bilinguals report feeling less emotional when using a non-native language. In psychotherapy settings, bilinguals are more likely to switch to a non-native language to discuss traumatic or distressing topics. Studies show that verbally induced fear conditioning decreases when using a foreign language and that literary works resonate differently in the native versus second language. In a functional neuroimaging study of bilingual brains, reading emotional passages from a Harry Potter book elicited stronger responses in several brain areas (including the amygdala, involved in emotion processing) in the native language than in the second language. One wonders, can wizards and witches still cast a spell in a second language? I'm standing by for an owl post with an answer to this question.

The patterns of decreased emotion when using a non-native language have also been corroborated by physiological evidence of less emotional reactivity when processing foreign-language stimuli. Skin-conductance response has been used to measure differences in emotional arousal across languages. When the nervous system is aroused, sweat-gland activity increases and skin conductance goes up. Two electrodes on, say, the fingers or hand of a person provide skin-conductance measures of physiological arousal. Skin-conductance responses show greater electro-dermal activity when participants hear or read emotionally charged words in a native rather than in a second language. In experiments with Spanish–English bilinguals, galvanic skin responses were stronger when participants' mothers were called insulting names in Spanish (the native language) than in English. So the next time you are abroad and about to insult someone in a language that is native for you but not for them, keep in mind that you're likely to get more riled up than they are.

Even when the content of a message is fully understood, receiving a reprimand, discussing a distressing experience, or reading an emotional passage are likely to be more evocative in a native language. When the artist Camila Cabello, in her hit song "Señorita," tells Shawn Mendes, "I love it when you call me señorita," she expresses what all speakers of multiple languages know—that words vary in the intensity and valence of the emotions they elicit in each language.

That different words or different ways of saying a word can elicit distinct emotions is something that happens within a single language as well, of course. One of my students asked me not to call her by her full name and to instead use an abbreviated version because, she said, her parents only used her full name when she was being reprimanded.

Many English speakers will similarly tell you that they knew when they were in trouble by the way their parents would use their middle name in addition to their first name.

A study of Chinese–English young adults in the United States found that bilinguals were more comfortable with English for sexual communication and that Chinese conveyed more intense emotions when expressing negative feelings. In some languages, different words express different kinds of love—say, one word for romantic love, another word for familial or parental love, and a different word for loving a pet or a food or item of clothing. Sex, too, is defined differently across languages, and sometimes within the same language by different people or groups. Anyone who lived through the '90s remembers President Bill Clinton's "I did not have sexual relations with that woman" raising a public discussion about what qualifies as sex.

The Japanese expression *akikaze ga tatsu* literally translates as "the autumn breeze begins to blow" but means "falling out of love." *Kenjataimu* is the Japanese word describing a "man's post-orgasm period when he can think clearly because his mind is free of sexual desire." The Japanese word for male masturbation translates literally to "a thousand rubs," whereas the Japanese word for female masturbation translates literally to "ten thousand rubs." As with cross-linguistic differences in how people describe color or time, the different words people use to talk about sex and love can both reflect and contribute to differences in how people think about their most intimate behaviors and relationships.

Not surprisingly, words for emotions are often not easy to translate. One of my favorites is the Icelandic word *sólviskubit*, referring to the feeling of guilt associated with choosing not to take advantage of the nice weather outside. I think of it when I am sitting at my computer looking out at a rare nice day in Chicago. Another word that captures multidimensional emotions in another language is the Chinese word 報復性熬夜 (*bàofù xìng áoyè*) for the feeling in which people who don't have much control over their daytime life refuse to go to bed early in order to regain a sense of freedom during late-night hours (a new English phrase denoting a similar idea, possibly as a result of increased online interactions between speakers of different languages, is "revenge bedtime procrastination"—I am guilty of it!). What else? How about the Icelandic word *flugviskubit*, which describes the feeling of shame associated with traveling by airplane due to its negative impact on the environment; the Japanese word *mononoaware* for the feeling of being simultaneously sad and appreciative of the nature of things; the Danish word *hygge* and Dutch word *gezellig* for feeling cozy and comfortable and content and experiencing conviviality and well-being; the Tagalog word *gigil* for the urge to squeeze or pinch something or someone that is unbearably cute; and the German word *Sehnsucht* for the feeling of inconsolable longing in the human heart for we know not what. There are also the emotions *amae* in Japanese (presumed indulgent dependency with a mix of sweetness and naïveté); *fago* in Ifaluk (a mix of love, compassion, and sadness); and *lajja* in Bengali (a version of shame and modesty).

It can be argued that multilinguals, as a result of having a larger repertoire of words for labeling emotions across their languages, are able to *experience* more emotions. Whether having a word to accurately label and capture a feeling influences how you actually feel remains a contested topic (the Sapir–Whorf conundrum raising its head yet again) in areas as diverse as child development, interpersonal relationships, and psychotherapy. Research on affect labeling finds that labeling your feelings disrupts amygdala activity in response to emotional stimuli. Participants who were asked to verbally describe how they felt before giving a public presentation showed greater reduction in physiological activation than control participants. This suggests that labeling our emotions can indeed influence how we feel. At the same time, emotions can transcend linguistic boundaries. A few years ago, I attended a wedding in Hong Kong between a mostly monolingual

English-speaking American man and a mostly monolingual Mandarin-speaking Chinese woman who communicated with each other primarily via Google Translate. You could say that their common language was love.

IN addition to shaping how we feel, perceive, and think about the world, language also shapes what we remember. My entry into academia and ultimately psycholinguistics was through memory, specifically through childhood amnesia, after reading an article about childhood amnesia in the *Journal of Experimental Psychology*. Childhood amnesia refers to our inability to remember events from the first months or years of life (the exact time frame is disputed, but it is typically considered to start from birth and last to approximately the age of two to four years, though it varies across people).

The limited language development in babies is thought to be one of the reasons behind childhood amnesia. Not having the linguistic knowledge and framework onto which to scaffold the memories of our lives in those first years may be contributing to our inability to remember them. Humans develop language and life memories in tandem: the two are coiled together, supporting each other.

The writings of Ulric Neisser—on cognitive psychology, on memory, on the self, on intelligence, on visual perception—influence how I think, write, and do research. His book *Memory Observed* brought the study of memory from the laboratory to real-world phenomena. It underscored the importance of doing ecologically valid research on memory that has relevance for daily life. Like Oliver Sacks's *The Man Who Mistook His Wife for a Hat*, *Memory Observed* makes readers fall in love with the study of the mind.

These books, like most popular science books, however, consider the mind and memory purely from a monolingual perspective. The mental experiences of the more than half of the world's people who use multiple languages are assumed to be identical to those of monolinguals, as if knowing another language does not change our memory and our remembered self. This is a blind spot in the study of human memory.

The language one speaks influences memory in at least three ways:

1. Through language co-activation at the time of encoding
2. Through language-dependent memory
3. Through the labels used in remembering

The first way in which multilinguals remember things differently is due to the co-activation of more than one language in the multilingual mind. When looking for a fly, an English speaker is more likely to remember seeing a flashlight because *fly* and *flashlight* overlap in word onset. A Spanish speaker, on the other hand, is not more likely to remember the flashlight because the Spanish names for *fly* and *flashlight* do not overlap. We find that English within-language overlap influences not only what English speakers look at when they hear a word, but also what they later remember. Objects that share either form or meaning are later remembered better than unrelated items. Because word overlap varies across languages, speakers of various languages will remember the things that were part of a visual scene differently. Similarly, bilinguals' memory is affected by whether the names of the things they see overlap across languages, with better memory for items that share form not only within languages but also across languages. When looking for the same *fly*, a Spanish–English bilingual may be more likely than an English monolingual to also remember seeing an arrow, because the Spanish word for arrow is *flecha*. In other words, bilinguals not only look at the world around them differently depending on linguistic overlap but also remember what they saw differently from monolinguals due to cross-linguistic co-activation.

The second way in which multilinguals remember things differently relies on the principle of language-dependent memory. Language-dependent memory refers to the idea that memories become more accessible when the language present at the encoding of a memory is reinstated again at the time of memory retrieval.

In psychology, the theories of Mood-Dependent Memory and Language-Dependent Memory suggest that the accessibility of memories at any given point in time is subject to the mood you're in or to the language you are using. When you are happy, the likelihood of remembering happy memories is higher, and when you are sad, the likelihood of remembering sad memories is higher (which is one reason depression can be such a vicious cycle). With language, in the same way, the likelihood of remembering something increases if you are using the same language that was used when the original event occurred.

When prompted in English with words like *doctor*, *birthday*, *cat*, or *dog*, Russian–English bilinguals were more likely to remember autobiographical events that happened in their lives when English was spoken and that included other English speakers, whereas when prompted with the translation equivalents of those words in Russian, they were more likely to remember autobiographical events that happened in their lives when Russian was spoken and that included other Russian speakers. Bilinguals also express more intense emotion when describing autobiographical memories in the language in which the memory took place. People who speak multiple languages remember different things about their lives and recall information about the world differently in their native versus their second languages because the accessibility of those memories varies. What comes to the forefront changes across languages. Bilinguals are more likely to recall events that happened in a certain language when the same language is used again. In turn, the memories accessed influence how we think about ourselves and our lives and how we interact with others.

Even recalling knowledge in subjects like biology, chemistry, history, and mythology can be subject to a match between the language used at the time of learning and the language used at the time of testing. When Spanish–English bilingual college students learned information in Spanish, they remembered it better when tested in Spanish than when tested in English. Likewise, when they learned information in English, they remembered it better when tested in English. In other words, memory was better when tested in the same language in which the information was learned. Of course, ultimately the goal of learning is to be able to access information in a decontextualized manner (it would do us little good if we only remembered things when tested in the same language, location, or mood in which we originally learned those things), and for the most part that is indeed the case—we do remember things across languages, contexts, and moods. Yet at the same time, slight variations in what and how we remember can be observed when the circumstances experienced at encoding are reinstated at retrieval. This is why when we return to a location we have not been to in a long time, we can be flooded with memories we thought were long forgotten. The same goes for language—when we once again use a language we have not used in a while, old memories come rushing back. Although perhaps not essential in most daily life situations, occasionally finding just the right cue to jog a much-needed memory can make a big difference, and language can be just the cue one might need.

In a study of immigration memories, we found that negative emotion words were more frequent than positive emotion words, especially for those who immigrated at a later age. We also found that bilinguals used more emotion words in their second language than in their first language. Perhaps the second language gives the speaker more distance from the emotional experience and one may need to use more emotion words to achieve emotional parity with the native language.

The third way in which memory is influenced by language stems from differences across languages in how things are labeled. For example, Spanish uses two different words to refer to a corner, one word for inside corner (*rincón*) and another word for outside corner (*esquina*). Speakers of Spanish have better memory for where items are presented in a display that involves corners than speakers of English because of the availability of two different words to refer to the spatial relations of objects relative to a corner. Similarly, Korean uses different words to refer to tight fit, as in the fit of a letter in an envelope (*kkita*) and loose fit, as in an apple in a bowl (*nehta*). This availability of different labels changes how precisely we remember exact aspects of our environment that our linguistic labels mark.

Multilinguals will often tell you that the accessibility of their memories is influenced by the labels that exist in their language. English has one single word for cousin, whereas Chinese has eight different words for cousin, depending on whether the cousin is on the maternal or paternal side, male or female, and older or younger. Simply by using the appropriate word for a relative, the additional information becomes immediately available, influencing what one accesses and remembers about the relative in a fraction of the time it takes a speaker of a language that does not make those distinctions. In some languages, like Bengali, the same word is used to refer to eating, drinking, and even smoking. Which may provide a convenient excuse for teenagers explaining the difficulty remembering who was and was not drinking or smoking at a party.

Tangible consequences of a multilingual's language use and their memory can be found in studies of culpability. Mock jurors render different judgments depending on whether they are using their native or second languages. For instance, the use of modal verbs that express possibility, such as "may" versus "might," did not change decision-making in native English speakers. However, such modal verbs were processed differently by non-native English speakers. When presented with statements such as "The man might have dropped the bag by the bushes," speakers of English as a second language considered events that were described using the word *may* as more likely than those described using the word *might*. The estimated certainty of a witness was significantly higher when *may* was used and lower when *might* was used.

Speakers of a single language are also susceptible to effects of labels on memory. Even within a single language, after seeing a film of a traffic accident and being asked how fast the cars were going, people report a higher speed if the word *smashed* is used than if the word *bumped* is used during questioning. Labels influence our memory daily, as advertisers well know when selecting just the right word for promoting their products. Notice the names of the pharmaceuticals in commercials next time you are watching TV. Research has shown that pharmaceutical drugs with names that are easier to pronounce are perceived to be safer and are recommended at higher doses.

The study of how language influences memory in legal settings was pioneered by Elizabeth Loftus, a trailblazer in research on ecologically valid, real-world memory phenomena. Her work (as well as that of Stephen Ceci and others) has had a major influence on how I think about memory—namely, that it is reconstructive and inexact, and that the linguistic labels used influence those reconstructions. When worded in a particular way, misinformation and leading questions can even lead to false memory.

In a now-classic study, Dr. Loftus and her collaborators interviewed people about memories that included the description of an event that did not happen (like getting lost in a mall) alongside several events that did happen. They discovered that many not only accepted the fabricated event as a true memory but also added details that they believed they remembered. I replicated this study with a fabricated event about hitting a dog with a car. I sent a questionnaire to parents of undergraduate students asking them to describe salient memories from their children's childhoods, and specifically asked whether a dog or any other animal had ever been hit by a car that their child would know about. I then interviewed the students about their childhoods using the authentic childhood memories their parents provided, along with the inserted fabricated event. Like in other studies of false memory, some not only accepted a fabricated event as a true memory but also claimed to remember details that were never provided (like the size or color of the dog, or the time of day).

In multilinguals, memory can be influenced by both the native and the non-native languages. Although human memory in general is susceptible to false intrusions and false memories, whether bilinguals are more susceptible to false memory in their native or non-native language is unclear. Some studies find greater rates of false memory in the native language, others in the second language, and still others find that it depends on levels of proficiency, relative dominance, age of the person when testing took place, and age at which the languages were acquired.

What is clear, however, is that the influence of language on the accessibility of memories has many real-world implications, including interviewing bilingual witnesses in legal cases, providing psychotherapy to bilingual clients, and creating optimal conditions for remembering important information. Dr. Loftus and I are currently serving as expert witnesses in an ongoing legal case involving questioning a bilingual person—just one of many real-world situations in which language and memory interact in ways that can have profound consequences for one's life.

DECISION-MAKING in real-world situations regularly involves ethical considerations. Which brings us to the question: Do those ethical considerations speak louder in a second language?

In the haunting story "The Ones Who Walk Away from Omelas," fiction writer Ursula K. Le Guin writes about a city whose residents live a life of joy and prosperity and happiness, knowing no hardship, every moment a celebration and a festival. That is, until the day comes when each of them learns the truth behind what powers their idyllic life—the suffering of one child, left alone in agony and misery and pain. Helping the child or any act of kindness toward the child, however small, would end the blissful life of the entire city. Upon learning the truth, some of the residents choose to walk away from the city of Omelas, into the unknown.

It's a short story with long-lasting resonance. What would you do? Would you turn a blind eye and acquiesce to this arrangement, sacrificing one child for the benefit of an entire city? Would you help the child and end their suffering even if that meant the end of Omelas's utopia? Or would you walk away? And would your decision change depending on the language in which you read the story and were asked to make your choice? (This is an experiment waiting to be run but also something we do every day as consumers, to a smaller and less dramatic extent.)

In ethics, *deontology* refers to the doctrine that the morality of an action should be based on whether the action itself is right or wrong rather than on its consequences. In contrast, *utilitarianism* refers to the doctrine that actions should be based on the greater benefit to the greatest number of people. It turns out that the language one speaks influences how deontological or utilitarian one's moral decisions are.

The Foreign Language Effect suggests that a foreign language yields more utilitarian decisions when faced with moral dilemmas, such as whether to sacrifice one person to save five, likely due to the increased psychological distance and decreased emotionality of a foreign language. Use of a second language decreases adherence to deontological values focused on the costs of sacrifice that are more closely tied to emotion and increases accessibility of utilitarian values focused on the benefits of sacrifice that are more closely tied to reflection and deliberation. People are more likely to make decisions that are of greater social benefit when using their non-native language, even when those decisions cause them internal emotional distress.

Using a second language leads to more logical and rational decisions than using a native language in moral judgments, financial allocations, and choices about health and medical care, and can even suppress superstition. Studies of speakers of multiple languages reveal that use of a foreign language can systematically alter bilinguals' judgments and preferences in domains such as taking risks, saving money, consumer decisions, environmental conservation, social identity, personality, and self-construal.

When Chinese–English bilinguals made gambling decisions that were each followed by positive or negative feedback and a monetary gain or loss ("Wonderful! +$10" or "Terrible! −$3"), positive feedback in the non-native language elicited fewer gambles and decreased the "hot hand" effect.

Use of a foreign language also reduces bias by how a problem is framed, as demonstrated by the 1979 "Disease Problem." The classic Disease Problem starts with the premise that if you do nothing, six hundred people will die from a disease. From there on, it proceeds in two ways, one framed in terms of gains and the other framed in terms of losses. In the version in which your options are framed in terms of gains, if you choose Option 1, two hundred people will be saved, and if you choose Option 2, there is a one-third chance that everyone will be saved and a two-thirds chance that no one will be saved. In the version in which your options are instead framed in terms of losses, if you choose Option 1, four hundred people will die, and if you choose Option 2, there is a one-third chance that no one will die and a two-thirds chance that everyone will die. Despite the two problems being formally identical, highlighting potential gains (two hundred people will be saved) tends to make people more risk-averse, resulting in a greater preference for the guaranteed outcome promised by Option 1. This emotionally driven bias is reduced in a foreign language, leading to more consistent risk preferences regardless of how the problem is presented. In other words, people's preferences are less affected by how the problem is framed in the foreign language compared to the native language.

In general, engaging with innovative but potentially aversive products (such as drinking recycled water or eating insect-based food) is perceived as less disgusting in a foreign language. When asked to judge the risks and benefits of nuclear power, pesticides, chemical fertilizers, and nanotechnology, bilinguals evaluated these as less risky and more beneficial when making the judgments in their second language. In a similar vein, bilinguals were more likely to drink certified-safe recycled water when asked in their second language than when asked in their native language.

Even medical decisions, such as the likelihood of accepting preventative care (like vaccinations) and medical treatments (like surgeries), differ depending on whether the questions and answers are given in the native or second languages. From immigrant families to foreign-born doctors, millions of practitioners and patients worldwide make healthcare decisions using a combination of native and non-native languages. Nearly 30 percent of all physicians in the United States are immigrants, working alongside millions of foreign-born nurses, technicians, and aides. Combined with the millions of multilinguals around the world who live their lives in a language other than their native tongue, it is clear that important decisions, such as those about our physical and mental health, are routinely made while using a foreign language.

When bilinguals were asked to evaluate a series of medical scenarios in either their native or non-native language, using a foreign language decreased the perceived severity of disease symptoms and treatment side effects and increased sensitivity to probabilistic information about personal risks. Medical conditions were perceived to be easier to cure, less physically painful, and less emotionally distressing in a second language. Using a second language also increased sensitivity to costs and benefits of preventative care and increased acceptance of experimental treatments.

The fact that use of a native versus foreign language changes how people evaluate the consequences of accepting and declining preventative treatment carries implications for millions of providers and patients who routinely make medical choices in their non-native tongue. Language experience and exposure can systematically alter how we interpret health-related information, with significant impact on individual and public health.

"My language is my awakening," says a Maori proverb of the Indigenous Polynesian peoples of New Zealand. What we believe in, how we vote, what we like, and who we are, are all subject to linguistic influences—we become somewhat different versions of ourselves when we use one language versus another. This is because each language is associated with somewhat different sets of experiences, memories, emotions, and meanings, and their accessibility differs across languages. As a result, different aspects of one's self come to the forefront depending on the language in use.

PART TWO

SOCIETY

For last year's words belong to last year's language
And next year's words await another voice.
—T. S. Eliot, "Four Quartets"

CHAPTER SEVEN

The Ultimate Influencer

When my children were about two years old, I used to shock family members, friends, other parents, or just random people who would overhear us in public with conversations with my toddler that went like this:

"What's four minus two?" I would ask.

"Two," they would answer.

"What's eighty-one divided by nine?" I would ask.

"Nine."

"What's seven hundred forty-five multiplied by zero?" I would ask.

"Zero," they would answer.

"What was the last territory to become a U.S. state, Alaska or Hawaii?"

"Hawaii."

"Who was the second U.S. president, Jefferson or Adams?"

"Adams."

And so on and so forth, on seemingly any topic, from math to politics, from physics to sports, my toddler seemed to know every-thing and have all the answers. It worked every time.

Was each of my children a little genius? Not any more than any other child is at that age. The only difference is that their mom studied and was teaching courses on language development, which means that I was able to use what I knew about language to my advantage in order to get the answers I wanted. The list of questions and answers has a revealing pattern, you may have already noticed.

The answer the child gave was always the last word in the list of options offered. No coach is needed for this performance. At a certain stage of language development, children repeat the last word they hear when presented with a choice. For them, this repetition is part of the word-learning process. Many parents around the world notice this without taking a language-development class as part of raising their child. For busy parents everywhere, knowing that their child will choose the last option presented (even if only for a brief period of their life) can change the dynamic on busy mornings or exhausting nights to get the child to wear the outfit the parent wants them to wear, eat the food the parent wants them to eat, or do the activity the parent wants them to do. Try it yourself sometime with a toddler; maybe even make it into a TikTok.

It is no surprise that language affects our choices, but such deci-sions are not just about our own lives. While the first part of this book considered the influence of language on the individual, the second part pans out for a wider shot of language from a broader social context. It is not only our brains, our bodies, our minds, and our feel-ings that are influenced by the languages we use. Society's structure and function are influenced to their core by language, linguistic di-versity, and multilingualism. From politics to who writes history to scientific advancement and discovery, the power of language is every-where.

Just like I used my knowledge of language development to get my kids to eat their vegetables or to shock an eavesdropping busybody, so do politicians, political commentators, and other public figures on both sides of the aisle use language to persuade—should I say manipulate?—their audiences.

Remember when the Republican Bush administration began calling the "Estate Tax" the "Death Tax," labeled the relaxed emission standards the "Clear Sky Initiative," and referred to drilling for oil as "responsible exploration for energy" and to logging as the "Healthy Forest Initiative"? Or when the Democratic Biden administration changed the terminology used to refer to immigrants, from "illegal" to "undocumented" and from "alien" to "noncitizen" or "migrant"? Just as different things come to mind when you hear "right to life" than "right to choose," so are you more likely to vote against a "death tax" than an "estate tax"—one bringing to mind taxation in times of grief and the other the taxation of the wealthy. This is not a uniquely American phenomenon. In international media, "closing the sky" elicits a very different reaction from the listener than "shooting down aircraft."

In countries all around the world, be they democracies or autocracies, words are selected and new labels are created not because they perfectly reflect what they label but to change the perception of what they stand for. The two most famous Soviet newspapers were called *Izvestia* (meaning "the news") and *Pravda* (meaning "the truth"), and the old joke about Soviet press propaganda was that "there was no truth in *Pravda* and no news in *Izvestia*." In a more recent example, the war in Ukraine was called "a special military operation" in Russia.

In George Orwell's dystopian novel *1984*, a totalitarian regime creates "Newspeak" as a mechanism for controlling the population of Oceania and suppressing subversive ideas such as self-expression and free will—the idea being that if there are no words for these thoughts, then the thoughts themselves will cease to exist:

The purpose of Newspeak was not only to provide a medium of expression for the world-view and mental habits proper to the devotees of Ingsoc [English Socialism], but to make all other modes of thought impossible . . . A person growing up with Newspeak as his sole language would no more know that "equal" had once had the secondary meaning of "politically equal," or that "free" had once meant "intellectually free," than, for instance, a person who had never heard of chess would be aware of the secondary meanings attaching to "queen" and "rook." There would be many crimes and errors which it would be beyond his power to commit, simply because they were nameless and therefore unimaginable.

Art doesn't just imitate life. It seems life imitates works of art like Orwell's novel.

When athletes from North and South Korea were on a joint Olympic team during the 2018 Winter Games, they found it difficult to communicate with one another, despite ostensibly speaking the same language. That's because many Korean words that have continued to be used in South Korea after the two countries became divided have since been eradicated by the North Korean regime (for example, words based on English or another foreign language) and have instead been replaced with original creations, to the extent that dictionaries are sometimes needed for South and North Koreans to communicate with one another.

In another countrywide "linguistic experiment," Soviet authorities changed the alphabet of the former Soviet Socialist Republic of Moldova from Latin to Cyrillic. Latin is the alphabet used by Romanians to the west of Moldova, whereas Cyrillic is the alphabet used by Russians to the east of Moldova. The population of the small southeastern country of Moldova is largely made up of Romanians, who were then forced for decades to use an alphabet that was ill-suited for their native language. Romanian is a Romance language that is the closest of the living languages to ancient Latin, hence its use of the Latin alphabet. The Soviet efforts to manipulate national identity were aimed at bolstering a more Russian and Soviet-oriented identity among Moldovans and building distance from a Romanian and Western-oriented identity.

Just as an individual's self is influenced by language, so is national identity shaped by the language its speakers share. Language channels culture, folklore, belief systems, values, history, and group identity. Which is why groups of people and entire nations at various points in history have been discouraged or even forbidden to speak their native language and had a different language imposed upon them. This happened in North and South America, in Europe, Asia, and Oceania, and continues to happen in several geopolitical regions today. Economic, political, and physical domination attract most of the attention, but dominating through language cuts to the heart of a nation and its people precisely because language and mind are so closely connected. To forbid not only certain words but entire languages is to forbid a certain way of thinking and of being in the world.

National-level language experiments affecting millions of people, like the ones in North Korea and the former Soviet Union, are rare. Instead, language is modified for political purposes in more subtle ways. Relabeling is not the only tactic used. Like children repeating the last word, adults, too, are affected by the order in which items are presented to them. For example, primacy and recency effects in memory suggest that the first and last items in a list will be remembered better than the items in the middle.

Another technique is alliteration, which refers to using the same letters or sounds at the beginning of adjacent or connected words, like "Build Back Better Budget" or "Save Social Security First!" for a more salient and memorable message. Metonymy, which refers to substituting the name of something with a related attribute or adjunct, like the White House for the executive branch of the U.S. government, or Wall Street for the financial sector, is another technique used to manipulate public opinion. Pronoun use (*we* versus *they*; *us* versus *them*), metaphors, and analogies are other ways in which language can be used to garner support, to create the illusion of choice, and to sow division or bring people together. To quote George Orwell again, this time from an essay, "Political language . . . is designed to make lies sound truthful and murder respectable, and to give an appearance of solidity to pure wind."

Politicians frequently use pronouns to manipulate. Using pronouns like *we, us, our/s* in contrast to *they, them, their/s* focuses on differences rather than on similarities, emphasizing distinctions between groups of people. This divide-and-conquer approach is not new. Julius Caesar and Napoleon Bonaparte both used it; as a military strategy it preceded the Roman Empire. But while winning for Caesar and Bonaparte meant conquering other territories, the definition of winning within the same national political landscape needs to be reconsidered.

Multilingualism inevitably raises the linguistic notion of *clusivity*. Speakers of different languages process pronouns differently because languages vary in clusivity. In its simplest explanation, clusivity refers to whether the pronouns *we* and *our/s* (as opposed to *you* and *your/s*) include or do not include the person you are speaking to. In some languages, when I am talking with you, you and I are part of the *we*, but others are not. In other languages, I and others are part of the *we*, but you are not. This is an interesting distinction, because depending on their language, listeners may or may not place themselves in the side intended by the politician's use of *we*. While English is not a language with clusivity distinctions, languages that have clusivity include Mandarin, Vietnamese, Malay, Gujarati, Punjabi, Tagalog, Malayalam, Tamil, Hawaiian, and many others. Politicians addressing voters that include speakers of these languages will want to make sure that they have the desired effect of including or excluding the audience in the intended grouping.

Politicians adjust the way they speak according to the audience they are speaking to. President Barack Obama spoke differently depending on whether he was trying to appeal to Black or white audiences. Vice President Kamala Harris during the Democratic Party primary debates similarly relied on subtle linguistic changes, including aspects of African American English phonology, morphosyntax, and prosody to reflect her positions.

Many political figures are fluent in multiple languages or dialects and use them on the political stage.

In one of the best-known Cold War speeches, President John F. Kennedy famously said, "Ich bin ein Berliner"—meaning "I am a Berliner"—to indicate solidarity with the people of Berlin and to signal the U.S. alliance with Western Europe and its objection to the construction of the Berlin Wall. What made these words so powerful at the time was that they were uttered in German, in the middle of a speech that was otherwise delivered in English. Most German citizens, of any age, young or old, are familiar with these words, and many students in other European countries still study this historic moment in school.

What Kennedy intuitively understood is that using the language of the people he was speaking to on that day in West Berlin carried greater weight and resonated more deeply with the listeners than if he had used English. Kennedy, like many effective public speakers, grasped that language influences not only our heads but also our hearts, something that is becoming increasingly clear through psycholinguistic research.

Decades later, during the war in Ukraine, Ukrainian president Volodymyr Zelensky seamlessly switched between Ukrainian and Russian in his speeches, using Ukrainian when addressing the people of Ukraine and Russian when appealing to the citizens of Russia. He used English in parts of his speeches and interviews with English-speaking media and policymakers, and incorporated words from other languages when addressing listeners from other nations.

Madeleine Albright, the first woman to serve as U.S. secretary of state, spoke English, Czech, French, and Russian. Former secretary of state Condoleezza Rice knows English and Russian. Former Florida governor Jeb Bush is fluent in English and Spanish. Even those who are not fluent in another language have given parts of their speeches in other languages when speaking in communities with a large proportion of voters who speak that language. But linguistically targeted political messaging can also backfire with the targeted group itself when it is perceived as disingenuous or pandering. In the United States, when it refers to the Hispanic voter or consumer, there is even a term for it, *hispandering*.

Spanish-targeted political campaigns in the United States tend to increase support among Spanish speakers but can reduce support among white English speakers. A survey of Republican voter attitudes toward a white Spanish–English bilingual candidate found that use of Spanish was viewed favorably among Latino voters, but negatively among Anglo voters (outside of Texas). A similar effect of more support among Latinos but less support among non-Latino whites was observed when political articles had Spanish-language versions available.

And although the role of language in politics is especially evident, politicians are not the only ones who use language to manipulate decision-making. Advertisers are paid to find the right linguistic combinations that will get us to pay the highest price for a commodity we can, or possibly can't, afford.

When advertising to multilinguals, marketing slogans are often perceived as more emotional in the native language than in the second language. In one study, using a foreign language elicited weaker feelings of ownership when pricing goods for sale. How favorably Hispanic Americans viewed Spanish versus English product ads depended on how favorably they felt Spanish speakers were perceived by other Americans. For those who felt there were negative cultural stereotypes, Spanish ads led to more negative product evaluations. The effectiveness of ad language appears to also vary depending on the product being advertised. Because in the United States Spanish is often associated with home and family and English is associated with work and government, ads related to the home were evaluated more positively in Spanish, while those related to work were evaluated more positively in English. Similarly, ads for luxury goods (like chocolate) in India were more effective in English than Hindi, while those for necessities (like detergent) were more effective in Hindi than in English. Who the advertiser is also makes a difference; the language of ads matters more for ads by multinational corporations than for ads by local firms or brands.

The language of advertisements will often differ when the same product is geared toward different consumers. Advertising of potato chips targeted toward consumers of high socioeconomic status differs from advertising of chips targeting consumers of lower socioeconomic status. For the upper class, the language of the advertising focused on food that is natural and not processed and without artificial ingredients. For the working class, the advertising was rooted in family recipes and located in the American landscape. Advertisements for expensive snacks used more complex language than inexpensive snacks; the former were written at about the tenth- to eleventh-grade level, whereas the latter were written at about the eighth-grade level. More generally, research on the language of food advertising reveals that advertising of more expensive foods focuses on what the product does not include (less fat, no artificial ingredients, never tested on animals), whereas the language of less expensive foods focuses on what is included (30 percent more, now bigger). The exclusionary language in descriptions of the product is intended to elicit sentiments of exclusivity in the consumer.

Multilingual experience may also make someone less susceptible to linguistic manipulation. A study in Norway found that speakers of two languages are better than monolinguals at detecting manipulative language. When presented with sentences that were intentionally designed to be misleading, like "More people have been to London than I have" and "More men have finished school than he has," bilinguals were more accurate than monolinguals in spotting the fallacy and rejecting these statements. The authors suggest that bilinguals are able to exert better top-down cognitive control processes to suppress intuitive answers and do the reasoning required to detect linguistic misdirection.

The effect of language in politics and advertising is so strong that the same person can even hold different political beliefs when using one language versus another. When multilinguals change languages, they often score differently on scales of conservatism versus liberalism. They can change their political opinions, influencing how they vote, their consumer behavior, and social relationships more broadly.

In a study with English–Spanish and Spanish–English bilinguals, political statements (like whether supporters of a president are racist) in a second language elicited less emotion than in the first language, and the decrease in emotionality neutralized the offense taken. More generally, using a foreign language evokes less extreme emotion when judging moral transgressions. In another study with bilinguals, after reading an article and online comments on it, people using their native language were more persuaded by civil than uncivil comments, whereas the civility of the comments had less impact when people were using their second language. Similarly, partisan signals in a second language are less effective at influencing people than partisan signals in a native language. When using their native language, bilinguals are more likely to choose compromise, to endorse moderation and caution, and to defer decisions.

Advertiser copy, speeches, TV and movie scripts, novels, even nonfiction books are written more or less to provoke an emotional response. Long before social media molded our thoughts into bite-size tweets, an apocryphal short story used only six words: "For sale. Baby shoes. Never worn." Packing the most punch into the fewest words is the subject of many marketing team meetings strategizing how to best advertise their products. Twitter did not invent reductionism. A catchy line from pre-Internet culture: "If I had more time, I would have written a shorter letter."

My fascination with languages was in part an accident of birth (being born into a majority-Romanian family), in part a historical artifact (a place of birth where Russian was the official language), in part an educational by-product (of a school where English instruction was mandatory), in part a geographical coincidence (bordering Ukraine and spending summers at the Black Sea), and in part an outcome of reading (my favorite writers growing up were French). I used to love listening to a radio program about how words change over time.

Did you know that a "jiffy" is an actual unit of time equivalent to one hundredth of a second? The etymology of various words across languages is fascinating. Etymology refers to the study of the origins of words and the ways in which their meanings change over time (not to be confused with entomology, which is the science of insects—as the nerdy joke goes, people who can't distinguish between etymology and entomology bug linguists in ways they cannot put into words).

No language is static. Every year new words are added to dictionaries while others are removed as obsolete. Here is an example of how English has changed over the course of just one thousand years, using the 23rd Psalm:

Modern Expanded Bible (2011)
The Lord is my shepherd; I have everything I need.
He lets me rest in green pastures.
He leads me to calm water.

King James Bible (1611)
The Lord is my shepherd. I shall not want.
He maketh me to lie down in green pastures.
He leadeth me beside the still waters.

Middle English (1100 to 1500)
Our Lord gouerneth me and nothyng shall defailen to me.
In the sted of pastur he sett me ther.
He norissed me upon water of fyllyng.

Old English (800 to 1066)
Drihten me raet ne byth me nanes godes wan.
And he me geset on swythe good feohland.
And fedde me be waetera stathum.

As much as each generation believes that it is the first to change language in a particular way or to come up with a new way to mark something linguistically, sometimes what seems new is only a superficially different version of something that came before. Or, as the French say, "plus ça change, plus c'est la même chose" (the more things change, the more they stay the same). Consider the neologism "dead," widely used online by young people today, sometimes in emoji or meme form, as a way to say *exceptionally, very, absolutely* (as in "she's dead beautiful") or that something is extremely funny (so much so that they've died laughing). About five hundred years before the cellphone generation started using it to express how they feel about something, their ancestors in the 1660s began to use the word *smite* in a similar way. *Smite*, which means "to strike with a firm blow" or to kill or severely injure someone, came to express feeling smitten, referring to liking someone very much or having strong feelings of attraction or infatuation.

Even within the same language, people use different words and talk differently at home than at work, or with their grandparents than with their coworkers, changing the way they speak in both vocabulary and tone. Linguists refer to these varieties within a language as *registers,* and most people have many registers at their disposal, to use as needed. If you are speaking to a baby, you are going to use what is known as the infant-directed speech register, elongating the vowels, raising the pitch, and making the contours and the breaks between words more distinct to help the baby learn.

Language variability carries a lot of meaningful information within itself. It can convey social status, identity, and affiliations. Language variation in speech communities is the norm. For example, sociolects are a type of language variety that can indicate social group and social class affiliation.

You may have read George Bernard Shaw's *Pygmalion* or seen the play performed. It was adapted into the musical film *My Fair Lady* starring Audrey Hepburn as the young woman who became the subject of a bet between two linguists. Professor of phonetics Henry Higgins claims that he can change someone's perceived social class and life circumstances simply by changing their speech patterns. After his language classes, a young woman transforms from speaking with a heavy Cockney accent to sounding like an upper-class socialite, with musical numbers and romance woven into the story along the way.

Modifying speech patterns to change perception happens not only in movies. Accent modification is one of the most lucrative services provided by speech and language therapists, despite the ethical questions inherent in changing how one talks to conform to narrow social stereotypes. Unlike clinical services to children with speech and language impairments or to adults who have suffered a stroke that receive minimal coverage by medical insurance and social services, accent-modification services are typically paid for out of pocket by businesspeople, media and entertainment personalities, or anyone wanting to learn to speak and sound a certain way. Before judging too harshly what you may think of as vanity, consider that how one speaks can influence employment opportunities, social connections, and life outcomes. People are regularly evaluated by the patterns of their speech, sometimes consciously and sometimes unconsciously. Accent profiling is real. Sounding like a person who speaks a language or dialect or a social variety of language in a stereotypical way elicits biases and prejudices that can contribute to or even drive discrimination.

Before the 1960s, variation in speech was largely ignored in research and was considered arbitrary and insignificant. Although some variation was studied (like regional change), because most linguists at the time were white men, a lot of variation was discounted because it happened in other social groups. In the 1960s, the linguist William Labov started using new methods, showing that variation is not arbitrary, but is socially significant as a way of signifying belonging to a group. Today, an entire field of sociolinguistics studies variation in language, and its social underpinnings.

Many sociolinguistic experiments that examined language variation were quite clever. In a well-known real-world study, salespeople at several New York City stores were asked about the location of a product that was on the fourth floor, to compare how the words *fourth floor* were pronounced. The salespeople varied in their pronunciation depending on how expensive the department store was. In the least expensive store that catered to the working class (S. Klein), the salespeople tended to delete both *r*'s (*fou'th floo'*). In the most expensive store that catered to the upper class (Saks Fifth Avenue), the salespeople consistently pronounced both *r* sounds. In the store that catered to the middle class (Macy's), the salespeople varied in their pronunciation, and many of them pronounced only one *r*. (Interestingly, in formal contexts, the lower middle class overcompensated, using more *r* pronunciations than the upper middle class.) This was a demonstration of real-world differences and similarities in language based on social class. Other sociolinguistic studies have since revealed systematic variation in language based on region, sexual orientation, political ideology, age, and other categories.

In addition to reflecting social class, pronunciation can also reflect attitudes. What has become known as the Martha's Vineyard study found that residents of Martha's Vineyard, an island off Cape Cod in Massachusetts, used speech that was indicative of how they felt about their affiliation with the island. Residents who had a positive affiliation with the island and intended to stay raised their vowels more when speaking. (The "height" of a vowel refers to the approximate position of the tongue when the vowel is produced—speakers display variation in vowels such as /ai/ in *light* and /au/ in *house*.) Residents who had a negative affiliation and wanted to leave the island had the lowest proportion of vowel raising in their speech. Residents who had a neutral affiliation with no strong views had a midrange proportion of vowel raising. The more an individual wanted to set themselves apart, the bigger the difference in vowel raising.

There are many examples of changes in vowel properties that reflect group identity. The Northern Cities Vowel Shift refers to a chain shift of vowels that is the defining accent feature of the Inland North dialect region of the United States. Think Minnesota. The Northern Cities Vowel Shift is thought to have started in the 1930s with a slight raising of the /ay/ sound. Over time, social learning drove the general vowel shift further, creating regional patterns of meaning. A score of movies and TV shows capitalize on this vowel shift to give a specific auditory texture and activate a cultural framework in the listener (see the feature film *Fargo* and/or the television series of the same name).

Patterns of language change tell us that even though linguistic variation appears random, it is not. Sound contrasts arise in groups to establish and mark an affiliation. At the same time, linguistic variability frequently engenders conflict between the need to identify with a community and not wanting to be categorized and stereotyped. Despite the existence of defined communities of linguistic practice, many people exist "between" categories, able to move across them as needed. Because language can be a source of prejudice and discrimination, studying the speech patterns of different linguistic communities delivers insights into social issues and social structure.

Language is highly effective in activating stereotypes. In one study, bilingual Arab Israelis were tested with the Implicit Association Test in either Arabic or Hebrew. Bilinguals had more implicit bias against Jewish people when using Arabic than when using Hebrew. In another study, Arabic–French bilinguals showed more pro-Moroccan attitudes when tested in Arabic than when tested in French. Similarly, Spanish–English bilinguals showed more pro-Spanish attitudes when tested in Spanish than when tested in English. This research on stereotype activation suggests that attitudes are affected by the language in which they are expressed, shifting in ways that reflect the cultural values embedded in that language.

The same words can carry different cultural connotations. When someone says "You don't need to bring anything," those words mean different things in different cultures. If the invitation comes from someone in Eastern Europe or Asia, the custom is typically to bring the host a gift, however small. For weddings, anniversaries, and major birthdays, the implicit expectation is that the guests will contribute in value at least the equivalent to the hosts' expenditure for the guest, be that in the form of a gift, a monetary contribution, or a special experience, trip, or entertainment. On the other hand, if someone from North America wants you to bring something, they will either create a gift registry or tell you directly what to bring, or perhaps even host the event as a potluck (an unheard-of thing in some cultures—to bring your own food to a special occasion). Whereas some cultures favor direct requests and find indirect expectations confusing and unclear, other cultures find direct requests tactless and impolite and indirect requests are the norm. Direct versus indirect requests vary depending on how much emphasis cultures place on social cohesion and harmonious relationships, and how they define politeness.

The Japanese culture is especially known for indirect requests and implicit cultural norms in language. The Japanese phrase *kuuki wo yomu,* meaning "read the air," is similar to the English "read the room," but carries a much stronger meaning. "Reading the air" is so much more important in the Japanese culture because one often can't rely on the words people say to know what they really mean. Some negotiation classes even teach that a statement such as "perhaps" from a Japanese person may very well mean the equivalent of the English "absolutely not."

In some countries—say, Moldova—when you are invited to a wedding, after traveling across the ocean from the United States, you are likely to discover that being invited to a wedding also means that the hosts will put you up in a place to sleep before and after the wedding, provide you with meals, and of course include you in the wedding ceremony, dinner, and party. In contrast, in, say, the Netherlands, you will discover that being invited to a wedding means being invited only to the ceremony itself and may not include being invited to the dinner and/or after-party, as the invitations to the wedding dinner and after-party are independent of whether the guests are invited to the ceremony.

Having now attended weddings in many countries, languages, and cultures, I have learned that a wedding invitation, although at first glance worded similarly and maybe even sharing a common language, can mean very different things. A Chinese wedding invitation typically involves being included in all wedding activities—ceremony, dinner, party—and not just one of the events. In the United States, the wedding invitation typically specifies the time of the ceremony and of the celebration separately, but it is unusual to invite guests to the ceremony and not the celebration. Even if the invitation is in English, its meaning often varies.

These are just some of the examples in which the meaning of a statement is subject to cultural norms. Although seemingly abstract at first glance, these differences directly affect interpersonal relations. The ambiance in my lab varies dramatically in use of direct versus indirect requests depending on the cultural background of its group members in different years. A majority European group twenty years ago (Ukraine, Germany, Russia); a majority American group (East Coast and Midwest) ten years ago; and a majority Asian group now (Japan, Thailand, Mauritius, China) have each required different interpersonal skills in mentoring and advising students and in managing and supervising projects.

The need to account for linguistic diversity and bridge the divides across languages and cultures is relevant to our personal relationships, our work, and our social systems. With the increased use of technology, interaction between speakers of different languages is becoming easier and more prevalent. Simply being aware that a person or group of people sees things differently in part due to their native language should increase the effort and thought devoted to cross-linguistic and cross-cultural communication.

ENGLISH is considered the official language of the skies. The international language of aviation is English, and regardless of origin or native language all pilots must identify themselves in English when flying and must have the ability to speak and understand English to a level specified by the International Civil Aviation Organization.

President Theodore Roosevelt proclaimed, "We have room for but one language here, and that is the English language," and "We must also have but one language. That must be the language of the Declaration of Independence, of Washington's Farewell address, of Lincoln's Gettysburg speech and second inaugural."

The founding fathers, however, did not favor having one official language for the United States. Thomas Jefferson argued strongly against the idea. Founded as a nation of immigrants, in addition to the languages spoken by the many nations of people native to North America, the American colonies spoke not only English but also Dutch, French, and German. Indeed, the majority of U.S. presidents have been bilingual or multilingual. Presidents John Quincy Adams, Thomas Jefferson, James Garfield, and Chester Arthur knew several modern and classical languages. For President Martin Van Buren and for First Lady Melania Trump, English was not even the native language—Martin Van Buren's was Dutch and Melania Trump's Slovenian. First Lady Grace Coolidge knew American Sign Language and had worked as a teacher of deaf students.

The United States is also home to many dialects. Linguistic varieties fall on a continuum and often result from contact between speakers of different languages. The boundaries between dialects and languages are somewhat arbitrary. Linguist Max Weinreich's tongue-in-cheek definition "A language is a dialect with an army and a navy" is not entirely wrong. The distinctions between languages and dialects are largely a matter of politics. Countries and governments often make distinctions between what to consider a separate language or a dialect of another language based on the sociopolitical dynamics of a region and the implications it would have on national identity, policy, and education. This sometimes leads to differences between dialects being greater than the differences between languages.

For example, Mandarin and Cantonese are sometimes incorrectly referred to as Chinese dialects, even though they are much more distinct from each other than the mutually intelligible Danish,

Norwegian, and Swedish, or than the modern Romance languages (French, Spanish, Portuguese, Italian, and Romanian), which are universally agreed upon as different languages.

In the former Soviet Union, Soviet authorities declared that Moldovan is a separate language, distinct from Romanian, even though linguists will tell you that Moldovan is a dialect of Romanian (Daco-Romanian, to be precise). Moldovan is no more its own language than Transylvanian, or Wallachian, or other dialects spoken in different regions of Romania. As separate languages, they are as real as the vampires who speak them. At the same time, Russian politics would have you believe that the Ukrainian language and nation are not really distinct from Russian, despite the Ukrainian and Russian languages differing more than Moldovan and Romanian. In other words, the statuses of the Moldovan and Ukrainian languages and national identities were not guided by the same standards, and were not rooted in linguistics, ethnography, or history. Rather, they were decided by political ideology. Languages and dialects have always been heavily politicized around the world and used to incite and subdue national movements and national identity.

In the United States, the dialect that elicits the most passionate feelings in both those who use it and those who do not, and is a source of fierce debate, is what is known variably as African American English, African American Vernacular, African American Vernacular English, African American Language, Black English, and Ebonics, although many find the last term offensive and the others objectionable on various grounds.

In the United States today, African American English (AAE) is spoken by many, though not all, of the approximately 13 percent of Americans who identify as African American, as well as by many Americans who identify as multiracial. And although there is some variation across geographical region, age, income, occupation, and education, for the most part African American English is surprisingly uniform across the country. It is rule-governed and follows patterns that are largely the same whether spoken in New York, Chicago, or Los Angeles.

Given that language, identity, and perception are tightly interconnected, it is disheartening to see the negative biases that continue to plague a lingua franca that is spoken by African Americans in the United States. Language researchers know that African American English is not "broken" or "lesser" English. Many of the grammatical and phonological structures of African American English that are in contrast to Standard American English are patterns that are present in West African languages.

To understand why African American English follows the patterns that it does, it helps to know its history. Enslaved people from various African regions and countries sometimes found themselves together on the same plantation without a common language. The human need to communicate is powerful and resulted in the evolution of a linguistic system that was influenced not only by the primary language of the plantation's owners but also by the words, grammar, and sounds that existed in the different native languages that the enslaved people knew and fused to communicate among themselves. Over time, these evolved to become pidgin and creole languages and dialects, including Jamaican Patois, Haitian Creole, Curaçao Papiamento, Mauritian Creole, and South African Afrikaans, among others. These examples of language evolution illustrate that humans need language to survive. When deprived of it, we generate languages ourselves. In a recently documented case in Nicaragua, deaf children created Nicaraguan Sign Language to communicate with one another in the absence of any other communicative code.

The evolution of dialects as a result of cross-linguistic contact between speakers of different African languages can be observed in many other places around the world where enslaved people were traded. Suriname, for example, is a well-studied example of how West Coast African languages interacted with Dutch (the language spoken by those who colonized the island) to produce a creole language.

Patois in Jamaica has many words of African origin, where English is filtered through a distinct phonetic system with fewer vowels and different consonant sounds. It is an amalgam of words and sounds and grammar of English and the languages of West Africa with which it has been mixed, as heard in Bob Marley and the Wailers' song "Trenchtown Rock": "Nuh wah yuh fi galang so / Wah come cold I up" meaning "I don't want you to behave like that / You are trying to keep me down."

As a linguistic system, AAE patterns are not arbitrary and follow clear phonological, syntactic, and semantic norms. The deletion of the copula in phrases like "She tall" or the omission of the third person marker or the possessive 's, although frowned upon in Standard American English, are common in many West African and other world languages. Such omissions can even be seen as efficiently reducing redundancy without sacrificing meaning.

One of the more remarkable skills that linguists have observed is how speakers of AAE can seamlessly switch across dialects from a very young age. Code-switching conceals impressive cognitive dexterity. It is not yet known whether bidialectalism has similar consequences for cognitive and neural function as bilingualism. Research and funding for studying linguistic, cognitive, and neural consequences of bidialectalism are scarce, due in part to the highly controversial discussion around AAE in the mid-1990s.

AAE is increasingly used in literature, popular music, and media to convey not only personal stories but also nuanced and/or urgent social messages. Hip-hop and rap, for example, are two genres of music that have been especially successful at using AAE to amplify messages about race, inequality, politics, history, and social justice.

AAE's strong oral traditions have transmitted essential information across generations. Before genetic testing was available to confirm that President Thomas Jefferson fathered children with Sally Hemings, the enslaved half-sister of his deceased wife, descendants conveyed that truth from generation to generation with no written documents to support it. (Sally Hemings and Jefferson's first wife, Martha, shared a white father who owned enslaved people, but had different mothers—Martha's mother was his wife and Sally's mother was an enslaved woman.)

My colleague Rachel Webster is working on a book about her ancestor Benjamin Banneker, whose story has also been passed across generations through oral tradition. The public mostly knows Benjamin Banneker as the African American almanac author, surveyor, mathematician, and naturalist; the Benjamin Banneker Historical Park and Museum in Catonsville, Maryland, and the Banneker-Douglass Museum in Annapolis, Maryland, are named after him. Banneker's statue is in the Smithsonian Institution's National Museum of African American History and Culture in Washington, DC, and his correspondence with Thomas Jefferson and other notable figures of their time is in the Library of Congress.

What official documents leave out is a story not unlike that of the Jefferson-Hemings descendants or that of millions of Americans with mixed racial ancestry. The family's oral tradition maintains that Benjamin Banneker's mother was the daughter of a white woman sold into indentured servitude named Molly Welsh and an enslaved African man named Bana'ka. According to the family's oral tradition, Molly was sold into indentured servitude as a young girl and, years later, bought two enslaved African men to help her work the land she came to own. After freeing them, she married Bana'ka and they had several children together. One of these children was Mary, Benjamin Banneker's mother, who herself went on to marry an enslaved African man who had been freed. The strong oral traditions of the African American language and culture helped preserve these stories over centuries before they could be confirmed by ancestry reports.

Some argue that AAE is "bad" English and that it limits opportunities for its speakers, ultimately restricting upward social mobility. But how can a language or dialect in itself be "good" or "bad"? These biases are rooted in phenomena that are independent of language. In the case of AAE, that phenomenon is racism. If we remove racism from the equation, AAE becomes just another English dialect spoken in the United States, one of many.

In all, over 350 languages and dialects are spoken in the United States. Other than English and the languages spoken by the Indigenous peoples of North America, the most frequently spoken languages are Spanish and Chinese (Mandarin, Cantonese, Hokkien). Other widely spoken languages in the United States include French and French Creole, Tagalog, Vietnamese, Korean, German, Arabic, and Russian. All of them are opportunities to examine how language shapes our identities and modifies our capacities while broadening our social perspectives.

CHAPTER EIGHT

Words of Change

In English, animate pronouns like *he* and *she* are reserved for humans, and occasionally for animals (and only some animals at that, not all, depending on our representation of the animal's biological sex); everything else gets an *it*. In many other languages, the boundaries between human personhood and non-human natural-world concepts are dissolved. In most of America's Indigenous languages, animals and plants are referred to with the same or similar animate pronouns as those used for humans, and the boundaries are placed not between humans versus everything else but between the natural world and everything else. In the essay "Speaking of Nature," a Potawatomi speaker and professor of environmental biology writes about her native language:

> You hear a blue jay with a different verb than you hear an airplane, distinguishing that which possesses the quality of life from that which is merely an object. Birds, bugs, and berries are

spoken of with the same respectful grammar as humans are, as
if we were all members of the same family. Because we are.
There is no *it* for nature. . . . Those whom my ancestors called
relatives were renamed *natural resources.*

Does the fact that we name our boats, cars, and guns ("Ain't she a
beaut?!") contribute to us treating them with more care than the water,
plants, and soil sustaining life itself? What we think influences the
language we use, and the language we use influences what we think—
and how we act.

In English, inanimate objects are generally referred to as *it.* But
in many other languages, inanimate objects are referred to with pronouns like *he* or *she.* Grammatical gender influences how we think
about the world in two ways. The first revolves around the concept of
animacy and inanimacy, and the linguistically placed differentiation
between animate and inanimate entities in the world. The animacy-
inanimacy distinction in language, as we just saw, is especially interesting from the perspective of ecological justice and how we see our
place within nature. The second revolves around the concept of a
masculine-feminine grammatical gender system.

While most languages have only two grammatical genders, masculine or feminine, others have more than two. Russian and German
have masculine, feminine, and neuter. Bantu languages range in having ten to twenty grammatical genders. Languages divide things into
categories in interesting ways. I have to admit that as a speaker of exclusively European languages that have at most three grammatical
genders, I do not have a clear understanding which of the twenty
grammatical categories goes with which inanimate object, just as
speakers of languages that do not have grammatical gender at all have
a hard time understanding which inanimate object is masculine and
which is feminine. When I used to tutor English-speaking students
learning Russian, they were perpetually puzzled by grammatical

gender assignments that seemed completely random to them. "Why is a pen feminine and a pencil masculine?" they would ask. "Why is thunder masculine but lightning feminine?"

Studies show grammatical gender influences how people think and talk about objects. In one study, German speakers and Spanish speakers were asked to describe objects that had opposite grammatical gender in Spanish and German. German–English bilinguals described a key (which has masculine grammatical gender in German) as *hard, heavy, jagged, metal, serrated,* and *useful.* Spanish–English speakers described a key (which has feminine grammatical gender in Spanish) as *golden, intricate, little, lovely, shiny,* and *tiny.* Once again, we see language altering the mental representations of objects.

In another experiment on grammatical gender, German speakers remembered the name given to an *apple* better if it was named Patrick than if it was named Patricia because the word for apple, *Apfel,* is masculine in German. Spanish speakers, on the other hand, remembered better if the apple was named Patricia than if it was named Patrick because the word for apple in Spanish, *manzana,* is feminine. Features of our language as seemingly minor as grammatical gender influence higher-order cognitive processes like memory.

When native English speakers were taught a fictional language with a distinction between male and female gender, gender effects emerged quickly. Participants were shown pictures of inanimate objects that were of either the "male" or "female" grammatical gender. Each object was assigned as either male or female for one half of the participants and the opposite for the other half. Participants were asked to describe pictures of the objects using adjectives that were later independently rated by a third party as masculine or feminine. The newly learned grammatical gender clearly drove the choice of adjectives participants used in their descriptions—just as the study of German speakers and Spanish speakers would lead us to expect.

Grammatical gender can also show up in baffling ways. In Russian, the days of the week have different grammatical gender, with Monday, Tuesday, and Thursday having masculine grammatical gender and Wednesday, Friday, and Saturday having feminine grammatical gender. Russian fairy tales, stories, pictures, and individuals personify Monday, Tuesday, and Thursday as males and Wednesday, Friday, and Saturday as females. We can only speculate why one of the seven days, Sunday, is neither masculine nor feminine, and instead is neuter. Perhaps it's because Sunday is a holy day in the Russian Orthodox Church and is above being gendered; perhaps it's to keep the number of masculine and feminine days balanced, perhaps it's a message in a linguistic bottle that gender is nonbinary, or perhaps it's an accident of language evolution over time.

Grammatical gender stereotypes have even permeated machine translation online. Anthropologist Alex Shams pointed that out on Twitter when attempting to use Google to translate from Turkish to English. Turkish is a gender-neutral language. But look at how Google translated these sentences from Turkish to English: *O bir doctor* became "He is a doctor," whereas *O bir hemsire* became "She is a nurse." *O evli* became "She is married," but *O bekar* became "He is single." *O çalişkan* became "He is hardworking," while *O tembel* became "She is lazy." Shortly after the collective gasps on social media, the translation algorithms were corrected to provide both gender options when translating *o bir* from Turkish to English—a testament to the powerful impacts of both language and social media.

Gender stereotypes influence our perceptions not only of inanimate items but also of people, including ourselves, and shape the lives we live. Would reproductive rights be perceived differently if "women's healthcare" was consistently replaced with "reproductive healthcare" and "women's rights" was changed to "human rights"?

In an attempt to push back against the gender stereotypes perpetuated through language, social movements in some Latin American countries like Argentina have even attempted to put an end to using gendered language and replace it with gender-neutral terms. But it is easier for a society to adopt new words or replace old terms than it is to eliminate grammatical gender for inanimate items. Indeed, efforts to eliminate grammatical gender altogether have not been successful, but efforts to use gender-neutral pronouns in addition to or instead of gender-binary pronouns are increasingly successful in countries around the world.

In Sweden, the non-gendered pronoun *hen* has recently been added to the traditional masculine pronoun *han* and feminine pronoun *hon*. In France, the new gender-neutral pronoun *iel* merges the masculine *il* and feminine *elle*. Similar changes have been adopted in other languages. In English, the gender-neutral pronoun *they* is becoming increasingly used instead of *he* and *she* as a third-person singular (like the second-person pronoun *you* that is both singular and plural). Spanish speakers are using the word *niñe* as a gender-neutral alternative to *niño* and *niña*. One argument for using gender-neutral pronouns is that they minimize gender-based biases and discrimination. Efforts to minimize the impact of gendered pronouns on how people are perceived and evaluated are met with a mixture of opposition and support from various groups, and it remains to be seen whether this is a transient trend or something that will forever change how we mentally represent gender.

Stereotypes about gender are also manifested linguistically through personal names. Experiments have shown that people whose names are perceived as softer-sounding (like Anne or Owen) are evaluated as being more agreeable, and people whose names are perceived as harder-sounding (like Kirk or Kate) are perceived as more outgoing. The likelihood of getting a job offer, as well as the salary amount, can be influenced by the person's name and the ethnicity, gender, and age information it carries. From the likelihood of getting into a preschool to the likelihood of getting an interview to how others perceive and evaluate us, our names can influence the associations activated in people's minds. Intelligence, competence, quality, and popularity are all likely to be perceived as higher when a résumé, lecture, or product is believed to come from a man rather than a woman, or from certain racial or national groups, even when everything else is held constant and even in studies where the thing being evaluated was entirely fictitious and manufactured by researchers.

Immigrants often change their names to better fit into their adoptive societies. I agonized over the decision of what name to use on the author byline for this book. Do I go with my Romanian name, Viorica, which sounds "ethnic" to a native English speaker and which in my thirty-plus years in the United States has frequently led to (let's call them "interesting") assumptions? For instance, because of my name, my accent, and my dark hair, whenever I would take my lighter-skinned, blue-eyed children to the playground, people would frequently assume that I was the nanny, which would lead to me learning private tidbits about my neighbors from other nannies who felt comfortable discussing them in my presence. I considered using only my first initial for the book, as well as using my last name as my first name. I thought back to reading an article about Ursula K. Le Guin being asked to publish her story "Nine Lives" without her full first name, using only the initials instead, U. K. Le Guin, so that readers would not know that it was written by a woman. And I thought back to reading novels as a young girl written by George Sand only to discover later that George Sand was the pen name for Amantine Lucile Aurore Dupin. In the end, recent social changes, including the publishing of more books by authors who not only have non-majority-culture names but also clearly are from non-majority cultures, led me to the decision to use the name given to me at birth (although it itself reflects Romanian gender stereotypes—my parents named me after a flower and my brother after a tree. My parents, like so many others, believed that a person's name can influence how they are perceived, their personality, and hence their life path—beliefs that both reflect and contribute to social biases).

DISCRIMINATION against non-native speakers in professional, clinical, and educational settings is common. Part of the reason why my academic home at Northwestern University is in a department of communication sciences and disorders is that the different communicative patterns of individuals who speak other languages are often mistaken for disorders. For more than twenty years, one of the primary aspects of my work has been to educate students, clinicians, and the public that *difference does not equal disorder.* Children from diverse linguistic backgrounds, whether another language or another dialect, are frequently overdiagnosed, underdiagnosed, or misdiagnosed as having a disorder. Diagnostic standards and most assessment and intervention resources are based on monolingual and monodialectal speakers. Speakers of other languages or dialects from diverse cultural backgrounds may communicate in ways that are in conflict with the norms of the mainstream culture.

For a child or adult to be diagnosed with a communicative disorder, it is not enough for the communicative pattern to call attention to itself, interfere with communication, and place an emotional burden on the speaker from the perspective of the mainstream culture. The same should be true from the perspective of the person's own culture as defined by their indigenous group. When a young child speaks differently, it is necessary to determine whether this difference reflects the norms of the child's native language or dialect before concluding that it is a communicative disorder. The position of the American Speech-Language-Hearing Association is that children with limited English proficiency are considered to have a communication disorder when the difficulty persists in both English and the language spoken most frequently by the child and that no English dialect should be considered a language disorder.

With the demographic trends in the United States and other countries, the changing patient population is becoming increasingly linguistically diverse, which means that the survival of many health-system practices is directly related to patient diversity. Mismatch in language, communication styles, cultural values, and expectations can cause underutilization, noncompliance, or premature termination of services by linguistically and culturally diverse individuals and families. Early intervention and family involvement are keys to successful outcomes, making it especially necessary to account for variations in approaches to services provided. The rationale for being linguistically and culturally competent makes not only moral and ethical sense for medical practitioners, it makes economic sense as well. Word-of-mouth references and reviews travel fast, online ones even faster and further, and the potential legal consequences can have costly ramifications.

For overcoming linguistic and cultural bias, the first and most important step is being aware of its existence. Simply the awareness that the language or culture of the person you are interacting with may be different from yours can shift social dynamics.

Second, clinicians and educators showing acknowledgment and respect for another's perspective, rather than minimizing it, can keep the window of communication open and increase receptiveness. Hearing the family's perspective and not dismissing it, even when that perspective goes against the cultural norms a clinician has been trained under, can help ensure the family will continue to bring the child in for treatment. This can be hard for a clinician when the specific treatment espoused by the family's culture is not effective. But unless that treatment is damaging and causing harm to the patient, it may be better to support a treatment that the family would like to pursue in addition to the treatment that is the norm in the mainstream culture than to have the family decline the effective treatment altogether. Before nixing a belief, it is best to reflect on whether it is harmless (the placebo effect is real!). The key is to keep the patient's interests in mind while showing sensitivity and understanding. In many cultures, the role of family and community may be stronger and more influential on one's decisions and choices.

Any advice to a person working in a diverse community should start with learning about its languages and cultures. Working with linguistically diverse populations should involve avoiding difficult words and idioms and erring on the side of being more formal rather than less (the United States is on average less formal). Other recommendations include avoiding asking yes-or-no questions, because you could have an entire conversation in which you keep talking and the other person keeps saying yes, only to discover later that your interlocutor does not speak your language and understood nothing you said. Be more specific rather than less specific—the definitions of statements like "keep the baby warm" or "eat a balanced diet" vary across cultures. If you are not sure about the person's proficiency, speak slower, not louder. Use culturally diverse materials so patients, especially children, can see others like them represented in the pamphlets and testing kits. Consider the appropriateness of certain exercises, especially those that require touching (as in touching the mouth of the speaker when working with a child that may have an articulation problem), which may be inappropriate in certain cultures.

Cultures vary in many ways, including nonverbal communication, eye contact, and interpretation of pauses and silence, not to mention in sense of humor and sarcasm. Narrow lists of dos and don'ts are of limited universal value; interpreter services typically surpass any such lists.

Of course, using interpreters comes with its own set of challenges. Regardless of whether the interpreting services are provided by a professional interpreter or by family members, having a third party present can complicate things. I was once asked to interpret for a physician and a mother with a teenage son. The son was embarrassed enough to have to see a doctor for his genital-area-related condition; having the mother *and* a female interpreter there made things even more traumatic for him. He definitely did not want to go into details or share information he could avoid sharing. Situations like those are not rare.

The advantages of using trained professionals are their mastery of both languages, knowledge of the content, and no role conflicts or negative family dynamics. The disadvantage is the cost, which proves prohibitive for most immigrant families. And although some hospitals now have speakers of other languages available on-site, usually it is only for the most frequently spoken languages in the community, and speakers of languages that are rare do not have access to an interpreter in clinical settings. Larger medical practices are now accessing interpreting services via video, phone, or online, which is helpful, but these remain rare as they still add to the cost of services beyond what most practitioners and patients can absorb.

In immigrant families, the children often serve as language brokers for their parents, grandparents, and other relatives. These children lack training as interpreters, they have limited knowledge and understanding of the material, and they may also not be sufficiently proficient in both languages. Imagine being a child who is interpreting for a parent whose diagnosis may be a terminal disease. A breakdown in communication across languages may take place because the child may not want to worry the parent, or may not understand the specifics, or may not want to communicate what the parent wants to say, or a host of other contingencies.

When a child is the language broker for a family member—in doctor appointments, job interviews, testing for school placements, the DMV, visa and citizenship meetings, or any number of administrative appointments—the child may be missing school, falling behind on schoolwork, and risking sleep deprivation, stress, and anxiety. The role reversal between the generations can lead to mutual resentment, and the complex family dynamics can have negative consequences for everyone. Being aware of the complexity of the interpreting dynamics, acknowledging them, and openly discussing them can help relieve some of the pressure experienced by all parties.

WHEN I took the Test of English as a Foreign Language at the age of sixteen, I knew that I had only one shot at it, because taking the one test cost more than the combined monthly salaries of both of my public-health-physician parents in the Soviet Union. Taking the test required a twenty-nine-hour train ride to Moscow. Moreover, I took practice tests at a Moscow library in preparation for the exam because that library was the closest one that had books with old practice TOEFL tests, so multiple trips were necessary. I would arrive to the library when it opened and stay until it closed. I was lucky to score above the required threshold for admission to an American university, just barely, surpassing it by only a couple of points. I am sure I wouldn't have passed had I not done the practice tests and familiarized myself with the exam format—only a couple of points lower would have meant an entirely different life. I probably would have scored higher had I not spent the previous night in the shared compartment of a train, looking out the window at the lights of villages and shadows of trees rolling by. My subsequent ten-day journey to the United States, through Siberia to Alaska, as difficult as it was, was still much easier than those of countless others who overcome wars, hunger, abuse, loss of loved ones, or all of the above. I did not have to risk my life swimming through perilous waters to escape the Ceaușescu regime in Romania or the Castro regime in Cuba. When I read about immigrants drowning or freezing on their journeys, I think, *There but for the grace of God go I*. I was fortunate to benefit from the end of the Cold War and the diplomacy between the Gorbachev and Reagan administrations that made it possible for me to study in the United States.

Stories of children who have to make their way in the world not only on their own but also in a language they do not speak and a country they do not know reveal the challenges that second-language students face. Even when children come with their families, the experience can be jarring. If you ever dropped your child off for the first day of kindergarten and remember the stress and emotions of that day, imagine how much more difficult and traumatic the experience of starting school can be for a child who does not speak the language of the school and cannot understand their teacher and classmates.

Some argue that bilingual education is expensive. However, by not supporting bilingual education, we may end up paying more over time. If a child cannot understand the teacher, is unable to learn, does not acquire literacy, ends up frustrated, and drops out of school, this pattern can end up costing far more over the long term. Dropping out of school is associated with a host of negative outcomes: there are correlations with underemployment and unemployment, substance abuse, poor health outcomes, lower income, changed family structure, and higher incarceration rates. Would we rather pay the salaries of teachers and school principals to support bilingual education or those of prison guards and wardens as the consequences of not doing the former? Investing in schools raises educational attainment and earnings and reduces the likelihood of both poverty and incarceration in adulthood.

Approximately 26 percent of school-age children in the United States speak a language other than English at home. In many states—Texas, New Mexico, Arizona, and Florida—the numbers are even higher. Places where immigrants settle, where Indigenous populations reside, or where multiple official languages are supported have higher proportions of speakers of multiple languages. In California, nearly half of school-age children are bilingual.

Some of these children grow up with one language at home and begin to learn English when they start school; these are known as sequential bilinguals. Others grow up with both languages, speaking one language with some household members (like grandparents) and the other language with other household members (like siblings); these are known as simultaneous bilinguals. Regardless of whether the learning of multiple languages is sequential or simultaneous, it is possible to achieve fluency and proficiency, including equal fluency and proficiency, in both languages.

But bilingual education continues to be a political lightning rod. If you'd guess that the argument is between political parties or races or depended on immigration status, you'd be wrong. Perhaps it is easiest to assume immigrants themselves are trying to push bilingual education into the mainstream, yet many immigrants would like nothing more than to assimilate, integrate, and be perceived as American above their original national identity. Some even argue against bilingual education. Partisanship on this issue defies familiar categories.

Not teaching American children another language is part of a larger problem in the education system. U.S. secondary schools currently lag behind other industrial nations in reading, science, and math. Most students in Europe must study their first foreign language by age nine and second foreign language a few years later.

The likelihood of learning another language is influenced not only by where you live but also by your socioeconomic class. Many children from upper- and middle-class families are encouraged to take foreign-language lessons at school, and some parents pay for private language tutors, support immersion programs, send students to study abroad, or take them on trips to destinations where other languages are spoken, under the assumption that learning another language is beneficial.

At the same time, families in the lower socioeconomic strata—often immigrants and frequently minorities—are instructed by educators,

Students Learning Three or More Languages in Europe

clinicians, and policymakers to abandon their native languages or
dialects and to use only the language of their adopted country. The
parents are often told that using their native languages and dialects
will hinder their children's language and cognitive development and
will result in academic difficulties, even though there is no research
backing up those claims. This contrast in how society perceives multilingualism in different socioeconomic classes is rooted in biases that
have nothing to do with the effects of multilingualism.

People who speak a language that is considered low-prestige are
well aware of the benefits of learning another language, ideally a dominant language that gives them access to the power dynamic of a glo-
balized world and economy. The opposite is less likely to be true,
where speakers of languages that are associated with countries that
have higher economic power do not always see the value in learning
another language.

Research shows that both minority- and majority-language children benefit from dual-language education. Yet, when it comes to dual-language education, there remains a disconnect between research and practice. The issue is frequently distorted and the term "bilingual education" is often used incorrectly in the United States to refer to education in a language other than English—instead of *in addition to* English.

The reason why bilingual education works so well is because it allows children to use their native language to continue learning new academic material and acquire more advanced knowledge and information in content courses during a period when they are still simultaneously acquiring a second language. This makes it possible for them to move forward academically. One of the most apt analogies is the Iceberg Model of bilingual education: What you see on the surface—words, grammar, pronunciation, speech comprehension—is just the tip. What is underneath—meaning, analysis, synthesis, evaluation—is much deeper, weightier, and more valuable.

Just like the small tip of an iceberg belies the enormous base underneath the water, so are the surface features of a language not always indicative of the deeper foundation and advanced critical thought of a bilingual. An education program that allows English-learners to continue growing the deeper cognitive skills in their native language—while learning English—makes it possible to gain a strong conceptual and academic foundation that transfers across both languages.

The other side of the coin is teaching a second language to native English speakers so they, too, can benefit from the cognitive, neurological, economic, and cultural advantages that knowing another language bestows. Actively encouraging and supporting all children to learn more than one language can further benefit the United States as it competes in a multilingual world economy.

Some of the differences in academic achievement between children with different linguistic backgrounds can also be explained through the linguistic and cultural discontinuities experienced by children from non-majority languages and cultures when they start formal schooling. There are subtle and not-so-subtle messages that are not intended to be part of the curriculum, but they are and they impact student performance.

Nigerian American anthropologist John Ogbu observed differences in the academic achievement of Native American children and immigrant Indian children studying in the same school. Both of these groups experience cultural discontinuity when starting mainstream American schooling compared to middle-class white peers. However, their average academic performance diverges, with the immigrant group performing better than the non-immigrant group. Ogbu proposed that minority groups differ on measures of academic achievement in part because of how they view schooling. He suggested that immigrant minorities are more likely to view schooling as an alternative model that allows for different behaviors in the school versus home settings and do not necessarily equate it with acculturation. Non-immigrant involuntary minorities, on the other hand, are more likely to view schooling as a one-way assimilation and acculturation into a dominant group and resist it either consciously or unconsciously.

Immigrant minorities can use a different frame of reference for themselves than the majority-culture frame of reference and consider themselves better off than before immigration or than their community in their home country. They may not always place themselves within the host country's stratification system, viewing themselves as strangers outside the prevailing system. They may also retain the option to go back to the country from which they emigrated. They usually hold the belief that one can participate in two cultures simultaneously, switching between the two, without a threat to group identity. Although immigrant minorities, too, experience barriers to advancement like segregation, inferior education, and jobs not commensurate with education and experience, they may reject or may not even understand the dominant status system and have not yet internalized discrimination.

Non-immigrant minorities, on the other hand, are caste-like and were incorporated into a society involuntarily through slavery, conquest, or colonization. Compared to immigrant minorities, non-immigrant minorities are more likely to use the same frame of reference and stratification system as the majority group. The internalized discrimination and exploitation over generations have led to the realization that their demeaning experiences, lack of opportunities, and generally unsatisfactory life situations are due to the dominant group's exploitation and not something inherently wrong with them. For non-immigrant minorities, going back to a home country is not a real option (although there is the history of Americo-Liberians who returned to the African continent after the American Civil War, with mixed outcomes).

As a result, in non-immigrant minorities, schooling sometimes becomes equated with the dominant culture and a feeling of having to choose between success in "the white way" versus affiliation with one's own group. Non-immigrant minorities experience the job ceiling and develop the belief that they cannot "make it" by following the same rules as the majority group. To be sure, non-immigrant minority groups still value education and view it as desirable and important for advancement and believe that it will improve status and lead to better jobs. At the same time, they receive contradictory messages when they see that their parents' and grandparents' words and overt encouragement are not commensurate with the parents' experiences in the real world. This contrast can highlight inequalities and injustices within the system and lead to becoming fatalistic, distrustful, and disillusioned.

In my classes, majority-culture students reading Ogbu's work are usually incredulous to learn about the drastic differences between the experiences of majority and minority students. Both immigrant and non-immigrant minority students typically agree that the descriptions are consistent with their own and their families' experiences. More recently, social media and social movements brought the experiences of minority students into mainstream conversation.

It should not be surprising, then, to realize that prejudice and discrimination are prevalent in schools, for schools do not exist in a vacuum. As society's beliefs change over time, schools continue to reflect what mainstream culture deems appropriate.

CHAPTER NINE

Found in Translation

When I first arrived in the United States as a teenager, I didn't always know the meaning of the words that my American friends used. Sometimes I would infer or guess the meanings based on the context around us or based on other words in the sentence, and sometimes I would just ask what the word meant. One close friend (who is now a military chaplain in the U.S. Navy) would ask me, "What does it sound to you like this word means?" I would venture a guess based on how the word sounded. Sometimes hilarity would ensue. But oftentimes my guess, based on context, would take me in the right direction.

This kind of guessing has a long history.

A 1933 study found that English speakers correctly matched Japanese word pairs to their English antonym word pair translations 69 percent of the time. So, for example, when given the Japanese words *heiwa* and *tatakai,* and the English words *war* and *peace,* they were able to correctly guess that *heiwa* means "peace" and *tatakai* means "war" more often than one would expect by chance. If you would like, you can make a few guesses yourself, using word pairs from the original study. Which of these two words—*tooi* and *chikai*—would you guess means "far" and which one means "near"? (If you guessed that *tooi* means "far" and *chikai* means "near," then you guessed correctly.) Which of these two words—*mikata* and *teki*—would you guess means "enemy" and which one means "friend"? (If you guessed that *mikata* means "friend" and *teki* means "enemy," then you guessed correctly.) Which of these two words—*tori* and *mushi*—would you guess means "bird" and which one means "worm/bug"? (If you guessed that *tori* means "bird" and *mushi* means "worm/bug," then you guessed correctly.) If you didn't get many—or any—right, that is frankly what I would have expected before trying out the twenty-five pairs on the list myself. I would have expected the guesses to be correct at about the 50 percent (chance) level.

Which is why I decided to replicate this study in my lab in 2022. Monolingual English speakers were asked to match the meanings of forty-five antonym pairs in nine different languages—French, Japanese, Mandarin, Polish, Romanian, Russian, Spanish, Thai, and Ukrainian—to their English translations. To our surprise, the likelihood of correctly matching antonym pairs in these languages to English translations (65 percent) was greater than predicted by chance (50 percent), even though the monolingual English participants were essentially guessing. The accuracy was lowest for Mandarin (55 percent), Japanese (55 percent), and Russian (56 percent), followed by Thai (57 percent), Polish (58 percent), and Ukrainian (58 percent), and highest for Romanian (74 percent), French (79 percent), and Spanish (81 percent).

In another study, Italian speakers and Polish speakers were asked to listen to words in Finnish, Japanese, Swahili, and Tamil and guess the meaning by choosing among three alternatives. For Finnish and

Japanese, participants' choices based on the sounds of words alone corresponded to the correct meaning more often than would be predicted by chance. The difference was significant for nouns and verbs, but not for adjectives, which in itself is interesting. Most likely, in the long run, sound-symbolism research will reveal mixed results, with patterns varying depending upon specific languages and participants' experience (how many languages they know, how similar the languages are, what their vocabulary size and literacy level are within a language).

Written evidence for the study of the relationship between form and meaning can be found even before the Common Era in the accounts of the Ancient Greek philosopher Socrates described in Plato's dialogues. In the dialogues, when asked by Cratylus and Hermogenes whether names are "natural" or "conventional," Socrates responds that combinations of sounds express the essence of a word's referent and that some sounds are best to describe the flow of water, others motion, and so on. Hermogenes counters that object names are a result of custom and convention and can be changed. Cratylus opines that names have divine origins, bestowed by the gods, which makes them inherently correct. These three positions, presented more than two thousand years ago, illustrate humanity's long history of fascination with words and their meanings and the range of disciplines that have considered these questions, from philosophy to religion to mysticism (mantras) to magic (invocations) to folklore to literature.

The idea of a "true name" that coincides with "true nature" can be found in many religions of the world. Ancient Judaism considered God's true name so powerful that to prevent abuse of its power, using it was taboo. The Bible, too, in Exodus 20:7 speaks against saying God's name in vain. The power of names is also present in non-Western schools of thought, including Daoism, Buddhism, and Sufism. Yogis consider the mantra *Ommm* to reflect the vibration of the universe.

While for the most part the relationship between form and meaning is largely arbitrary, it is not entirely random. The form of a word can influence the representation of its meaning, and the meaning of words can influence their form.

Most people, when hearing about the relationship between sound and meaning, think of onomatopoeia, which refers to words that themselves sound like the thing they describe, like the ticktock of a clock or the honk of a car. Words for animal noises are the most prevalent example of onomatopoeia. Curiously, these words differ across languages. In English, pigs *oink-oink* and dogs *woof-woof*, while in Russian, pigs *hriu-hriu* and dogs *ghav-ghav*, and in Romanian pigs *koveets-koveets* and dogs *hum-hum*. In Japanese, the same word is used to describe the sounds made by multiple animals—the verb *naku* is commonly used to refer to the sounds of dogs, cats, sheep, frogs, birds, and insects. Before I start making nerdy jokes about how Japanese animals are able to communicate better across species or go on a tangent about bidialectal goats—yes, there is such a thing—let me return to form and meaning.

Direct evidence for the relationship between form and meaning can be found in nonspoken languages. Sign languages often represent the meaning of a word by visually tying it to an aspect of its meaning, either by the location or motion of the sign or by the hand shape or palm orientation. The sign for *book*, for example, resembles opening the pages of a book, and the sign for *tea* emulates swirling a teabag or a teaspoon in a cup. Gestures and signs are used as one of the first forms of communication during language development.

Beyond sign languages, the relationship between form and meaning can also be seen in logographic languages like Chinese, where the written form of words is made up of signs that oftentimes constitute other words on their own. The Chinese name for *America* (美国) includes two signs, one for *beauty* (美) and one for *nation* (国). The literal combination of these two signs can be translated to "nation of the beautiful" or "the beautiful country." The Chinese words *jealous*

(嫉妒) and *slave* (奴隶) both include the character for *female* (女) as one of their components. Do the individual meanings influence the mental representation of Chinese speakers' actual translation? Does the form of a label—auditory or visual—influence how people mentally represent this concept and think about it?

For alphabetic languages that rely on meaning-free letters rather than logographic signs that carry meaning like in Chinese, the evidence has been mixed.

My academic grandfather (advisor of my advisor), psychologist Wolfgang Köhler, first demonstrated sound symbolism in 1929 with what has since become widely known as the bouba-kiki effect.

The bouba-kiki effect refers to experiments in which people are presented with two shapes, like the ones in the figure below, and asked which one is a bouba and which one is a kiki. You try.

People are consistently more likely to decide that the rounded shape is a bouba and the jagged, spiky shape is a kiki. This finding holds for college students, older adults, and very young children, and for speakers of not only English but other languages as well. Köhler first conducted the experiment in Spanish on the island of Tenerife using the words *baluba* and *takete*, but the study has since been widely replicated. A preference for these associations has been found in infants as young as four months.

A study with Tamil speakers and with American college students found the preference rates are as high as 95 to 98 percent; across all studies the rates seem to be on average around 88 percent, lower but still significantly higher than chance. (These rates are lower in individuals with autism, around 56 percent, although the reasons for this are unclear.)

A neuroscience experiment using functional neuroimaging found that the prefrontal activation of the brain was stronger when there was a perceived mismatch between the name and the object (when *bouba* was paired with the spiky shape) than when there was a perceived match between the name and the object (when *bouba* was paired with the round shape), likely because people needed to devote more cognitive resources in the mismatch condition. Interestingly, the cortical activation differed not only in the frontal cortex responsible for higher-order cognition but also in the auditory and visual brain networks, suggesting that sound symbolism may be embedded in early stages of sensory processing as well.

It is not yet clear what is responsible for effects like these, nor whether they are present for other codes, like mathematics (which shape refers to a bigger number, 1 or 2? Infinity or zero?). Several hypotheses have been put forward. It has been suggested, for example, that the association is related to the shape of the mouth when producing the sounds—the more rounded shape of the lips when saying *bouba* and the more taut shape when saying *kiki*. It has also been suggested that the association is tied to the proportion of vowels and consonants and the phonemic qualities of the sounds in the words. It seems that individuals base sound-symbol judgments on the acoustic cues of the sounds, but exactly how they do so is unclear.

The relationship between meaning and the phonemic qualities of vowels and consonants has been of interest in many parts of the world and across centuries. Mikhail Lomonosov, the Russian scientist, philosopher, writer, and polymath who in 1755 founded the Moscow State University now named after him (about a dozen other institutions in the former Soviet Union were named after him) wrote about sound symbolism of vowels and consonants in the eighteenth century. He proposed, for instance, that front vowel sounds like /e/, /i/, and /yu/ should be used when denoting tenderness, and back vowel sounds like /o/, /u/, and /y/ should be used when denoting fear.

The strongest connection to sound symbolism can be found in poetry. Using euphony (sounds that are perceived as pleasant, harmonious, comforting); alliteration (repetition of identical initial sounds); rhyme (repetition of similar final sounds); and other linguistic tools, poetry capitalizes on the idea that specific sounds evoke certain emotions and thoughts.

To what extent does a poet's perception of the world shape their language, and to what extent does a poet's language shape their perception? There is likely some of both, with a feedback loop between the two. A poet's lyricism is a reflection of their cognition, but their lyricism also changes their cognition. In the words of Edgar Allan Poe, "Those who dream by day are cognizant of many things which escape those who dream only by night."

What makes the language of poetry so unique is the density of meaning encapsulated in each linguistic unit. Unlike prose, where the writer has pages of room to move, a poet's wordsmithery must be precise not only in selecting just the right word but also the right vowels and consonants. These vowels and consonants create sounds that siphon out the physical experience of the poem. Like a painter mixing colors on the palette, a poet or a lyricist must mix sounds to evoke just the right mental state.

Poetry is one of the oldest forms of communication. It predates written language, with poetry about hunting believed to have been used already in prehistoric times. Poetry therefore can be seen as a link between the auditory experience of language and its written form. Early poems kept track of wars and victories, ferried information through time, and were memorized by entire groups of people as part of the national folklore.

Poems come as short as Aram Saroyan's four-legged version of the letter *m* described as a "close-up of a letter being born," or George MacDonald's two-word poem titled "The Shortest and Sweetest of Songs" that simply reads "Come Home." And they come as long as the *Iliad* and the *Odyssey*, or the Indian *Mahabharata*, with 1.8 million words.

In translating poetry, the challenge is not just about relaying the meaning but also reflecting the sounds, the syntax, the structure, the cadence, the rhyme, the meter, the texture, the associations, the affect, the allusions, and the layers of meaning—all of which vary across languages. Re-creating them while staying true to the artistry typically means that the translation is an approximation or an imitation of the original poem, arguably becoming its own poem. How do you translate Lewis Carroll's "Jabberwocky," for instance, into another language, with verses like "All mimsy were the borogoves, / And the mome raths outgrabe"?

A translator of poetry must have mastery of two languages to at least the same extent as the poet had of the language they wrote in, for translating poetry in essence means transforming it, creating it anew in another linguistic realm. With translation being its own field of study, translation of poetry is a subfield of study within it.

In *Nineteen Ways of Looking at Wang Wei*, a four-line Chinese poem was translated into nineteen different English versions. Even just the title of the poem itself, "Lù zhái," was translated into "The Form of Deer," "Deer Fence," "Deep in the Mountain Wilderness," and "Deer-Park Hermitage," and the same opening line translated variably into "There seems to be no one on the empty mountain," "Through the deep wood, the slanting sunlight," "Not the shadow on a man on the deserted hill," and sixteen others. No two versions were exactly the same. Such poetic variability only grows when translating into other languages.

I have been asked whether one language yields itself to poetry more than another. I think there is no language that is better suited to poetry than others, for speakers of no language are more soulful than speakers of another language, and if you believe otherwise, it is probably only because you have not yet fully mastered that other language. I say this having heard innumerable times from speakers of one language complaining about the paucity of lyricism in their second (or third or fourth) language. Speakers of many languages—Greek, Mandarin, Spanish, Irish—will rhapsodize about how lyrical and soulful their language is relative to others, and all these languages are indeed poetic, lyrical, and soulful, but not any more so than Hindi, Japanese, Urdu, Swahili, or any other language spoken in the world. Although laboratory studies measure multilinguals' linguistic proficiency by measuring language abilities using objective scales with predetermined reliability and validity, outside the laboratory a multilingual's ability to enjoy poetry of varying complexity can be a pretty good indicator of their proficiency in that language.

What distinguishes the language of poets is not the country they originate from but the way in which they unshackle their writing from the conventions and norms of language, changing it as they write, giving it their own unique voice and way of seeing the world. Because languages have different rules, poets in each language must decide which rules to break, and part of what makes translating poetry difficult is that different sets of rules need to be broken across languages. In a way, poetry is its own language, or rather, it creates a language—and with it, a universe—of its own. Like learning another language, the language of poetry shapes one's mind, brain, senses, emotions, and memories.

In the words of Nietzsche's Zarathustra, "This, however, all poets believe: that whoever pricks up his ears as he lies in the grass or on lonely slopes will find out something about those things that are between heaven and earth." Never mind Nietzsche's later musings that "poets . . . muddy their waters to make them appear deep." For poets are less guilty of that, in my experience, than writers of scientific articles, student papers, and political speeches.

Poets are not alone in their hypersensitivity to language nuances. Writers, filmmakers, musicians, artists, and just about anyone else who makes a living by connecting with, influencing, or moving people through language are known to have agonized over finding just the right word (as have lovers composing love letters and texters on the other end of the dancing dots on an incoming text).

OVER the years, I worked a variety of jobs to support myself while I was in school. Some of these included working as a translator of documents required for international adoptions of children from orphanages in Romania, Ukraine, Russia, or other former Soviet republics, or of love letters and other correspondence for mail-order brides from those countries. Others included working as an interpreter, for example, for the 1996 Olympic Games in Atlanta, or for political and economic ventures between Alaska and Russia's Far East in Siberia, like the 1993 Conference of the Four Regions that brought together U.S. senators and political leaders and Russian politicians and executives from companies in the petroleum industry.

The difference between interpreters and translators is not strictly defined, but typically interpreters work with spoken language and translators work with written language. The people who translate Chuck Lorre's "vanity cards"—the snippets of text that flash on the screen for a second or so at the end of each episode—for *The Kominsky Method*, *The Big Bang Theory*, and other shows into various languages for their airing in other countries are translators. They work with written text and have a relatively flexible amount of time at their disposal to translate the messages. It's hard to say how much of the message and how much of the unique way in which the author's mind works is lost in their translation into other languages.

A good translator is a wizard with words and language. When translating into another language, a good interpreter or translator does not use word-for-word or direct translations but instead tries to find substitutes that are culturally, linguistically, and experientially appropriate. This is true not only for idiomatic expressions or specific sayings but also for examples, stories, and cultural references. In writing this book in English, I have to select from a repertoire of phrases, anecdotes, and references that are appropriate for an English reader. If I were to write for a reader in Romanian or Russian, I would have to draw on a different set of cultural references, anecdotes, and phrases. Writers who write in more than one language, like Vladimir Nabokov or Haruki Murakami, have somewhat different voices in each of the languages they write in.

My experiences of working as an interpreter and translator offer insights into how challenging the job of an interpreter is, especially that of a simultaneous interpreter who must translate speech into another language in real time. This is the kind of interpreting you witness when you see United Nations meetings. Most of the time, as the listener, you are not even aware that simultaneous interpreting is happening unless you notice the small and almost invisible earpiece in the listener's ear, through which the simultaneous interpreter is translating the information into the other language even as the speaker is still speaking. Sometimes the speaker pauses to allow the interpreter to translate what was just said, which is known as consecutive interpreting. Other times there is no pause and the interpreter has to simultaneously listen to what the speaker is saying and translate it into the other language while the conversation continues to unfold, which is known as simultaneous or synchronous interpreting. I am in awe every time I witness the ability to synchronously decode incoming speech, reformulate the content into the lexically, semantically, and syntactically valid forms of another language while incorporating language- and culture-specific terms and connotations, and express the reformulated information into the target language, all while new speech continues to stream in. The cognitive load on working memory, attention, language comprehension, and language production is incredible!

My experiences as an interpreter and translator came full circle when, twenty-five years later, I served on the dissertation defense committee for a PhD student at the University of Geneva who studied simultaneous interpreters working at the United Nations, as well as trainees preparing to become simultaneous interpreters. She was part of a larger Swiss research group that studies the eye movements, neural function, and cognitive abilities of simultaneous interpreters.

This research on simultaneous interpreters suggests that intense language control may be associated with more widespread connectivity between different areas of the brain. Even more than in other multilinguals, the repeated engagement of attentional control and working memory in simultaneous interpreters improves executive function and makes efficient use of neural structures. Simultaneous interpreters outperform multilingual controls in dual-task and task-switching experiments. They also have greater gray-matter volume in the left frontal pole, and more functional connectivity between the frontal pole and the left inferior and middle frontal gyri. Simultaneous interpreters have greater connectivity in alpha-frequency oscillations in the prefrontal cortex shown to be associated with attention, inhibitory control, and working-memory processes.

Research on the brains of simultaneous interpreters revealed that the extreme language control required for simultaneous interpreting changes not only the brain areas involved in language processing but also areas involved in learning, motor control, and general executive functions. When the brains of interpreters were compared before and after an intensive training program in simultaneous interpreting, the interpreters' brains showed reduced activation in several brain areas, suggesting that with training, the processes engaged during simultaneous interpreting become more automatic and require fewer cognitive resources. Intensive training in simultaneous interpretation also produced increased cortical thickness in brain regions implicated in speech comprehension and production and in brain regions implicated in attentional control. Increased cortical thickness in simultaneous interpreters suggests that a high degree of language control may serve as a protective factor contributing to cognitive reserve.

Brain comparisons before and after training and experience with simultaneous interpreting reveal brain plasticity in contrast to other studies that simply compare the brains of interpreters to the brains of non-interpreters. This research is similar to neuroimaging studies that show changes to the brain as a result of learning a second language, but are a more extreme form of acquiring multilingual experience.

The number of simultaneous interpreters and translators, however, is minuscule when compared to the number of bilinguals and multilinguals who engage in interpreting and translating in their daily lives, either by choice or out of necessity. Every multilingual has engaged in some form of interpreting or translating at some point in their life.

When done right, interpreting can make the difference between correctly assessing and properly treating a patient to full recovery versus operating on the wrong body part, giving the incorrect treatment or no treatment at all, or even death. Incorrect translations can have serious medical and legal consequences and can also influence economic and political outcomes, all of which are far more serious than the occasional lost tourist.

Failed translations can also be funny. There are pictures online of a Chinese restaurant called Translate Server Error. It seems the owner attempted to translate the Chinese name into English, the machine translation produced an error, and the text of the error was printed on the sign. A quick search for failed translations will yield thousands of pictures and stories of signs and experiences of a similar ilk. Perhaps a good alternative to cat videos on days your mood needs a quick lift.

Humor can be particularly hard to translate across languages. In addition to everything else, one needs to get the timing right and be familiar with the many experiences speakers of the target language live through in their daily lives. I still remember the first joke I heard in English that relied on wordplay: "The odds are good, but the goods are odd"—a remark about the likelihood of single women finding a mate in Alaska. I knew my proficiency in English was finally decent when I was able to make jokes in English: "I once taught an eight a.m. English class. So many grandparents died that semester. I then moved my class to three p.m. No more deaths. And that, my friends, is how I save lives." Still, to this day I mix up proverbs and metaphors across languages or start with the beginning of a proverb from one language and finish with the end from another. My best advice to non-native speakers whose sense of humor is not yet working perfectly—laugh it off.

IT appears there is no limit to the number of languages a human brain can hold. A search for the world's most extraordinary language learners revealed many historical and living figures who could speak multiple languages. The nineteenth-century Italian priest and university professor Giuseppe Mezzofanti, the son of a Bolognese carpenter, is said to have known seventy-two languages and was able to learn a new language to fluency in two weeks. It is impossible to now know his level of proficiency in those languages based on historical and literary texts, but people who spoke a seemingly exceptional number of languages can be found throughout history. The former governor of Hong Kong, Sir John Bowring, was said to have known two hundred languages and been able to speak one hundred. French linguist Georges Dumézil, who died in 1986, was said to have been able to speak or read more than two hundred languages with varying degrees of proficiency. The well-known Victorian explorer, geographer, diplomat, spy, and cartographer Sir Richard Francis Burton was said to have known twenty-nine languages and many dialects, which he used during his explorations.

A famous thought experiment by philosopher W. V. Quine illustrates how tricky learning another language can be (or even a native language, for that matter). In the Gavagai thought experiment, a linguist is visiting a nation that speaks a language the visitor does not know. When a rabbit goes by, one of the native speakers exclaims, "Gavagai!" The linguist's initial assumption is that *gavagai* means "rabbit," but that assumption may not be correct. *Gavagai* could mean "look," "animal," "long ears," "something just went by," "it's getting dark out," "let's catch this for dinner," and it could be one word or two or a complete phrase. This indeterminacy is to some extent present in all new language learning. It is also why many locations named by explorers or colonizers after hearing words from populations native to those places carry names that either mean something entirely different or are tautological, like Mountain Mountain or Lake Lake. The Hatchie River in the southern United States literally is River River, with *hatchie* meaning "river" in the Muskogean Native American language family. Walla Walla River is River River River, after the Sahaptian Native American language branch in which a word (like *walla*, which means "river") is repeated twice to express the diminutive form. In Norway, the Filefjell area literally is Mountain Mountain from Old Norse, and Bergeberget is Hill Hill.

Successful language learning depends on a constellation of variables in both the content being learned and the learner. How well we learn new words depends on properties at multiple levels of representation, including how a word sounds, how it is spelled, how it is represented mentally, and how it is used. New words are easier to learn if they refer to concrete concepts (like dog) than abstract ones (like freedom). The mental representations of what a word refers to differ on a number of dimensions, including our ability to visualize them.

Our research shows that phonological and orthographic neighborhood size and phonotactic and orthotactic probabilities influence word learning. Phonological neighborhood size refers to how many other words in a language differ by only one sound, and orthographic neighborhood size refers to how many other words in a language differ by only one letter. Phonotactic probability refers to how likely sounds are to occur together based on the patterns of the learner's native language, while orthotactic probability refers to how likely the letters are to occur together in a language. Both across and within languages, some sounds are more prevalent than others. Knowing the likelihood of letters and sounds co-occurring makes a difference when playing Wordle and other word games that rely on letter and sound frequencies, and figuring out those probabilities is part of the fun in those games.

If you are wondering why we differentiate between sounds and letters, the answer is because often the letter-to-sound correspondence is not exact. In languages that are considered to have more opaque spellings, like English, the same sound can be spelled with different letters and the same letter can map to different sounds. For instance, /e/ is the most frequently used sound in the English language and can be spelled seven different ways, as you can count for yourself in the sentence "He believed Caesar could see people seizing the seas."

Another factor that influences learning is frequency. Words vary in how often they are used in a language. High-frequency words in a language are typically easier to learn. It is not clear whether easier words become used more frequently over time or if words that are more frequently used over time acquire an easier form. It is also possible that common reasons drive both frequency of use and ease of learning simultaneously, making words that are more likely to be used also easier to learn. In English, the top one thousand most frequent words make up 90 percent of all English texts.

Hand in hand with word frequency is word length. In most world languages, there is a relationship between word length and frequency of use, with shorter words used more often than longer words. The shortest English word is *I*, and the longest English word is the 45-lettered *pneumonoultramicroscopicsilicovolcanoconiosis* and refers to a lung disease contracted from the inhalation of silica particles from a volcano.

Understanding what makes word learning easier can provide theoretical insight into how the mind organizes knowledge and can serve a practical function by informing teachers and students about what is likely to work best in classrooms and learning settings. Emotional processes and cognitive factors like motivation also influence the acquisition of another language. Positive moods and use of various strategies (such as associating a word in the new language with a word in the native language that sounds similar to it) benefit new language learning. For learners with lower moods, using a strategy is especially helpful. In other words, affect and strategy interact to shape successful language learning.

One of the findings that consistently emerges across studies is that it is easier for bilinguals than monolinguals to learn new languages and symbolic systems. People who already know two or more languages learn new languages faster and better than speakers of only one language. One explanation is that this could be due in part to bilinguals' practice with inhibitory control, which is key to learning. When learning new words, you must be able to suppress the activation of the name you already know for an object to prevent it from interfering with the new name. Using mouse tracking, we found that because bilinguals have experience managing competition across languages, they are better at inhibiting competition from known languages, making it easier to learn new ones.

Another piece of the puzzle is that it becomes easier to learn new languages the more languages you know because, with each additional language, you have less new information to acquire. Think about it in terms of a Venn diagram. When you learn a first language, all the information you learn is entirely new, a full circle in the diagram. But when you learn a second language, part of your two circles will overlap, because even though you learn a lot of new information, some of the information (grammatical rules, sounds, maybe even the alphabet) overlaps with your native language. With a third language, you still learn some new information, but now part of the third circle overlaps with your other two circles. With each additional language, the total

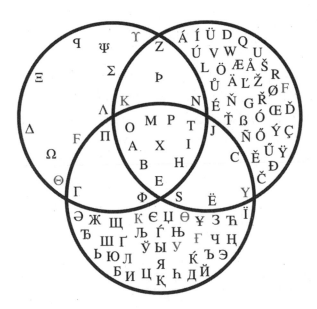

Venn diagram showing the uppercase letters shared by the Greek, Latin, and Cyrillic alphabets.

surface that the circles occupy grows, but the part of the circle that constitutes completely new information gets smaller, making every new language easier to learn.

If knowing another language makes it easier for you to learn a new language, which in turn makes it easier for you to learn yet another language, then more language(s) equals more learning equals more language(s) equals more learning, with language and learning advancing further and further together in a mutually reinforcing pattern, ad infinitum.

Interestingly, as this overlap makes additional languages increasingly easier to learn, it simultaneously becomes increasingly more demanding to cognitively manage the competition across all of them, in ways that keep challenging and optimizing your brain. Moreover, as we have seen in the chapter on the multilingual brain, changes to one area of the brain as a result of language learning have cascading effects in other areas—better cognitive control can enhance auditory processing, for instance, creating a virtuous cycle in which it becomes easier to learn additional languages, which in turn further changes brain activity, which continues to improve cognitive function, and so on. Given the importance of both sensory and executive functions for language learning, one of the consequences of bilingualism is a greater capacity to learn new languages, thereby perpetuating the cycle of neural reconfiguration resulting from exposure to multilingual speech. The mind's potential for learning languages may be limitless, at least in some people.

This is why language is such a powerful tool for progress and humanity's advancement. Even after nonlinguistic communication between minds becomes possible (which new neuroscience discoveries on the recording and transmission of neural activity suggest may no longer be science fiction), symbolic systems will remain essential to our ability to acquire, encode, decode, and share information.

CHAPTER TEN

The Codes of Our Minds

The most famous artifact in the history of multilingualism is the Rosetta Stone, found in 1799 in the Egyptian town of Rashid (Rosetta). Before the Rosetta Stone, nobody knew how to decipher ancient Egyptian hieroglyphs. The Rosetta Stone contained the same text written in three different codes—ancient Greek, Egyptian demotic, and Egyptian hieroglyphs. The ancient Greek reflected the Greco-Macedonian writing system used by the rulers of Egypt after the conquest of Alexander the Great, at the time of the Rosetta Stone's creation. The Egyptian demotic was the script used by the people of Egypt for daily purposes. The Egyptian hieroglyphs were used by priests and the religious class. All three were used in Egypt when the Rosetta Stone was created, which means that at that point in history (over 2,200 years ago), at least some Egyptians knew more than one script.

It took Egyptologists years to decipher Egyptian hieroglyphs with the help of the Rosetta Stone and the other two scripts. It similarly took decades to decipher the Linear B script of Mycenaean Greek.

Since then, machine learning and artificial intelligence have made deciphering codes much faster. Researchers at Macquarie University in Australia and data scientists at Google, for example, combined efforts to translate ancient Egyptian hieroglyphs into English and Arabic in a fraction of that time. Deciphering and enciphering codes is a valuable skill and a matter of national and international security.

During the Second World War, decrypting messages sent by opposition forces was instrumental in securing victories and directing the course of the war. The German Enigma code was especially significant. Enigma used a cipher machine that scrambled the letters of the alphabet and made it possible for the Germans to transmit messages securely in an enciphered way without being understood by the Allied forces. Cryptologists from the U.K., France, Poland, and elsewhere worked for years on solving the Enigma, which the Germans continuously altered, improved, and strengthened. It was the brilliant British mathematician Alan Turing who famously cracked the code. The 2014 historical drama *The Imitation Game* tells the story of how the Enigma code was cracked and influenced the outcome of the Second World War.

Turing himself has entered public knowledge through "Turing completeness," a term used in computer science to describe programming languages, and through the famous "Turing test," which refers to whether a computer at the other end of a conversation could pass for a human. Initially, recognizing a machine was easy due to the rather primitive nature of the conversations. With advances in symbolic notation, symbolic systems are constantly evolving in their ability to follow complex rules. Modern computers engage in conversations that increasingly resemble those of a human, leading to speculations that AI could eventually pass the Turing test and be able to converse in a way indistinguishable from a human.

The codes used nowadays are complex languages that rely on symbols and rules to both safeguard and open up national secrets, control

access to large-scale infrastructures, and operate financial conglomer-
ates. In recent years, code breakers were responsible for some of the
largest data breaches of the twenty-first century, in companies (like
Alibaba, Microsoft Exchange, and Adult Friend Finder) and government agencies (like the 2020 United States federal government data
breach) alike. In 2021, the cyberattack on the Colonial Pipeline disrupted gas supply along the East Coast of the United States, causing
chaos and panic, impacting a critical infrastructure system, and
threatening safety. In another attack, a code breaker was able to breach
the Florida water system and briefly increase the amount of sodium
hydroxide from 100 parts per million to 11,100 parts per million in an
attempt to poison the water supply. For minds that relish a linguistic
challenge, code breaking can be as satisfying as playing a game. In
1999, a fifteen-year-old hacked the computers of the U.S. Department
of Defense and intercepted thousands of internal messages from government organizations. And then of course there is the kind of hacking that tricks people into giving access to restricted information.

This is to say that while some languages are created to enable and
facilitate communication, others are created to limit and restrict information access.

HUMANS have been creating languages for millennia. These are known
as "natural languages"—they evolved over time and are used for communication. Depending on where one draws the line on what is a natural language, there are more than 7,000 natural languages used by
people in the world today. They span more than 140 language families,
with about 80 languages serving as official languages of the world's
approximately 190 nation-states (the exact number of nation-states
and the exact number of official languages fluctuates based on geopolitical changes). This is only a small fraction of all the languages
that humans have used over time, and more languages are becoming
extinct every year.

It is impossible to know the first spoken word that was uttered by a human or by a human ancestor, because there are no records of spoken words and because it depends on where we draw the line on what qualifies as a word and as a prehistoric ancestor. At best, we can make guesses based on studying the anatomy of the articulatory system in early hominids and by statistical analyses of frequency and overlap of words across different world languages.

Even when it comes to writing, figuring out the first written language depends on how one defines written languages and whether cave drawings, pictographic images, and glyphs count as writing. The earliest uncovered written script is believed to be the cuneiform wedge-shaped characters of the Sumerian language of Mesopotamia circa 3500 BCE. The roots of modern writing, where a sound corresponds to a specific symbol, are typically traced to the proto-Sinaitic script that was developed between 1800 and 1500 BCE. The first known linear alphabet that most closely resembles modern alphabets was the Phoenician alphabet developed circa 1050 to 150 BCE. It consisted of twenty-two letters, all of which were consonants, leaving vowel sounds implicit.

In theory, the human body can create a virtually unlimited number of sounds to use in a language. The number of potential language sounds depends on how we control the air flow coming from our lungs when we speak and how we shape our mouth and position our tongue. The vowels are determined by a combination of height and "frontness" or "backness" of the tongue's position in the mouth, by lip rounding, and by how tense or lax the sound production is. The consonants are determined by a combination of place of articulation (where in the vocal tract the tightening happens), manner of articulation (how narrow the constriction is, how the air is flowing, and where the tongue is), and voicing (whether and how the vocal folds are vibrating). Anatomically, there are an infinite number of options for generating different sounds by varying just one of these variables in each combination, even by just a little. But despite the potentially limitless repertoire of sounds we could produce anatomically, in actuality only a few combinations exist in each language.

The exact number of consonants and vowels varies across languages. At one end of the spectrum, Hawaiian has 5 vowels and 8 consonants, and Pirahã is believed to have 3 vowels and 7 or 8 consonants. At the other end of the spectrum are languages like Lithuanian with 12 vowels and 47 consonants and Danish with 32 vowels and 20 consonants. The Khmer Cambodian alphabet has 74 characters, whereas the Rotokas language on the island of Bougainville in Papua New Guinea has only 12. Languages also vary drastically in what sound combinations are allowed. In Spanish, for example, words cannot start with /st/ or /sp/ unless an /e/ sound is added before them. In English, words cannot start with /kj/ or /gb/. In Hmong, the only final consonant is /h/. Georgian can have as many as 8 consecutive consonants in a row, and Polish can have as many as 6 initial consonants in a row. To make it possible to record and reproduce all sounds of all human languages, an alphabet was created called the International Phonetic Alphabet, or IPA. The IPA is used by linguists, speech-language pathologists, language teachers, and other scientists, clinicians, and educators to transcribe the sounds of all languages.

Some variances are so minuscule that they are imperceptible to speakers of other languages. It is common for speakers to be unable to hear the differences between sounds that do not exist in their native language but exist in other languages. Many Japanese speakers have difficulty distinguishing between the sounds /r/ and /l/ (because the two map to one equivalent in Japanese), and many Spanish speakers have difficulty distinguishing between the sounds /v/ and /b/ (the two are pronounced similarly in Spanish). These difficulties are not immutable, and it is possible to train speakers to perceive and pronounce new sounds. Functional neuroimaging studies of the brain show changes in neural activity as a result of learning new sound distinctions.

Creating language is not a rare phenomenon for the human brain. We "google," "crowdfund" and create new words every year. Young children spontaneously invent words all the time. Leo Tolstoy wrote in 1936, "[The child] realizes the laws of word formation better . . . because no one so often thinks up new words as children." In the Russian classic on children's language, *From Two to Five*, children's book author Kornei Chukovsky describes examples of children spontaneously inventing words that turn out to exist in other parts of the world or were used at other times in history:

> At times the child creates words that already exist in the language but are unknown to him or to the adults around him. I heard, for instance, a three-year-old in the Crimea spontaneously use the word "bulleting" [puliat], and he "bulleted" from his tiny rifle all day long, not even suspecting that this word has been thus used for centuries in the faraway Don region. In a story by L. Pantileev, a Yaroslavl woman says several times: "And so they bullet and they bullet!" Another child, whose exact age I did not know, created the words "shoeware" [obutki] and "clothesware" [odetki]; this youngster lived in the steppes near Odessa, not far from the Black Sea. He, too, was completely oblivious of the fact that these two words had existed for a few centuries, in the past, in the distant north, in the Olenets District.

Some children go beyond coming up with individual words and invent entire mini languages to communicate with a best friend or a special group of friends or to write secrets in their diaries so that others may not understand them—from pig Latin to entirely new and unique languages. Perhaps you were that child yourself, or parented such a child, or have known one.

My oldest daughter was exactly the kind of child who invented a language in preschool, and then in elementary school developed a writing code so she could pass secret notes with her best friend. By middle school she asked for a book on hacking for Christmas. She eventually went to high school at the Illinois Mathematics and Science Academy, a residential three-year state-funded high school that *Wired* magazine called "Hogwarts for Hackers." As a parent, I remember that, unlike other high schools that have different levels of repercussions for students depending on the severity of infractions—from dress code to alcohol to drugs—IMSA's different levels of repercussions varied in severity depending on the seriousness of hacking the student took part in—from changing a grade on a report card to breaking into a government agency.

The IMSA teenagers of yesterday went on to become today's YouTube co-founder Steve Chen, PayPal co-creator Yu Pan, Yelp co-founder Russel Simmons, SparkNotes and OkCupid co-founder Sam Yagan, Hearsay Social founder Clara Shih, and many other technology-sector innovators. Traditionally, the Pentagon and more generally the defense sector led the way in advancing technology in the interests of national security. Some of those technologies eventually became widely used by society, most notably the Internet and the GPS, which are now part of everyone's daily experience. Increasingly, however, Silicon Valley and the private sector more generally are successfully competing for the best talent and leading the way in discovery and innovation. Private companies are advocating for the adoption of commercial technologies by the U.S. government and defense agencies, like Google's partnership with the Pentagon to improve object recognition on video or Microsoft's $21.9 billion contract to build custom augmented-reality headsets for the military. While some point to the risks of outsourcing military capabilities to private, for-profit companies, others counter with the necessity of doing so to stay competitive with nations like China and Russia. Regardless of whether it is the government or the private sector, success will depend on the ability to recruit and train the best learners, users, and creators of multiple symbolic systems.

When I was on sabbatical at Stanford, I met several multilinguals who came from other countries and were now developing computer languages in the technology sector. One of them got his undergraduate degree from MIT at sixteen and his PhD from Stanford at nineteen, and he is not as exceptional in that community as you may think. The influx of talent from around the world that is multilingual in natural and computer languages represents invaluable intellectual capital for Silicon Valley and the academic and governmental organizations that compete to drive innovation and discovery.

It's a creativity loop: multiple languages beget more creative minds, and more creative minds beget more advanced languages.

JUST as microscopes revealed the role of germs in diseases, and just as telescopes showed us the existence of other planets and galaxies, so do artificial languages help us understand the codes of our minds.

The relationship between natural human languages and artificial languages is a symbiotic one, meaning they mutually benefit each other. To understand what leads to successful language-learning outcomes, we need to understand the mechanisms behind language learning—and many important discoveries in this area come from careful experimentation with artificial languages. Artificial languages and artificial intelligence build on knowledge generated by human language and thought, and, in turn, generate new information that makes it possible to further advance human thought and learning.

Artificial languages have a long history, starting with Lingua Ignota, created in the 1100s by a German abbess named Hildegard von Bingen. The world's most widely known artificial language is

Esperanto, created by a Polish doctor in 1887 and intended to be a universal language for international communication. Esperanto has highly regular morphological and syntactic rules that could arguably be learned in a couple of hours, at least by speakers of Indo-European languages.

Unlike natural human language, artificial languages are constructed based on formal logic and are used primarily for scientific, technological, or entertainment purposes. Depending on how one defines artificial language, the estimates for the total number of artificial languages range from fifty commercially supported general-purpose languages to more than nine thousand artificial languages (depending on whether the definition includes syntax and grammar or vocabulary only). When it comes to counting artificial languages, the number is essentially meaningless, because any coder out there could "create" a new computer language at any moment or modify an existing language to generate a new language, and any aspiring writer can give his characters a made-up language, so the number of languages is theoretically infinite.

Artificial languages can be broadly divided into three types. The first are computer languages like Python, Java, JavaScript, C, C++, and C#. The second are languages created for entertainment, for movies and books and games, like Na'vi (*Avatar*); High Valyrian (*Game of Thrones*); Klingon (*Star Trek*); and Sindarin (*The Lord of the Rings*). And the third are languages used in research, like Brocanto, Láadan, and Colbertian. Artificial languages like Esperanto and Interlingua fall between the second and third categories. Several artificial languages, like Klingon, are offered by online language-learning platforms such as Duolingo.

I will only briefly remark on computer languages here to not only demystify their similarity to natural languages but also to drive home the point about the power of language to advance learning and progress. Like natural languages that people use, computers use languages made up of symbols. These symbolic systems organize knowledge and information. Both artificial intelligence and human brains are focused on encoding, decoding, and acquiring new information—in other words, on communicating and learning. Also like natural languages, computer languages make it possible to efficiently encode large volumes of information into smaller units. And again, like natural languages, computer languages can be "translated" from one language to another. For example, archaic computer languages like COBOL frequently need to be translated to modern computer languages. Such translations enable companies and systems to continue to access information from decades ago even as new and more sophisticated computer languages are being developed. The rapid evolution of artificial languages as they encode increasingly large chunks of information into smaller symbolic units is what is accelerating the pace of scientific discovery exponentially over time. Progress in programming, mathematics, and artificial intelligence historically has gone hand in hand with progress in symbolic notation.

Beyond technological advancement (as with computer languages), and beyond building imaginary worlds (as with Klingon, Sindarin, or Dothraki), artificial languages can be used to gain insight into how we acquire natural languages and into the codes of our mind and of the universe. Even Klingon has been used to assess language-learning aptitude, showing that the ability to map Klingon sounds to symbols can predict English-language proficiency.

As we saw earlier, natural languages vary in the sounds they include, writing systems they employ, modalities they rely on, grammar systems and rules, and a slew of other parameters. There is also variability within each language (words differ in concreteness, frequency, pronounceability, and other variables), as well as among language users (proficiency, cognitive abilities, exposure, where one lives and whom one interacts with, and so on). As a result, isolating the influence of any one variable when studying natural languages can be difficult, if not impossible.

This is precisely why a good way to study language is to create artificial ones and manipulate their properties as needed. Artificial languages are useful tools for studying language acquisition by controlling for the immense variability that exists within natural languages. With artificial languages, we can study multilingualism, the mind, and communitive codes more generally in carefully controlled ways that are not possible with natural languages. Researchers can control not only the learners' prior experience with that language, but also the properties of the language itself, to disambiguate related effects, and to simulate the emergence and learning of natural languages. By developing carefully controlled languages, it is possible to manipulate how different or similar they are to known languages in various ways and to study the relative contribution of variables like probability frequencies, writing systems, language experience, and even language development in babies and children.

For instance, numerous studies of language acquisition have used the Wug Test of language development in children. The Wug Test uses nonsense pseudowords to study how children acquire morphology, like the marking s for plural. Children see images of a cute little blue Wug creature and are asked to finish incomplete sentences about the Wug. The children's ability to generalize rules to new and previously unheard stimuli showed that humans do not learn language by simply memorizing what they hear and repeating it, but that they extract patterns from the input around them and their brains deduce rules and generalize the deduced rules to new stimuli.

In my laboratory, we learn a lot about how language and the mind work by teaching people artificial languages like Morse code. In one line of research, we developed a mini artificial language called Colbertian. We named it Colbertian after Northwestern alum Stephen

Colbert, a comedian and wordsmith himself, inventor of such neologisms as "truthiness" and "lincolnish." We use Colbertian to vary things like frequency of co-occurrence of letters and sounds in a word and degree of similarity to words in known languages, to better understand how various word properties influence word learning in a second or third language. Other labs use artificial languages like Brocanto to study the learning of grammar.

One may question, however, whether learning artificial languages stripped of idiosyncrasies can truly inform us about learning natural languages. And certainly, even a well-formed artificial language is bound to pale in comparison to the rich and vivid constellation of sensory inputs, linguistic structures, motor executions, thoughts, beliefs, and memories that become associated with natural languages. Nevertheless, just as physicists can collide particles to study the origins of the universe, psycholinguists can use artificial languages to study language and mind. The substantial overlap between neural activation when processing natural and artificial languages speaks to the utility of using artificial languages in multilingualism research.

Artificial languages in the laboratory, so far, have primarily been used to study how we learn sounds, written forms, words, and grammar, but have not yet been used to study higher-order processes like analogical reasoning or learning event structures. These are the types of learning with which artificial intelligence still has difficulty. Moving forward, future research may address the open question of whether artificial languages can be profited from to better understand the development of higher-order cognitive functions. With their capacity to distill complex processes down to their critical components, artificial languages may hold the key to understanding uniquely human abilities that confound even the most advanced forms of artificial intelligence.

Could our mental constructs, what we currently think of as "thoughts," potentially be rewritten in computational terms, similar to the mathematical descriptions that define layers in artificial neural networks? Research that merges neuroscience with machine learning to train neural nets attempts to do just that.

We have entered a unique age in language research, created by the combination of large linguistic corpora and advanced computational power. The result is that scientists have unprecedented abilities to conduct research on a large scale and span multiple variables within a language or across many languages. These capabilities to do precise, well-controlled research using large, corpus-based analyses are contributing to scientific and technological advances at a pace that is faster than ever before. It also democratizes science and discovery as it enables all of us to take advantage of the tools available online and develop new ways to expand human knowledge.

It is in part because computer science and artificial languages use universal mathematical symbols that they may possibly be able to transcend the limitations of human languages. They don't yet. For now, computer languages use symbols (keywords) from natural language together with mathematical notation. They use formal semantics that can be described in mathematical terms. To date, math and computer science go hand in hand. One need only consider the Curry–Howard isomorphism to see the direct correspondence between a computer program and a mathematical proof (isomorphism refers to a one-to-one correspondence when mapping two sets that preserves the relationship between the elements of the sets).

Whether the current state of affairs, where math and artificial intelligence are two sides of the same coin, will continue indefinitely, or whether the two will potentially diverge in the future is a question nobody has the answer to yet. Some see the relationship between math and artificial intelligence as analogous to the relationship between language and human intelligence, with the limits of that similarity and the differences between the two types of mappings intensely debated.

Is mathematics the language in which God has written the universe, as no less than Galileo Galilei proposed?

Symbolic systems are one of the most amazing tools that humans have at their disposal. You can do all sorts of amazing things with symbols. You can use the symbol "apple" to offer someone something to eat, to describe what things are made of (as in sauce or pie), to tell stories (like the one about Adam and Eve), or to pass along wisdom (what it takes to keep the doctor away), or you can use it figuratively (like saying that someone is the apple of your eye to express how fond you are of them). You can use symbols to communicate your wants and thoughts and plans and past to others, you can use symbols verbally with one person or many people, or you can write them down to communicate across space and time—like I am doing here.

In line with Wittgenstein's *Sprachspiel* idea of a "language-game," language itself is, then, its own example of a language game to which we all agree. In that sense, what constitutes language is a matter of definition and one that is not universally agreed upon. For example, is chess a language? Chess has rules and specific notations and chess players may argue that it is indeed a language in itself.

One of the most powerful symbolic systems developed by the human mind is mathematics. It is said that the Greek mathematician Archimedes was engaged in solving a mathematical problem when he was killed by a Roman soldier. Mathematical symbols carry meaning and follow a set of rules that are organized into structures that can be understood by others. Many features of the physical world as we know it can be described and predicted using mathematical models. Mathematical equations can model the motion of boundaries between ice and water to prove that melting ice stays smooth. Even the shape of leaves is prescribed by fractals and follows mathematical rules. The predictive power of mathematics has made our technical and scientific progress possible. Math allowed Albert Einstein to predict many phenomena theoretically that are only now validated by observation. Einstein famously believed that "God does not play dice with the universe" and that nature and the universe can ultimately be described by mathematical models.

Like poetry, mathematics is a language in itself and is a code that shapes our minds and brains in powerful ways. Unlike poetry, math is the closest thing we have today to a universal language. Math is considered the queen of the sciences because it can describe, explain, and predict so much in our universe. Its history goes hand in hand with the history of language and humanity. Starting with the use of zero to denote a quantity and all the way to quantum physics, math is the language we tie most closely to scientific progress.

Mathematical symbols were first used to estimate the circumference of the Earth more than two thousand years ago by Greek thinker Eratosthenes. Although humans have been able to represent quantities, lengths, and time since prehistory, most mathematical symbols known today did not enter common use until the sixteenth century. Before that, words were used to write mathematical problems. The word *calculus* originates from the Greek word for pebbles because ancient Greeks used pebbles to represent numbers. Even the famous Greek philosopher Pythagoras, whose theorems students still study in school today, used pebbles to work out mathematical equations. The lack of symbolic notation is one of the main reasons for the slow progress in the history of math early on. Only with the development of symbols did the field of mathematics take off.

If math is the language of the universe, then it is not surprising that other species have mathematical abilities as well. Researchers studying animal cognition found competence for counting and numerosity even in insects. Despite the small size of their brains, honeybees count landmarks and ants keep track of the number of steps taken. Ravens and crows are known to have quite sophisticated mathematical abilities, including an understanding of the concept of zero—not as nothing but as a quantity, as a mental representation of something. This is an ability that human children do not develop until approximately the age of six. Recording a crow's brain activity as it performed numerical tasks revealed that neurons in the crow's brain represent zero as a quantity similar to other numerosities, which is also what the prefrontal cortex does in humans and other primates. We are still not sure how deep or sophisticated the mathematical knowledge of other species is. In a 2018 study, after individual honeybees were trained to the numerical concepts of "greater than" or "less than" using stimuli containing one to six features, the bees could order numbers, including the abstract concept of zero, on a numerical continuum. The remarkable abilities of bees have even won researchers who study them a Nobel Prize in Physiology or Medicine.

Math, even counting, can be a form of communication, including in other species. Some species of frogs and toads rely on numbers during their mating ritual. In the mating competitions of túngara frogs, a male calls out by placing a brief pulsing note (a chuck) at the end of his call, a rival frog responds by placing two chucks at the end of his call, to which the first frog then responds with three chucks, the second with four, and so on up until they run out of breath. This turn-taking to add one sound to their calls is not only a demonstration of being able to keep track of the number of calls and therefore count and perform simple arithmetic but also an example of using math as a form of communication in other species.

Even more remarkable, neurons in the auditory midbrain of the túngara frogs selectively respond only if a threshold number of sound pulses has occurred with the correct timing, and these interval-counting neurons represent neural correlates of some of the behavioral counting abilities of the frogs. The responses of these neurons in the frogs appear to reflect a counting process.

In humans, how many digits one can remember and the speed with which one performs mathematical computations is affected by the length of number words in one's language. Other things held constant, speakers of a language with longer words for numbers take longer to perform a mental arithmetic problem than speakers of a language with shorter words for numbers.

Not surprisingly, number systems vary dramatically across languages. For example, English uses a base-ten number system, also known as the decimal system. That is not the case for all languages, however. French uses base ten when counting to seventy, but then switches to a mixture of base ten with base twenty, with the number 70 verbally encoded as "sixty plus ten"; 80 as "four times twenty"; and 90 as "four times twenty, plus ten." Danish is similar to English until you get to 50, and then switches to a fraction system, where instead of 50 it is verbally stated as "two and a half times twenty"; 70 is "three and a half times twenty," and 90 is "four and a half times twenty." Some claim that the optimal mathematical base is base 12 (also known as duodecimal or dozenal or uncial). Natural languages that use base-12 systems are rare, but they do exist. In a duodecimal language that uses 12 as the basic number word around which the number system is built, 29, for example, would be pronounced using the verbal description of the formula $(12 \times 2) + 5$, and 95 is $(12 \times 7) + 11$. You can see why these number systems are not as common, although they can still be found today in some of the languages spoken in Nigeria and Nepal.

Other languages are even more interesting. Oksapmin in New Guinea relies on a base-27 counting system where the words used for counting are the names for body parts, starting at the thumb of one hand, going up to the nose, then down the other side of the body to the pinky of the other hand. Tzotzil, the Mayan language spoken in Mexico, uses the base-20 counting system that relies on the names of fingers and toes. Ancient Babylonians used a base-60 numerical system, known as sexagesimal. Sexagesimal systems are used today to measure time (60 seconds in a minute, 60 minutes in an hour), geographic coordinates, and angles.

Even when the number systems are not so dramatically different, learning another language often entails learning another number system. For multilinguals, math proves to be a special case. Most multilinguals, even highly fluent ones and those who have used their second language as their primary language for many years, will often revert to their first language when performing mathematical computations. The language in which math is initially learned is likely to be the default language for mathematical operations throughout one's life, even when proficiency in another language is fully attained and is greater than in the native language, including for simple math tasks like basic arithmetic.

A brain-imaging study at the University of Luxembourg suggests that bilinguals are more likely to recruit brain regions normally involved in spatial and visual thinking when solving math problems in their second language. This may be because the brain areas are more interconnected in multilinguals, or it could also be that bilinguals resort to visualizing the problems more because they are less automated in each language.

Experience with the rules and vocabulary of different languages may be training the brain to recognize and process new arithmetic information as well. In one study, the basal ganglia in bilingual brains responded more to new math problems than to old ones, and bilinguals were about half a second faster than monolinguals at solving new math problems, but performed similarly on familiar problem sets. Half a second may seem insignificant when you are lying on the couch watching TV, but it is quite a meaningful amount of time in neural and computational terms (think of how fast your electronic devices refresh and download information).

Research on the brain networks of expert mathematicians suggests that high-level mathematical thinking recruits neural circuits initially involved in space and number, and not traditional language areas. When the brains of professional mathematicians were scanned across various math tasks, no overlap was found between the math-responsive network and the areas activated by sentence comprehension and general semantic knowledge. This suggests that the differences in math performance between bilinguals and monolinguals observed in other studies are likely not due to quantitative differences with bilinguals knowing more words or having "more" language but due to qualitative transformations to the cognitive system as a result of being multilingual—a reconfiguration of the brain beyond language alone. An interesting corollary finding from that study is that expert mathematicians showed reduced activation to faces in the right fusiform gyrus—a finding curious because research on reading experts also suggests that they shift responses in that area away from faces and toward letters, just as mathematicians do toward numbers. This finding from mathematics illustrates yet again the plasticity of the brain and how it can be rewired by experience—be it with multiple languages, math, or reading.

The exponential learning-begets-more-learning growth axiom is not limited to natural languages but applies to artificial languages and to math and logic as well. For Christmas last year, my daughter got a set of stackable rings. I took three, put them on my ring finger, and said, "Look, Mommy has three rings. Each of them can be turned with the pointy side up or down. And I can also change the order of the three rings. How many different designs can Mommy create with these three rings?"

If you answered forty-eight, as my daughter did, then you are right (or seventy-eight if you include designs with only two or one ring in addition to designs with all three rings). My kids can solve permutation problems like this faster than me these days (even though I grew up with the most classic permutation puzzle of them all—the Rubik's Cube). They have surpassed me just like they have at skiing and technology use. I attribute it to the neural agility of their young brains but also to playing mental puzzle games with them since they were little. My grandparents made up brain teasers all the time when I was growing up. Just this past weekend at the family dinner, my father asked the younger grandkids, "How can you tell that forty-five minutes have passed if you don't have a watch but have matches and two ropes that each take an hour to burn if you light them from one end?" And of course most people are familiar with the many variations of the wolf, goat, and cabbage river-crossing problem: How do you bring the three across a river in a boat if you can only carry one at a time but cannot leave the wolf with the goat or the goat with the cabbage, because they will get eaten? These may be silly, but with each, the brain learns how to problem-solve. With each problem solved, new ways to solve problems come easier.

CHAPTER ELEVEN

The Future of Science and Technology

We are still trying to understand where language ends and language-free thought begins, and whether there is a boundary between the two at all. The psycholinguistic version of the chicken-and-egg question is what comes first—thought or language? While some say thought precedes language, when later asked how they know it to be so, the answer they give usually relies on some form of linguistic measurement of thought. In other words, we usually know what someone is thinking based on language. Because we use language to assess thought, and because the two are tightly interconnected, it is extremely difficult to separate them.

With the advance of mathematical notation, computer science, and artificial intelligence, we have been able to separate logic and knowledge from verbal language by using math instead. However, as previously discussed, math itself is a language, a symbolic system. Like the words you and I use to communicate our thoughts with each other, mathematical notations are used to communicate ideas, instructions, and plans. In other words, math is not a demonstration of language-free thought but another symbolic system to encode, communicate, and discover.

Because we typically use language to study thinking, measuring thought is nearly impossible without the confounding influence of language. One potentially fruitful avenue for separating language and thought empirically has been the study of prelinguistic babies. Using simple measures of behavior, like sucking rates or direction and duration of eye movements or head turning, scientists have been studying infant cognition in an attempt to get to the origins of thought and language. It turns out that very young infants have sophisticated cognitive abilities long before they can speak.

But even that line of research can be resisted by showing that before babies can speak, they already understand some aspects of the language spoken to them, and even before they can understand it, they have been exposed to it, including in utero before birth, which means that language is already shaping their minds even before they are born. Because babies are exposed to and sensitive to linguistic input while they are still in the womb, separating thought and language is not as easy as you may think.

At one point, we thought that using new methodologies like fMRI, EEG, or eye tracking would give us access to language-free thought, because we would not use language but measure neural activity or saccadic eye movements to index thought instead. But that, too, has proven misguided, because we still use language-based criteria against which to compare the observed patterns of brain activity or eye movements.

Studying the relationship between language and thought inevitably leads to the question of where language comes from. And for that matter, where thought comes from. If language and thought are two sides of the same coin (an arguable view, as we saw in the discussion of linguistic determinism), then language would have to be derived from a source outside the human realm, because thought is impossible without language and before language there would have been no thought.

And even when you identify a behavior that cleanly eliminates language, what you are left with is something that can then be found in other animal species as well, at which point we are left with the question, What is thought? If what we consider nonlinguistic thought can also be found in other, nonhuman species, does it then mean that these nonhuman species are also capable of thought, logic, consciousness, and sentience? And if animals think and communicate as well, then what is thought, and what is language, and what does it mean to be human? Is symbolic language unique to our species on this planet?

Examples of language (depending on how one defines it) and communication in other species are frequent, as are examples of cognitive phenomena. A 2021 study in the journal *Science* reported that the babbling of baby bats of the *Saccopteryx bilineata* species is characterized by the same features as babbling in human infants, including reduplication and rhythmicity. Ants communicate with their guests, and their language can be analyzed.

If we define language as electrical signals used to communicate with other entities, then by that definition organisms as unexpected as fungi communicate with each other. Mushrooms can use up to fifty different electrical impulses to share information. These impulses can even be transmitted underground to communicate about food or injury, making these fungi "champignon" communicators. Computer scientists go as far as proposing that these electrical signals are similar to human words. But mycologists (biologists who study fungi such as mushrooms, molds, and yeast) pump the brakes on adding Fungusese to Google Translate and suggest instead that these neural spikes may be nutrient pulses, which are seen in other plants.

There may even be reason to believe that the ability to use and switch between multiple codes of communication is not unique to humans and can also be observed in other species, from goats to birds and even naked mole rats. Naked mole rats, rodents that live underground and are functionally blind and nearly deaf, use unique dialects of chirps that differ across colonies. Mole rats recognize social information conveyed through the chirps and modify their behavior in response. When pups are transplanted to other colonies, the fosters learn the dialect of their adoptive families. The dialect is influenced by the colony queen, and when the queen is replaced, the dialect changes. In a research study, after a colony underwent a series of coups in which two consecutive queens were killed and replaced by new females, the dialects quickly became less stable and more variable. Studies like these point to the greater value of being able to use multiple communicative codes for survival, not only at an individual level, but also at a group and species level. If we have anything in common with naked mole rats (and we do), our ability to flexibly use different languages—to learn them and communicate in them—may determine, at least in part, whether humanity thrives or perishes.

As a dog lover, I can joke that my dog understands some of what I am saying—not as much as my students, but sometimes more than my kids. But as a scientist, I have to say that it depends on how you define language and whether you consider rote learning and the creation of associations to be language, as opposed to spontaneous generation of new linguistic combinations, which is a different thing entirely. There is captivating research on the communicative and cognitive abilities of other species, and you can spend a good chunk of time on YouTube watching videos of adorable and not-so-adorable animals performing all sorts of linguistic and cognitive feats.

Advances in science and technology can have dramatic consequences for humanity and our ability to communicate, but the positive effect is often tied to negative repercussions as well. Consider the fact that it is now possible to marry neuroscience and computer science to create technology that can be implanted in the brain to translate neural activity into language. It is no longer the domain of science fiction. Neuroscientists can now use machine learning to transform the brain's electrical signals into synthetic speech, a technology that is beginning to be used to help people with communicative disorders. For example, patients with anarthria, which is the loss of the ability to speak resulting from a stroke or from illnesses and vocal paralysis, can already benefit from implantable devices in clinical research that enable communication. At this point, the technology is still very rudimentary, allowing the thought-to-language conversion only at the level of simple single words and requiring invasive brain surgery, but it provides proof of concept that the ability to generate sentences and complex natural speech with minimal medical intervention is feasible in the not-too-distant future.

Cutting-edge brain-computer interfaces today include so-called neurograins. Neurograins are tiny microchips scattered throughout the brain that can record and transmit brain activity to a computer and can be used to stimulate the biological brain matter itself. Right now, these chips are about the size of a grain of salt, are made primarily from silicon microchips, and are still only experimented with in species like rats and other rodents. Before they can be used with humans, smaller sensors would be needed so that implanting them causes less damage to the brain and so that the immune system is less likely to detect and reject them as foreign objects. Better technologies would also need to be developed for placing them in the brain (right now the surgical techniques used with neurograins are crude). The safety and longevity of the neurograins still needs to be established, and we don't yet have the capacity to fully and meaningfully decode and interpret the data sent by the neurograins.

Our ability to garner one's neural activity and use technology to translate it into language that can be communicated to others is groundbreaking. It can be used to do a great deal of good, for example to help people who have lost the ability to communicate or were born without it, as well as to automatically translate thoughts into another language the speaker does not know, to dictate or communicate without having to type or speak or move at all, and to work in many other positive ways that make it easier and faster to communicate between minds. Neurograins, for example, could potentially be used to restore movement in people with brain and spinal injuries. These technologies will be part of our human future and will change us as individuals and as societies, modifying our language and how we communicate along the way.

If the ability to one day record our neural activity remotely and decipher the thoughts it reflects for communicating between minds without verbal or written language seems farfetched, remember that the ability to transmit our language across large distances through a telephone seemed just as miraculous not long ago. In his masterpiece *In Search of Lost Time*, Marcel Proust once quipped, "The telephone, a supernatural instrument before whose miracles we used to stand amazed, and which we now employ without giving it a thought, to summon our tailor or order an ice cream." Another such "supernatural" example is the theremin, a musical instrument controlled by the player without physical contact but instead by moving one's hands near it. Even though it follows clear principles of physics and electronics, if you ask people how they think a theremin works, many will incorrectly say that the hand emanates an energy that plays the instrument. This is to say that just because something seems opaque to us, that does not make it miraculous or farfetched.

At the same time, like any other discovery, there is the possibility of using this knowledge and technology for nefarious purposes, of which there could be many if one has access to others' thoughts by way of recording their brain's neural activity, potentially remotely and potentially without consent. The legal regulation of how that may work in a society will be a quagmire, and success will require establishing and enforcing strict rules for the use of these technologies. We are getting a glimpse of the kind of ethical and legal violations that such technological developments will entail in current attempts to regulate social media and technological access to personal data, including search histories, consumer behavior data, and medical, financial, political, and personal information. The legal cases and political ramifications surrounding technological privacy and social media are but a drop in the bucket relative to what access to our thoughts and neural activity may bring. Although still remote, this technology is now not only theoretical but also demonstrably realistic for humanity's future, with proof-of-concept options already available. Personalized brain implants are currently being tested for clinical use in treating epilepsy, Parkinson's, and even severe depression.

Of course, scientific advances can have both positive and negative ramifications, as history shows. Most notably, nuclear energy can be used to provide a nearly inexhaustible source of sustainable power (for example, to generate electricity, heat, and so on), but it can also be used to create the atomic bomb and other nuclear weapons. Einstein admitted, "I made one great mistake in my life—when I signed the letter to President Roosevelt recommending that atom bombs be made. But there was some justification—the danger that the Germans would make them." Although the technology of nuclear weapons has changed since Einstein's time, the ethical questions continue to have direct relevance for scientific research today.

Unfortunately, the study of ethics lags behind the technological and methodological advancements of the twenty-first century. Because of where we choose to allocate our financial support, some branches of science advance faster than others, sometimes before we can fully grasp their long-term implications. While we are beginning to understand the links between language as symbolic system and thought as neural activity, as well as how to measure and benefit from that connection, we do not yet fully understand either the limits or the risks associated with doing so. To quote science-fiction writer Isaac Asimov, "The saddest aspect of life right now is that science gathers knowledge faster than society gathers wisdom."

This should not prevent us from continuing to invest in science and technology that can benefit our planet and advance humanity in ways that make it more likely to survive when faced with challenges, be they natural to our planet or extraterrestrial. It does, however, underscore the need to invest more in and support equally the study of ethics, morality, philosophy, social science, humanities, the arts, and spirituality, because they are just as essential to humanity's survival as technology. Immanuel Kant, the philosopher who believed in an uncompromising principle of morality, wrote, "Two things fill the mind with ever new and increasing wonder and awe—the starry heavens above me and the moral law within me."

What those who are anti-science do not grasp is that, to quote Carl Sagan, "Science is not only compatible with spirituality; it is a profound source of spirituality." To be a scientist is to constantly marvel at the universe and to try to understand it, be it the universe of the cosmos or the consciousness within us, at the level of stars or at the subatomic level, or in my case, at the language-mind interface.

We still understand very little about our linguistic and our neural potential. Just as cosmology and astrophysics provide ways to understand outer space, psycholinguistics and cognitive science provide ways to understand our inner world. The study of language and mind is also the study of consciousness. And we do not yet understand how cosmos and consciousness interact beyond being aware of the existence of both within a universe we are part of.

But even more frustrating than realizing how little we humans know is realizing how little many wish to know, including some who are in positions of power. The value of basic science, for example, is misunderstood and underestimated dramatically. Yes, neuroscientists record brain activity in crows and other species to study the functions, origins, capacities, and potential of the brain. Yes, biologists study what other species, and even cells, can do. Basic science lays the foundation for applied uses and eventual benefits to society, and is instrumental in making discoveries whose impacts and utility and significance we may not yet fully comprehend. This is something that policymakers who decide on how to allocate research funding frequently do not understand. I still remember how disappointing it was to hear crowds cheer when Sarah Palin criticized the National Institutes of Health in speeches during her vice-presidential run for allocating federal funding to studying the drosophila fly, showing a complete lack of appreciation for the contribution that can be made to understanding human disease by genetic research on the drosophila model. The drosophila fly has 60 percent of its genome homologous to that of humans and about 75 percent of genes responsible for human disease. Unlike humans, who take decades to go from birth to reproduction to death, the drosophila's life cycle is much shorter, speeding up the possibilities of research across the life span and making progress in curing many human diseases much faster. (To be fair, Sarah Palin is not the only politician to speak against things she does not understand, and not nearly the worst. Perhaps the reason why I am holding Palin to higher standards is because anything Alaska-related holds a special place in my heart. I would expect a better understanding of the natural world from someone who has spent their entire life fishing, hunting, and living with nature.)

Economic estimates suggest that for every dollar invested into research and development, society receives at least $5 back, with some estimates putting the number as high as $20 in social benefits per $1 spent. It is like having a proven engine for human progress and national interest. And yet, currently, the United States invests 2.8 percent of GDP in research and development, a number lower than, for example, Israel (at 4.9 percent), South Korea (at 4.6 percent), or Japan and Germany (at 3.2 percent). China's investment in research and development has grown 16 percent per year since 2000. Progress in science and innovation is proportional to the investments made into them. Underinvestment in the curiosity that drives science affects a nation's strength and its people's standard of living, health, and capacity to respond to crises, as well as the nation's competitiveness in the world.

While chairing the National Institutes of Health Study Section that evaluates research proposals on language and communication, I routinely saw brilliant research applications go unfunded because the funding allocated to the NIH is so low that sometimes only around 10 percent of highly competitive applications are funded and 90 percent of studies do not receive funding and cannot be conducted. Think about how much progress we could make if those numbers were reversed!

I *chose* to immigrate to this country precisely because of the appreciation I have for its systems of government, its laws, its Constitution, its scientists, its people, its spirit. My being an American is not an accident of luck or birth. I considered my options carefully and made a conscious decision, as do many other immigrants in what has been a centuries-long brain drain from countries around the world into the United States. The high number of foreign-born doctoral students in the United States and the high number of companies started by innovative immigrants are well-known facts around the world. Immigrant-founded firms employ more people in total than there are immigrants in the U.S. workforce. And even though mobility between socioeconomic classes in the United States is relatively low, as a *New York Times* "Class Matters" interactive site demonstrates, it is still higher than in other countries. But to choose to become a naturalized U.S. citizen and to love this country does not mean to ignore the areas that need strengthening for its benefit. Investing in research and development is one such area that would carry benefits far greater than the costs.

When it comes to training a diverse research-and-development workforce, much is being written today about diversity, equity, and inclusion in the sciences. There's the concept of WEIRD groups—Western, Educated, Industrialized, Rich, and Democratic. In addition to the acronym, they are weird because they constitute only 12 percent of the world's population but represent about 80 percent of research populations and have a disproportional impact on shaping the scientific and social narrative.

Neurotree is a web-based database for academic genealogy that is similar to a conventional genealogy or family tree, but instead of showing connections among individuals who are kin (like parents to children), it shows connections among scholarly mentors and disciples (like doctoral advisors and their trainees) and contains hundreds of thousands of scholars going back centuries. When I look at Neurotree, I continue to be shocked at the minuscule number of women relative to men in my academic lineage, which goes back hundreds of years. As I trace my academic genealogy to my PhD dissertation advisor, Ulric Neisser, to his advisors, S. S. Stephens and Wolfgang Köhler, to Edwin Boring to Edward Titchener to Wilhelm Wundt to Karl Hasse and Johannes Müller and Hermann von Helmholtz, to scores of other brilliant and hardworking men who have dedicated their lives to science and discovery and humanity's advancement, I wonder—where are the women? Surely there were women who were at least as brilliant and hardworking as the men, yet they did not have a seat at the table. In many places around the world, they still don't. When kids draw pictures of scientists, they are still more likely to draw men, and most people cannot name any women scientists, despite the influence on every branch of science they have had throughout history. Hypatia of Alexandria, a brilliant philosopher, mathematician, and astronomer who lived nearly two thousand years ago, exemplifies that the story of science is also the (undertold) story of women, even if it cost many their lives and even if most of their names never made it to the rosters of national academies. Philosopher Umberto Eco starts his book *Kant and the Platypus* with "The history of research into the philosophy of language is full of *men* (who are rational and mortal animals), *bachelors* (who are unmarried adult males) . . ."

It is only in the last few years that the National Institutes of Health have made it a point that research it funds should include not only men but also women, consistently and on equal footing. There is currently a major social movement to increase the representation of racial and ethnic minorities in science and technology as well. To discussions of diversity, we must add linguistic diversity. Most scientific articles are written in a handful of languages. Which means that more than half of the world population neither has access to the body of knowledge shared in those articles, nor can contribute to that knowledge. As a result, a broad swath of the population is left out of these conversations. The discovery of a treatment for malaria was cited only once outside of China prior to Tu Youyou winning a Nobel Prize for it (Tu Youyou is the first Chinese woman to win a Nobel Prize, and one of only fifty-eight women out of nearly a thousand Nobel laureates). Imbalances in who gets cited depending on authors' backgrounds are pervasive in the reference lists of scientific papers. Think about how much faster scientific and technological advances could progress, how much further humanity could advance, if access to knowledge and participation in the knowledge economy were more equitable. The intellectual resources of the majority of the world population are currently untapped due to linguistic, racial, gender-based, and other forms of exclusion; capitalizing on these will help solve the global climate crisis and treat COVID, cancer, heart disease, and countless other ills and perils.

In a study financed by the Swiss National Research Program, economists at Geneva University looked at foreign languages in professional activities and concluded that Switzerland's multilingualism gives it an economic advantage equivalent to $38.15 billion. Switzerland has four national languages—German, French, Italian, and Romansh, and English is spoken by many and studied in schools as well. Media outlets were quick to interpret the study as saying that multilingualism is behind one-tenth of Swiss GDP.

The findings from Switzerland are consistent with a study on multilingualism and economic competitiveness by the European Commission. The European Commission reported that 11 percent of European small- and medium-sized businesses were losing out on exports because of a lack of language and intercultural skills. In the United Kingdom, the government estimates that the U.K. economy is losing approximately £50 billion a year due to poor foreign-language skills.

Training a multilingual workforce can have direct economic benefits both at the level of the employer and at the national level. In science and technology, inclusion of people who speak multiple languages can help find answers to questions about the human condition that are otherwise unattainable, with knowledge advancing further and faster when linguistically diverse populations are not excluded.

Leaving linguistically diverse populations out of research means an incomplete understanding of humanity and the stunting of scientific discovery and progress.

Mysteries, famous and obscure, are waiting to be solved. Most people know that the ears are used for hearing incoming sounds. But few people know that the ears also produce outgoing sounds, and that if you put a very sensitive microphone, such as those used in hearing research, next to your ear, you can actually record the sound that your ear emits. These sounds are called otoacoustic emissions and are a modern-day scientific puzzle. What is their function? Do they have any utility at all or are they evolutionary artifacts like the vestigial tail?

It wasn't until Sumit Dhar's Auditory Research Lab (which studies otoacoustic emissions) and my Psycholinguistics Research Lab (which studies bilingualism and multilingualism) combined forces and included bilinguals in a study of otoacoustic emissions that an accidental discovery was made. It turns out that otoacoustic emissions are influenced by higher cognitive processes and are related to the brain's executive function. The magnitude of otoacoustic emissions changed when multiple sensory channels, like hearing and vision, received redundant versus nonredundant input. Individuals with bilingual experience had larger changes in otoacoustic emissions in response to speech stimuli. What these findings tell us is that otoacoustic emissions are shaped by experience and influenced by top-down cognitive processes. And while it remains unknown why exactly humans and other mammals evolved to produce sounds that cannot be heard with the naked ear, it appears that otoacoustic emissions likely serve a function, even if we don't yet know exactly what that function is. If what we know now about otoacoustic emissions still leaves you unsatisfied ("OK, you've just told me that human ears produce sounds, but you didn't tell me why and what they can be used for—how anticlimactic!"), welcome to science!

Who knows how many discoveries like this or of greater value have not yet been made because multilinguals are routinely excluded from research samples? Bilingualism and multilingualism may act as a hidden moderator driving findings in studies of child development, aging, and health. Taking into account linguistic diversity regardless of whether language and/or bilingualism are the focus will improve the replicability of research and our understanding of the human condition. The innate language ability we all have can and should be capitalized upon to optimize our brain, expand human capacity, and accelerate the velocity of discovery and progress, with linguistic diversity becoming an integral part of the quest rather than an afterthought, a key factor rather than a complicating one.

The multilingual mind is a paragon of this marvel of the universe, and it provides a wonderous and surprising new view of human cognition. But although multilingualism is the norm in the world rather than the exception, lack of research on it has resulted in its devaluation.

The value of multilingualism exists not only at the level of the individual, but also at the level of society. The connection between language and thought and the multilingual mind can be, at a minimum, a propeller that advances humanity to new heights, and at a maximum, the -key to its survival.

Even more mind-bending, not only do we live in a world of codes, we *are* code, literally, down to our body's DNA. We are made of language. Our genetic code can be read in a universal language encoded in DNA base pairs. Like the language we use to combine a limited number of symbols (words, or letters, or other notations) into an unlimited number of thoughts and ideas, the DNA code combines a limited number of DNA pairs into complex and varied organisms and species that represent all life on this planet. The human faculty of language and the genetic code of all life on Earth include many similarities, like hierarchical structure, generativeness, recursion, and a virtually limitless scope of expression.

We can use one language (that of mathematics as used by artificial intelligence) to access information from the other language (that of our DNA as used by genetics). It is because of computational advances that we were able to sequence the entire genome. The Human Genome Project, although technically completed in thirteen years, in actuality took decades to achieve and is a discovery as grand as that of exploring outer space, giving us access to the language that writes the formula for all life on Earth.

In addition to DNA, there is also RNA. RNA stands for ribonucleic acid. While DNA is responsible for genetic information transmission, RNA transmits genetic codes necessary for protein creation. Messenger RNAs have recently entered public conversation after being used in some of the COVID-19 vaccines, such as those developed by Moderna and Pfizer. Messenger RNAs carry instructions for the cells to make the protein that causes the body to create antibodies to a virus, and after delivering the message they are broken down without entering the cell. Messenger RNA is just another way to communicate across systems and life-forms, a message in yet another language. Both DNA and RNA are written in a language of four nucleotides, adenine (A), guanine (G), cytosine (C), and thymine (T, in DNA) or uracil (U, in RNA). This nucleotide language can be translated into other languages (like the language of proteins, which includes twenty amino acids) by sequences called codons. Understanding the language of our genes and of our cells, just like understanding natural, artificial, and mathematical codes, opens the door to new knowledge and new worlds unbeknown to us otherwise.

The codes of the universe and our ability to learn them will, to a large extent, determine humanity's future. Our languages have the power to transcend the limitations of both the human mind as we use it now and the artificial intelligences we currently have at our disposal. We may not know where languages and their evolution will take us, but one thing is certain: we cannot get far without them.

If symbolic systems are codes for our minds, and our minds are windows into the universe, then languages hold the key to unlocking the mysteries of the universe. Multilingualism gives us a greater chance of finding the right key to the right lock. To not yet know exactly what all the locks are is part of the discovery process. Humanity may be most successful not when answers to existing questions are obtained but when new questions come into focus, questions we have not yet thought to ask and ideas we have not yet conceived.

What will we—and our languages—do next?

In Conclusion—or Happy Trails!

I am frequently asked what happens to languages we once knew, perhaps as children, but have not used due to migration to another country, adoption, or sociopolitical changes. You will be happy to hear that those languages are not entirely lost. Languages once learned and later forgotten still leave traces in memory. If you knew or were extensively exposed to a language early in life, it becomes easier to learn that language later.

One of the areas of research in the field of multilingualism focuses on language attrition, which is the loss of a previously known language, for example in adopted children or in children of immigrants. In one study, the influence of a language not spoken for decades could be detected long after a child was adopted and even despite the child not knowing what language and culture they were adopted from.

TJ was adopted through a closed-case adoption that did not disclose her linguistic and ethnic background. She was placed in foster care at the age of three and after changing foster families a few times was adopted by an American family and moved to another state. She knew that she was born in the United States to a mother who was not American-born and spoke a language other than English. At the age of thirty-three, as an American English-speaking woman going through psychotherapy, she approached a language-learning expert at Ohio State University to see if it might be possible to unlock some of the secrets of her linguistic past and learn more about her background. As a result of psychotherapy, TJ had accessed some childhood memories that included traces of individual words, and wanted to see if she could also access linguistic information that was once known. During the initial conversation, TJ gave several word forms, some of which the researchers were able to identify as having Slavic origin. The research team then used the well-known "savings paradigm"—a learn-and-relearn technique that compares the rate of learning old, previously known words to new, previously unknown words to identify the lost childhood language. TJ's performance was compared to that of a control group of twelve English-speaking females. Based on TJ's learning rate of words likely known by a child before the age of three compared to words that are unlikely to be known by a three-year-old, and compared to the control group, the researchers were able to establish that TJ's lost childhood language was either Russian or Ukrainian. This study showed that the loss of a childhood language, as often happens in adoptees, can be reversed with greater ease than learning a new language from scratch.

THERE is evidence that some people have a predisposition toward languages and are naturally better at language learning from birth. There are even theories of multiple intelligences. Linguistic intelligence is proposed to be the type of intelligence that multilinguals and those who excel at language learning are especially endowed with.

The theory of multiple intelligences, however, is not universally agreed upon. Seven types of intelligence were proposed initially—

musical-rhythmic, visual-spatial, linguistic-verbal, logical-mathematical, bodily-kinesthetic, interpersonal, and intrapersonal. Later, naturalistic intelligence (classification and use of plants and animals) and existential intelligence (big-picture thinking about human existence) were added. Since then, other types of intelligences have been proposed. But who ultimately decides what qualifies as a type of intelligence and what doesn't? What are valid and reliable measures of each type of intelligence? Some interpret intelligence as one's worth based on potentially innate characteristics one cannot be held responsible for. No surprise this theory is controversial.

The theory of multiple intelligences is right to note, however, that some people are better at language learning than others, just as some people are better at music or sports. But innate ability does not explain geographic and national bilingualism. National policies and social frameworks directly influence linguistic diversity. It is much easier to adopt a lifestyle habit if it's supported by your community, be it healthy eating, exercise, or multilingualism. When second languages are taught in schools and linguistic diversity is appreciated rather than marginalized, multilingualism becomes as common as literacy.

Other than a natural predisposition toward languages or social policies that help establish multilingual communities, the experience of language learning itself makes people better at language learning. Like anything else, the more you do it, the better you get at it.

If you already speak another language or if your parents speak another language, don't let others extinguish that part of you because of the discomfort your language or your accent causes them. Think of the languages you know as your own personal superpowers that enable you to do amazing things, including little fun things like understanding what people are saying when they are speaking behind your back, unaware that you understand them.

The language app Babbel reports that 71 percent of Americans and

61 percent of Britons say that they find someone who knows more than one language more attractive. Knowing another language can also boost one's income. A study in Florida reports that Hispanic Americans who are fully bilingual in both English and Spanish earn nearly $7,000 more per year than their English monolingual counterparts. Economists at the University of Guelph in Canada found that English–French bilingual men earn 3.6 percent more than men who speak only English, and English–French bilingual women earn 6.6 percent more than their English monolingual counterparts. In the Quebec province of Canada, French–English bilingual men earn 7 percent more than monolingual French men, and this difference jumps to 21 percent for those who speak English at work.

At this point, having covered the powerful changes to our brain, perception, memory, decision-making, emotions, and creativity that result from multilingualism, some readers may decide to venture into learning a new language themselves or into having their children learn a new language. But how? When? How can you peek behind the monolingual curtain for yourself? If you are wondering when one should learn another language, the answer is that the best time is from birth. The second best time? Now.

Although it was once thought that learning a new language to fluency after a certain age and beyond a "critical period" was difficult if not impossible, we now know that is not true. The idea of a critical period dates back to a 1967 study that proposed the cut-off point to be puberty. Later, a large-scale analysis of 669,498 people pinpointed that age to be 17.4 years, with hundreds of other studies suggesting a multitude of other age points. Most recently, a reanalysis of the large data set found no evidence for a critical age. Instead, it seems that the effects reported previously were driven by personal and social factors that disrupted patterns of language learning, including schooling effects and differences in living circumstances and in socialization.

Through my decades of research with speakers of multiple languages, I have seen that people can learn another language at any age, with almost immediate benefits. It is true, however, that those who learn a second language post-puberty or from other non-native speakers will often retain a foreign accent when speaking in their new language, in part because their articulation and perceptual systems have already been influenced by their native language. An accent is a minor tradeoff to being able to speak another language, and some may even consider it a plus.

You may be interested in learning another language for brain health, travel, romance, or personal growth. You may be someone who in the past googled "How to learn Spanish" or "fluent in 3 months" or bought *Italian for Dummies*. Maybe you are someone who buys books on self-improvement, on professional development, on keeping the mind sharp, on improving relationships, or on travel. Maybe you are a teacher. A businessperson. A marketer. A life coach. A retiree. A student. Learning another language is a gift you can give yourself.

When it comes to learning languages, it is entirely possible to have a greater aptitude for learning some languages but not others. Someone may find it a breeze to learn Latin-based languages, harder-but-still-manageable to learn Germanic-based languages, extremely difficult to learn computer languages, and impossible to learn any languages that rely on tonal information to convey meaning (such as Mandarin). Writers may find natural languages easier than artificial languages; coders may find artificial languages easier than natural languages; musicians may be better at languages that rely on tones.

No matter what preferences we as individuals have, anyone can make progress in learning a new language, even if the ultimate measures of success vary. Based on data from the U.S. Department of State from foreign-language training provided to diplomats and government employees with job-related needs, it is estimated that the number of hours English-native speakers need to learn a language ranges from 600 to 2,200, depending on the language—a timeline based on over seventy years of teaching languages to U.S. diplomats. A native English speaker can learn Spanish in about 600 hours but would take nearly four times as long to learn Japanese. Below is a table of the DoS breakdown of languages taught and how long it takes to acquire them.

Category I Languages 24–30 weeks to learn (600–750 class hours)	24 weeks: Danish, Dutch, Italian, Norwegian, Portuguese, Romanian, Spanish, Swedish 30 weeks: French
Category II Languages Approximately 36 weeks to learn (900 class hours)	German, Haitian Creole, Indonesian, Malay, Swahili
Category III Languages Approximately 44 weeks to learn (1,100 class hours)	Albanian, Amharic, Armenian, Azerbaijani, Bengali, Bulgarian, Burmese, Czech, Dari, Estonian, Farsi, Finnish, Georgian, Greek, Hebrew, Hindi, Hungarian, Icelandic, Kazakh, Khmer, Kurdish, Kyrgyz, Lao, Latvian, Lithuanian, Macedonian, Mongolian, Nepali, Polish, Russian, Serbo-Croatian, Sinhala, Slovak, Slovenian, Somali, Tagalog, Tajiki, Tamil, Telugu, Thai, Tibetan, Turkish, Turkmen, Ukrainian, Urdu, Uzbek, Vietnamese
Category IV Languages 88 weeks to learn (2,200 class hours)	Arabic, Cantonese, Mandarin, Japanese, Korean

The good news is that you can begin to experience changes after just a short time of learning. One semester of study abroad is sufficient to produce some of the effects of multilingualism, suggesting that just a few months of experience immersed in another language can change how your brain works.

After only six months of taking an Introduction to Spanish course, monolingual undergraduate students performing an executive-control task had electrophysiological brain responses that resembled those of bilinguals. Another study found improvements in attention switching after an intensive one-week Gaelic course, relative to a control group, in participants between the ages of eighteen and seventy-eight. Swedish Armed Forces Interpreter Academy recruits showed increases in cortical thickness in language-processing areas after three months of language training.

Once you have decided which language to learn, you may be eager to get some tips for how to do so effectively. Below you will find several strategies you may want to consider when embarking on learning another language as an adult, as well as for raising bilingual children. To help you on your journey:

1. Take a class.

Foreign-language classes are now widely available at universities and community colleges. Many community centers, retirement homes, and places of worship offer evening and weekend classes.

2. Use language-learning apps.

If taking a formal class is outside your budget or doesn't fit your schedule, you can use modern technology instead. Pandemic lockdowns saw a surge in use of language-learning apps. There are many digital platforms to choose from and clinical trials report that language learning through smartphone apps improves executive function in older adults. What many of these apps do especially well is incorporate gaming designs to capitalize on the brain's release of serotonin and dopamine, which keeps language learning engaging, fun, and exciting. Many of them, like Duolingo, hire language scientists and researchers who have a strong foundation in the cognitive and neural aspects of language learning and rely on evidence-based science and practices.

3. Travel.

Immersion in another culture provides an excellent opportunity for learning another language. Not only are you exposed to native speakers, you are also exposed to a diversity of speakers. Study-abroad programs in secondary schools and colleges can be especially valuable during the years when the brain is still most pliable. If financial or life circumstances prevented you from doing so when you were younger, it is not too late to benefit from immersive language experiences later in life. Sometimes you may not need to travel to the other side of the world, but can visit another province or state in your home country, or even a neighborhood or area in your own city.

4. Develop relationships with speakers of another language.
Many years ago, my brother made an arrangement with a Swedish speaker—he would help her with her English, and she would help him with his Swedish. Long story short, that Swedish speaker has now been my sister-in-law for over a decade. Interacting with people who speak other languages, be they friends, coworkers, or dates, is one of the easiest and often most enjoyable ways to learn another language while at the same time strengthening your social network.

5. Make it a habit.
Like with anything else—be it exercise, playing a musical instrument, or investing—consistency and a long-term approach are key. Incorporate another language into your daily schedule and routines. You can do that both by actively studying the language and by passively exposing yourself to it through listening to music and consuming visual and other entertainment in that language. You can play video games and online games with speakers of other languages. If you have the option, select the new language for the movies you are watching, or on your phone or computer interface.

7. Use mnemonics.
Mnemonics refers to techniques that improve and assist memory. There are many mnemonic techniques available to choose among, but

one that language learners find especially helpful is creating connections between the words they already know and the new words they are learning. Here is an example from a multilingual student in one of my seminars: "When I was learning the word for 'dangerous' in Spanish, which is *peligroso*, the way I learned it was that it sounded similar to the English word *pelican*. I have a fear of pelicans, so it reinforced my way of learning the word and its meaning. Meanwhile, when I learned the Chinese word for 'dangerous,' which is 危险, I learned it because 险 looked like the Chinese word for 'sword,' which is 剑, and so I had it encoded in my brain that the word means 'danger' because swords are dangerous. I now have this really weird link between pelicans, swords, and *dangerous*."

8. Find a pattern that works for you.

There are many paths to bilingualism and you can try them all until you find one that works for you. Some choose to speak a different language on different days of the week. Others speak a certain language to specific friends or family members, like grandparents. Others incentivize themselves by speaking another language as either a reward or a penalty. You could resolve to spend ten minutes on a language-learning app every time you feel the urge to argue with someone on social media—you'll be fluent in no time!

IF you want to raise a bilingual child, here are seven evidence-based suggestions:

1. Increase language *quantity*.

The quantity of linguistic input children receive in each of their languages predicts vocabulary and grammatical development. The richer the input, the higher the likelihood of successful language acquisition. Children who hear a lot of words have a larger vocabulary size. Verbally describe activities you are engaging in together, read to and with your child, and expose your child to two languages as often as reasonably possible.

2. Increase language *quality.*

Quality of linguistic input influences children's language outcomes. Having stimulating face-to-face interactions with caregivers is crucial in helping children acquire language. For example, interacting with and reading books to children supports language development, whereas language exposure via television has minimal benefits. While adults may benefit from consuming media in the foreign language, low-quality television exposure has actually been associated with lower vocabulary scores in bilingual children. Aim for more face time.

3. Enlist the help of family and friends.

Variability in language input is another key predictor of language growth. Having regular interactions with many *different* speakers of the two languages can help boost bilingual proficiency, as children are exposed to more diverse inputs. Interacting with multiple family members and friends, grandparents, and extended family who speak the other language benefits children's language development.

4. Select a strategy that works best for your family.

There are many different ways to expose your child to multiple languages, depending on the household. Although no single approach has been identified as the best for raising bilingual children, several have been found to support bilingual language development. There is the "one person, one language" approach, commonly used by two parents who speak different languages (Parent A speaks one language; Parent B speaks another language). In another common approach, a child is exposed to one language (typically a minority language, referred to as a heritage language when this is the native language of the parents) in the home and a second language (typically the majority language) in school. You can also develop your own strategy that works best for your child and you.

5. Let your child lead the way.

Pay attention to cues from your child and follow their interests. Language development is most successful when children interact with attentive and sensitive adults. A child is more likely to learn new words when an adult focuses on things that the child is interested in, as opposed to what the adult is interested in. Your child will have a higher chance of success acquiring two languages if they are engaged. To encourage learning, try to find activities involving two languages that interest your child.

6. Consider bilingual education.

During early development, there may be an option of having babysitters or caregivers who speak another language or enrolling children in preschools where another language or more than one language is spoken or signed. Once your child is of school age, consider schools with two-way immersion programs, which include students of two different native languages in the same classroom and teach content classes in those two languages. If two-way immersion programs are not available in your school district, there may be other alternatives. After-school or weekend language lessons can provide a formal instructional setting that promotes second-language acquisition. Places of worship can also be useful resources if you are trying to raise your child to speak a language that is associated with your faith. Similarly, summer camps, exchange programs, or studying or traveling abroad, if they fit into the family budget, can provide wonderful language-learning opportunities.

7. Continue educating yourself about bilingual language development.

Learn more about bilingualism yourself. There are numerous misconceptions surrounding raising a bilingual child. Good starting points on this topic include resources shared by the Bilingualism Matters network and books written by experts in this area.

Although there are no universal rules to follow when it comes to raising a bilingual child, the most important thing to do as a parent is to provide nurturing support. The approach that you end up taking will depend on the nature of your household, the temperament of your child, the area you live in, and the resources that are available to you. At the end of the day, focus on raising a happy child. The ability to speak two or more languages and the cognitive and social benefits that come with it are a bonus.

Finally, if you are wondering whether you should speak your native language with your child or use a second language instead, the answer is *you should speak the language that will provide your child with the richest linguistic input.* Instructing parents to speak to their children in a second language that they do not know well instead of a fluent native language in which they have a larger vocabulary and better grammar is ill-informed advice, however well-intentioned it may be. Telling parents not to use the native language with their children eliminates use of the native proficient language, and the size and richness of language input provided to the child is compromised. If the parent is not proficient in this second language, asking them to use a language they lack dexterity in means replacing a rich input of vocabulary, grammar, and storytelling with an impoverished input, perhaps even with only passive input from television and the Internet instead of interactive and rich in-person communication. Richness of input is one of the best predictors of a child's language and cognitive development. It is more important for the child to receive a rich linguistic input—a kaleidoscope of sounds, words, and grammar—than it is for them to receive these inputs in one language over another. The richer the input the child receives—auditory, visual, tactile—the more neurons are firing and the more active the brain is. The brain's wiring is largely shaped by the input it receives.

In my own family, because we spoke so many different languages (Romanian-Russian-speaking mother, Dutch-German-speaking father, English in the Midwest area of the United States, and sprinklings of Spanish and French during travel), we did not insist that our children learn one specific language. Instead, we exposed them broadly to all these languages so that when they choose to, they can more easily learn them to proficiency. That approach seems to have worked, as languages come easily to all three of my children and they learn them with ease when they need to. (None of them are fully functionally multilingual, to be honest. In part this is because their own individual passions lie elsewhere. And in part it is because my kids went to school in the United States, where the education system does not support multilingualism, and grew up in a community where monolingualism is the norm. This contrasts with their parents' and their grandparents' experiences of growing up with multiple languages in Europe and going to schools where education included at least one, but usually two or more foreign languages.) Of course, because it is not a controlled experiment, it is impossible to know to what extent this proclivity for languages comes from a genetic predisposition as opposed to extensive exposure to multiple languages during childhood. But as anecdotal evidence, it reflects the recommendation to expose children to, and surround yourself with, a rich linguistic environment of multiple languages. Exposure to more than one language, even if fluent multilingualism is not attained, provides an enriching experience likely to yield long-term benefits.

It is never too early or too late to start learning another language. It may even be fun.

ACKNOWLEDGMENTS

I thank Stephen Morrow for bringing me to Dutton, Giles Anderson for bringing me to Stephen, Art Markman for bringing me to Giles, and Dedre Gentner for bringing me to Art. To the team at Dutton—Stephen, Grace Layer, Sabila Khan, Rachelle Mandik, Rick Ball, Alice Dalrymple, Vi-An Nguyen, Sarah Thegeby, Nicole Jarvis, Hannah Dragone, and Tiffany Estreicher—thank you!

I thank the current and past members of my Bilingualism and Psycholinguistics Research Lab who have conducted many of the studies discussed in this book. Special thanks to Ashley Chung-Fat-Yim, Sayuri Hayakawa, Sirada Rochanavibhata, Anthony Shook, Wil van den Berg, and Rachel Webster, as well as Rina Magarici and Matt Schiff, for their contributions and suggestions.

I thank Northwestern University, the National Institutes of Health, the National Science Foundation, and the Delaney Foundation for supporting my research.

I thank the students, mentors, and colleagues in the fields of psycholinguistics, cognitive science, communication sciences and disorders, psychology, linguistics, neuroscience, philosophy, education, and world languages who have helped shape my work and ideas over the years.

I thank Grace, Nadia, Aimee, and Aswin van den Berg, my parents, Nicolae and Natalia Marian, and my family and friends for their love.

And I thank you, the reader, for connecting with me across time and space on these pages.

NOTES

Introduction

2 **"A Tranquil Star":** Primo Levi, "A Tranquil Star," *The New Yorker,* February 12, 2007, https://www.newyorker.com/magazine /2007/02/12/a tranquil star.

2 **neuroscientists at Stanford University:** Russell A. Poldrack, Yaroslav O. Halchenko, and Stephen José Hanson, "Decoding the Large-Scale Structure of Brain Function by Classifying Mental States Across Individuals," *Psychological Science* 20, no. 11 (2009): 1364–1372, https://doi.org/10.1111/j.1467-9280.2009.02460.x.

3 **constructs that emerged from machine learning:** Russell A. Poldrack and Tal Yarkoni, "From Brain Maps to Cognitive Ontologies: Informatics and the Search for Mental Structure," *Annual Review of Psychology* 67 (2016): 587–612, https://doi.org/10.1146/annurev-psych -122414-033729.

4 **perceive and describe a bridge:** Lera Boroditsky, Lauren A. Schmidt, and Webb Phillips, "Sex, Syntax, and Semantics," in *Language in Mind: Advances in the Study of Language and Thought,* eds. Dedre

Gentner and Susan Goldin-Meadow (Cambridge: MIT Press, 2003), 61–79.

4 **grammatical gender of inanimate objects:** Steven Samuel, Geoff Cole, and Madeline J. Eacott, "Grammatical Gender and Linguistic Relativity: A Systematic Review," *Psychonomic Bulletin & Review* 26, no. 6 (2019): 1767–1786, https://doi.org/10.3758/s13423-019-01652-3.

5 **NASA's Mars Climate Orbiter:** National Aeronautics and Space Administration, "Mars Climate Orbiter," last modified July 25, 2019, https://solarsystem.nasa.gov/missions/mars-climate-orbiter/in-depth/.

5 **"The word has other meanings":** National Security Agency, "Mokusatsu: One Word, Two Lessons," accessed February 18, 2022, https://www.nsa.gov/portals/75/documents/news-features/declassified -documents/tech-journals/mokusatsu.pdf/.

6 **delays Alzheimer's:** Ellen Bialystok, Fergus I. M. Craik, and Morris Freedman, "Bilingualism as a Protection Against the Onset of Symptoms of Dementia," *Neuropsychologia* 45, no. 2 (2007): 459–464, https://doi.org/10.1016/j.neuropsychologia.2006.10.009.

Part One: Self

9 **"the limits of my language":** Ludwig Wittgenstein, *Tractatus Logico-Philosophicus* (London: Routledge & Kegan Paul, 1922).

Chapter 1: Mind Boggling

14 **other than English at home:** Karen Zeigler and Steven A. Camarota, "67.3 Million in the United States Spoke a Foreign Language at Home in 2018," Center for Immigration Studies (2019): 1–7, https://cis.org /sites/default/files/2019-10/camarota-language-19_0.pdf/.

16 **new methods:** Sayuri Hayakawa and Viorica Marian, "Studying Bilingualism Through Eye-Tracking and Brain Imaging," in *Bilingual Lexical Ambiguity Resolution,* eds. Roberto R. Heredia and Anna B. Cieślicka (Cambridge: Cambridge University Press, 2020), 273–299.

16 **Experiments in my lab:** Northwestern University, "Bilingualism and Psycholinguistics Lab," accessed February 18, 2022, http://www .bilingualism.northwestern.edu/.

16 **influenced by the languages we know:** Viorica Marian, "The Language You Speak Influences Where Your Attention Goes," *Scientific American,* December 5, 2019, https://blogs.scientificamerican.com /observations/the-language-you-speak-influences-where-your -attention-goes/.

16 **eye movements are recorded:** Viorica Marian, "Bilingual Language Processing: Evidence from Eye-Tracking and Functional Neuroimaging," (PhD diss., Cornell University, 2000).

16 **objects with names overlapping in English:** Viorica Marian and Michael Spivey, "Competing Activation in Bilingual Language Processing: Within- and Between-Language Competition," *Bilingualism: Language and Cognition* 6, no. 2 (2003): 97–115, https:// doi.org/10.1017/S1366728903001068.

16 **overlap across the two languages:** Michael J. Spivey and Viorica Marian, "Cross Talk Between Native and Second Languages: Partial Activation of an Irrelevant Lexicon," *Psychological Science* 10, no. 3 (1999): 281–284, https://doi.org/10.1111/1467-9280.00151.

17 **parallel activation of the other language:** Viorica Marian and Michael Spivey, "Bilingual and Monolingual Processing of Competing Lexical Items," *Applied Psycholinguistics* 24, no. 2 (2003): 173–193, https://doi.org/10.1017/S0142716403000092.

17 **Stroop task:** Ellen Bialystok, Fergus I. M. Craik, and Gigi Luk, "Cognitive Control and Lexical Access in Younger and Older Bilinguals," *Journal of Experimental Psychology: Learning, Memory, and Cognition* 34, no. 4 (2008): 859–873, https://doi.org/10.1037 /0278-7393.34.4.859.

17 **pay attention to the ink color:** Viorica Marian, Henrike K. Blumenfeld, Elena Mizrahi, Ursula Kania, and Anne-Kristin Cordes, "Multilingual Stroop Performance: Effects of Trilingualism and Proficiency on Inhibitory Control," *International Journal of Multilingualism* 10, no. 1 (2013): 82–104, https://doi.org/10.1080 /14790718.2012.708037.

17 *Statue of Liberty* **when speaking English:** Viorica Marian and
Margarita Kaushanskaya, "Language Context Guides Memory
Content," *Psychonomic Bulletin & Review* 14, no. 5 (2007): 925–933,
https://doi.org/10.3758/BF03194123.

19 **accessibility of memories varies across languages:** Viorica Marian
and Margarita Kaushanskaya, "Language-Dependent Memory:
Insights from Bilingualism," in *Relations Between Language and
Memory,* ed. Cornelia Zelinsky-Wibbelt (Peter Lang, 2011), 95–120.

19 **Language-Dependent Memory:** Viorica Marian and Ulric Neisser,
"Language-Dependent Recall of Autobiographical Memories," *Journal
of Experimental Psychology: General* 129, no. 3 (2000): 361–368, https://
doi.org/10.1037/0096-3445.129.3.361.

19 **"I love you" feels different:** Jean-Marc Dewaele, "The Emotional
Weight of I Love You in Multilinguals' Languages," *Journal of
Pragmatics* 40, no. 10 (2008): 1753–1780, https://doi.org/10.1016
/j.pragma.2008.03.002.

19 **can provide more emotional detachment:** Viorica Marian and
Margarita Kaushanskaya, "Words, Feelings, and Bilingualism:
Cross-Linguistic Differences in Emotionality of Autobiographical
Memories," *The Mental Lexicon* 3, no. 1 (2008): 72–91, https://doi.org
/10.1075/ml.3.1.06mar.

20 **Foreign Language Effect:** Sayuri Hayakawa, Albert Costa, Alice
Foucart, and Boaz Keysar, "Using a Foreign Language Changes Our
Choices," *Trends in Cognitive Sciences* 20, no. 11 (2016): 791–793,
https://doi.org/10.1016/j.tics.2016.08.004.

20 **classic trolley dilemma:** Albert Costa, Alice Foucart, Sayuri
Hayakawa, Melina Aparici, Jose Apesteguia, Joy Heafner, and Boaz
Keysar, "Your Morals Depend on Language," *PloS ONE* 9, no. 4 (2014):
e94842, https://doi.org/10.1371/journal.pone.0094842.

20 **this time on cheating:** Yoella Bereby-Meyer, Sayuri Hayakawa, Shaul
Shalvi, Joanna D. Corey, Albert Costa, and Boaz Keysar, "Honesty
Speaks a Second Language," *Topics in Cognitive Science* 12, no. 2
(2020): 632–643, https://doi.org/10.1111/tops.12360.

Chapter 2: The Parallel-Processing Super-Organism

24 **recording these unconscious eye movements:** University of Western Ontario, "Lab Tutorials," accessed February 18, 2022, https://sites .google.com/site/kenmcraelab/lab-tutorials/.

26 **integrated with the visual input:** Viorica Marian, "Audio-Visual Integration During Bilingual Language Processing," in *The Bilingual Mental Lexicon: Interdisciplinary Approaches,* ed. Aneta Pavlenko (Clevedon, UK: Multilingual Matters, 2009), 52–78.

27 **Evidence for such "covert co-activation":** Anthony Shook and Viorica Marian, "Covert Co-Activation of Bilinguals' Non-Target Language: Phonological Competition from Translations," *Linguistic Approaches to Bilingualism* 9, no. 2 (2019): 228–252, https://doi.org/10.1075 /lab.17022.sho.

28 **parallel activation for syntax and grammar:** Holger Hopp, "The Processing of English Which-Questions in Adult L2 Learners: Effects of L1 Transfer and Proficiency," *Zeitschrift für Sprachwissenschaft* 36, no. 1 (2017): 107–134, https://doi.org/10.1515/zfs-2017-0006.

29 **activates the written and spoken forms:** Margarita Kaushanskaya and Viorica Marian, "Bilingual Language Processing and Interference in Bilinguals: Evidence from Eye Tracking and Picture Naming," *Language Learning* 57, no. 1 (2007): 119–163, https://doi.org/10.1111 /j.1467-9922.2007.00401.x.

29 **differ in letter-to-sound mappings:** Viorica Marian, James Bartolotti, Natalia L. Daniel, and Sayuri Hayakawa, "Spoken Words Activate Native and Non-Native Letter-to-Sound Mappings: Evidence from Eye Tracking," *Brain and Language* 223 (2021): 105045, https://doi.org /10.1016/j.bandl.2021.105045.

30 **parallel co-activation across both languages:** Anthony Shook and Viorica Marian, "The Bilingual Language Interaction Network for Comprehension of Speech," *Bilingualism: Language and Cognition* 16, no. 2 (2013): 304–324, https://doi.org/10.1017/S1366728912000466.

31 **thresholds of activation:** Henrike K. Blumenfeld and Viorica Marian, "Constraints on Parallel Activation in Bilingual Spoken Language Processing: Examining Proficiency and Lexical Status Using

Eye-Tracking," *Language and Cognitive Processes* 22, no. 5 (2007): 633–660, https://doi.org/10.1080/01690960601000746.

31 **Co-activation is even found across different modalities:** Anthony Shook and Viorica Marian, "Language Processing in Bimodal Bilinguals," in *Bilinguals: Cognition, Education, and Language Processing,* ed. Earl F. Caldwell (Hauppauge, NY: Nova Science Publishers, 2009), 35–64.

32 **ASL–English bimodal bilinguals:** Marcel R. Giezen, Henrike K. Blumenfeld, Anthony Shook, Viorica Marian, and Karen Emmorey, "Parallel Language Activation and Inhibitory Control in Bimodal Bilinguals," *Cognition* 141 (2015): 9–25, https://doi.org/10.1016/j.cognition.2015.04.009.

32 **An illustration of the ASL experiment:** Anthony Shook and Viorica Marian, "Bimodal Bilinguals Co-Activate Both Languages During Spoken Comprehension," *Cognition* 124, no. 3 (2012): 314–324, https://doi.org/10.1016/j.cognition.2012.05.014.

33 *even when no words are used:* Sarah Chabal and Viorica Marian, "Speakers of Different Languages Process the Visual World Differently," *Journal of Experimental Psychology: General* 144, no. 3 (2015): 539–550, https://doi.org/10.1037/xge0000075.

33 **when a mental load was added:** Sarah Chabal, Sayuri Hayakawa, and Viorica Marian, "Language Is Activated by Visual Input Regardless of Memory Demands or Capacity," *Cognition* 222 (2022): 104994, https://doi.org/10.1016/j.cognition.2021.104994.

33 **multilingualism affects not only the language system:** Judith F. Kroll, Paola E. Dussias, Cari A. Bogulski, and Jorge R. Valdes Kroff, "Juggling Two Languages in One Mind: What Bilinguals Tell Us About Language Processing and Its Consequences for Cognition," *Psychology of Learning and Motivation* 56 (2012): 229–262, https://doi.org/10.1016/B978-0-12-394393-4.00007-8.

34 **parallel activation has repercussions:** Viorica Marian, Sayuri Hayakawa, and Scott R. Schroeder, "Memory After Visual Search: Overlapping Phonology, Shared Meaning, and Bilingual Experience Influence What We Remember," *Brain and Language* 222 (2021): 105012, https://doi.org/10.1016/j.bandl.2021.105012.

34 **manage the competition across languages:** Henrike K. Blumenfeld
and Viorica Marian, "Bilingualism Influences Inhibitory Control in
Auditory Comprehension," *Cognition* 118, no. 2 (2011): 245–257,
https://doi.org/10.1016/j.cognition.2010.10.012.

Chapter 3: On Creativity, Perception, and Thought

36 **relationships with someone from another country:** Jackson G. Lu,
Andrew C. Hafenbrack, Paul W. Eastwick, Dan J. Wang, William W.
Maddux, and Adam D. Galinsky, "'Going Out' of the Box: Close
Intercultural Friendships and Romantic Relationships Spark
Creativity, Workplace Innovation, and Entrepreneurship," *Journal
of Applied Psychology* 102, no. 7 (2017): 1091–1108, https://doi.org
/10.1037/apl0000212.

37 **features of 1,010 word meanings:** Bill Thompson, Seán G. Roberts,
and Gary Lupyan, "Cultural Influences on Word Meanings Revealed
through Large-Scale Semantic Alignment," *Nature Human Behaviour*
4, no. 10 (2020): 1029–1038, https://doi.org/10.1038/s41562
-020-0924-8.

38 ***kli*, in Hebrew:** Tamar Degani, Anat Prior, and Natasha Tokowicz,
"Bidirectional Transfer: The Effect of Sharing a Translation," *Journal
of Cognitive Psychology* 23, no. 1 (2011): 18–28, https://doi.org/10.1080
/20445911.2011.445986.

39 **how related in meaning two objects were:** Siqi Ning, Sayuri
Hayakawa, James Bartolotti, and Viorica Marian, "On Language and
Thought: Bilingual Experience Influences Semantic Associations,"
Journal of Neurolinguistics 56 (2020): 100932, https://doi.org/10.1016
/j.jneuroling.2020.100932.

39 ***"Fight was what I did":*** Li-Young Lee, "Persimmons," in Li-Young Lee,
Rose: Poems (Rochester, NY: BOA Editions, 1986), 17–19.

40 **ambiguous-figure task:** Ellen Bialystok and Dana Shapero,
"Ambiguous Benefits: The Effect of Bilingualism on Reversing
Ambiguous Figures," *Developmental Science* 8, no. 6 (2005): 595–604,
https://doi.org/10.1111/j.1467-7687.2005.00451.x.

40 **experiments with younger children:** Marina C. Wimmer and
    Christina Marx, "Inhibitory Processes in Visual Perception: A
    Bilingual Advantage," *Journal of Experimental Child Psychology* 126
    (2014): 412–419, https://doi.org/10.1016/j.jecp.2014.03.004.

40 **drawing nonexistent objects:** Annette Karmiloff-Smith, "Constraints
    on Representational Change: Evidence from Children's Drawing,"
    Cognition 34, no. 1 (1990): 57–83, https://doi.org/10.1016/0010
    -0277(90)90031-E.

40 **drawings of bilingual children:** Esther Adi-Japha, Jennie Berberich-
    Artzi, and Afaf Libnawi, "Cognitive Flexibility in Drawings of
    Bilingual Children," *Child Development* 81, no. 5 (2010): 1356–1366,
    https://doi.org/10.1111/j.1467-8624.2010.01477.x.

42 **Torrance Test of Creative Thinking:** E. Paul Torrance, "Predicting the
    Creativity of Elementary School Children (1958–80)—and the Teacher
    Who 'Made a Difference,'" *Gifted Child Quarterly* 25, no. 2 (1981):
    55–62, https://doi.org/10.1177/001698628102500203.

42 **evaluated again fifty years later:** Jonathan A. Plucker, "Is the Proof in
    the Pudding? Reanalyses of Torrance's (1958 to present) Longitudinal
    Data," *Creativity Research Journal* 12, no. 2 (1999): 103–114, https://doi
    .org/10.1207/s15326934crj1202_3.

44 *Sprachspiel,* **or** *language-game:* Ludwig Wittgenstein, *Philosophical
    Investigations,* trans. Gertrude Elizabeth Margaret Anscombe (New
    York: Macmillan, 1953).

46 **"Perhaps it is the suggestion":** John B. Carroll, *Language, Thought,
    and Reality: Selected Writings of Benjamin Lee Whorf* (Cambridge,
    MA: MIT Press, 1956).

46 **language a "prisonhouse":** Erich Heller, "Wittgenstein and
    Nietzsche," in *The Artist's Journey into the Interior and Other Essays*
    (London: Secker & Warburg, 1966), 199–226.

47 **treating a woman with anterograde amnesia:** Édouard Claparède,
    "Récognition et moiïté," *Archives de psychologie Genève* 11 (1911):
    79–90.

50 **language shapes the representation of time:** Lera Boroditsky, "Does
    Language Shape Thought?: Mandarin and English Speakers'
    Conceptions of Time," *Cognitive Psychology* 43, no. 1 (2001): 1–22,
    https://doi.org/10.1006/cogp.2001.0748.

51 **words of Edward Sapir:** Edward Sapir, "The Status of Linguistics as a Science," *Language* 5, no. 4 (1929): 207–214.

52 **Sensory perception can be nudged:** Peiyao Chen, Ashley Chung-Fat-Yim, and Viorica Marian, "Cultural Experience Influences Multisensory Emotion Perception in Bilinguals," *Languages* 7, no. 1 (2022): 12, https://doi.org/10.3390/languages7010012.

54 **multilingual experience alters multisensory integration:** Viorica Marian, Sayuri Hayakawa, Tuan Q. Lam, and Scott R. Schroeder, "Language Experience Changes Audiovisual Perception," *Brain Sciences* 8, no. 5 (2018): 85, https://doi.org/10.3390/brainsci805008.

54 **shape sensory processing:** Sayuri Hayakawa and Viorica Marian, "Consequences of Multilingualism for Neural Architecture," *Behavioral and Brain Functions* 15, no. 1 (2019): 1–24, https://doi.org/10.1186/s12993-019-0157-z.

54 **Using swearwords:** Richard Stephens, John Atkins, and Andrew Kingston, "Swearing as a Response to Pain," *NeuroReport* 20, no. 12 (2009): 1056–1060, https://doi.org/10.1097/WR.0b013e32832e64b1.

Chapter 4: The Word Made Flesh

57 **started to study multilingual brains:** Viorica Marian, Michael Spivey, and Joy Hirsch, "Shared and Separate Systems in Bilingual Language Processing: Converging Evidence from Eyetracking and Brain Imaging," *Brain and Language* 86, no. 1 (2003): 70–82, https://doi.org/10.1016/S0093-934X(02)00535-7.

57 **functional magnetic resonance imaging:** fMRI 4 Newbies, "fMRI 4 Newbies: A Crash Course in Brain Imaging," accessed February 18, 2022, http://www.fmri4newbies.com/.

59 **alternate antagonism aphasia:** Michel Paradis, Marie-Claire Goldblum, and Raouf Abidi, "Alternate Antagonism with Paradoxical Translation Behavior in Two Bilingual Aphasic Patients," *Brain and Language* 15, no. 1 (1982): 55–69, https://doi.org/10.1016/0093-934X(82)90046-3.

59 **Neurologist Albert Pitres:** Albert Pitres, "Etude sur l'aphasie chez les polyglottes," *Revue de Médecine* 15 (1895): 873–899.

60 **multilingual aphasia has been studied:** Franco Fabbro, *The Neurolinguistics of Bilingualism: An Introduction* (London: Psychology Press, 1999).

61 **sound transformed into meaningful words:** Liberty S. Hamilton, Yulia Oganian, Jeffery Hall, and Edward Chang, "Parallel and Distributed Encoding of Speech Across Human Auditory Cortex," *Cell* 184, no. 18 (2021): 4626–4639, https://doi.org/10.1016/j.cell.2021 .07.019.

62 ***Modularity of Mind* removed the notion:** Jerry A. Fodor, *The Modularity of Mind* (Cambridge, MA: MIT Press, 1983).

62 **complex system explained by emergence theory:** Steven Johnson, *Emergence: The Connected Lives of Ants, Brains, Cities, and Software* (New York: Scribner, 2001).

63 **described mathematically by Alan Turing:** Alan Turing, "The Chemical Basis of Morphogenesis," *Philosophical Transactions of the Royal Society of London B* 237, no. 641 (1952): 37–72.

63 **automatic self-organization and self-replication:** Marvin Minsky, *The Emotion Machine: Commonsense Thinking, Artificial Intelligence, and the Future of the Human Mind* (New York: Simon & Schuster, 2006).

64 **words *sleep* and *green*:** Noam Chomsky, *Syntactic Structures* (The Hague: Mouton, 1957).

64 **rewires your brain and transforms it:** Sayuri Hayakawa and Viorica Marian, "Consequences of Multilingualism for Neural Architecture," *Behavioral and Brain Functions* 15, no. 1 (2019): 1–24, https://doi.org /10.1186/s12993-019-0157-z.

64 **higher gray-matter density:** Andrea Mechelli, Jenny T. Crinion, Uta Noppeney, John O'Doherty, John Ashburner, Richard S. Frackowiak, and Cathy J. Price, "Structural Plasticity in the Bilingual Brain," *Nature* 431, no. 7010 (2004): 757, https://doi.org/10.1038/431757a.

64 **subcortical sensory and motor regions:** Jennifer Krizman and Viorica Marian, "Neural Consequences of Bilingualism for Cortical and Subcortical Function," in *The Cambridge Handbook of Bilingual Processing*, ed. John W. Schwieter (Cambridge: Cambridge University Press, 2015), 614–630.

65 **brain structures involved in language processing:** Viorica Marian, James Bartolotti, Sirada Rochanavibhata, Kailyn Bradley, and Arturo E. Hernandez, "Bilingual Cortical Control of Between- and Within-Language Competition," *Scientific Reports* 7, no. 1 (2017): 1–11, https://doi.org/10.1038/s41598-017-12116-w.

65 **gray- and white-matter regions:** Christos Pliatsikas, Elisavet Moschopoulou, and James Douglas Saddy, "The Effects of Bilingualism on the White Matter Structure of the Brain," *Proceedings of the National Academy of Sciences* 112, no. 5 (2015): 1334–1337, https://doi.org/10.1073/pnas.1414183112.

65 **differences in metabolite levels:** Christos Pliatsikas, Sergio Miguel Pereira Soares, Toms Voits, Vincent DeLuca, and Jason Rothman, "Bilingualism Is a Long-Term Cognitively Challenging Experience that Modulates Metabolite Concentrations in the Healthy Brain," *Scientific Reports* 11, no. 1 (2021): 1–12, https://doi.org/10.1038/s41598-021-86443-4.

66 **heritability due to epigenetics:** Sharon Begley, "Was Darwin Wrong About Evolution?" *Newsweek,* January 1, 2009, https://www.newsweek.com/begley-was-darwin-wrong-about-evolution-78507/.

67 **passed down for two generations:** Brian G. Dias and Kerry J. Ressler, "Parental Olfactory Experience Influences Behavior and Neural Structure in Subsequent Generations," *Nature Neuroscience* 17 (2014): 89 96, https://doi.org/10.1038/nn.3594.

67 **"language of the cell":** Biao Huang, Cizhong Jiang, and Rongxin Zhang, "Epigenetics: The Language of the Cell?" *Epigenomics* 6, no. 1 (2014): 73–88, https://doi.org/10.2217/epi.13.72.

68 **an enriched stimulating environment:** Richelle Mychasiuk, Saif Zahir, Nichole Schmold, Slava Ilnytskyy, Olga Kovalchuk, and Robbin Gibb, "Parental Enrichment and Offspring Development: Modifications to Brain, Behavior and the Epigenome," *Behavioural Brain Research* 228, no. 2 (2012): 294–298, https://doi.org/10.1016/j.bbr.2011.11.036.

68 **children of trauma survivors:** Rachel Yehuda, "Trauma in the Family Tree," *Scientific American* 327, no. 1 (2022): 50–55, https://doi.org/10.1038/scientificamerican0722-5.

68 **Epigenetic influences play a role:** Shelley D. Smith, "Approach to Epigenetic Analysis in Language Disorders," *Journal of Neurodevelopmental Disorders* 3, no. 4 (2011): 356–364, https://doi.org /10.1007/s11689-011-9099-y.

68 **DNA double-strand breaks:** Shaghayegh Navabpour, Jessie Rogers, Taylor McFadden, and Timothy J. Jarome, "DNA Double-Strand Breaks Are a Critical Regulator of Fear Memory Reconsolidation," *International Journal of Molecular Sciences* 21, no. 23 (2020): 8995, https://doi.org/10.3390/ijms21238995.

Chapter 5: Childhood, Aging, and In-Between

74 **four extra years of education:** Jana Reifegerste, João Veríssimo, Michael D. Rugg, Mariel Y. Pullman, Laura Babcock, Dana A. Glei, Maxine Weinstein, Noreen Goldman, and Michael T. Ullman, "Early-Life Education May Help Bolster Declarative Memory in Old Age, Especially for Women," *Aging, Neuropsychology, and Cognition* 28, no. 2 (2021): 218–252, https://doi.org/10.1080/13825585.2020.1736497.

74 **is about the same as the effect of exercise:** Ellen Bialystok, "Bilingualism as a Slice of Swiss Cheese," *Frontiers in Psychology* (2021): 5219, https://doi.org/10.3389/fpsyg.2021.769323.

75 **Neural reserve:** Jubin Abutalebi, Lucia Guidi, Virginia Borsa, Matteo Canini, Pasquale A. Della Rosa, Ben A. Parris, and Brendan S. Weekes, "Bilingualism Provides a Neural Reserve for Aging Populations," *Neuropsychologia* 69 (2015): 201–210, https://doi.org/10.1016/j.neuropsy chologia.2015.01.040.

75 **with an average age of eighty-one:** Scott Schroeder and Viorica Marian, "A Bilingual Advantage for Episodic Memory in Older Adults," *Journal of Cognitive Psychology* 24 (2012): 591–601, https://doi .org/10.1080/20445911.2012.669367.

75 **trilinguals show even larger advantages:** Scott Schroeder and Viorica Marian, "Cognitive Consequences of Trilingualism," *International Journal of Trilingualism* 21 (2017): 754–773, https://doi.org/10.1177 /1367006916637288.

75 **Alzheimer's is lower in multilingual countries:** Raymond M. Klein, John Christie, and Mikael Parkvall, "Does Multilingualism Affect the Incidence of Alzheimer's Disease?: A Worldwide Analysis by Country," *SSM-Population Health* 2 (2016): 463–467, https://doi.org/10.1016/j.ssmph.2016.06.002.

76 **grow up with two or more languages:** Viorica Marian, Yasmeen Faroqi-Shah, Margarita Kaushanskaya, Henrike K. Blumenfeld, and Li Sheng, "Bilingualism: Consequences for Language, Cognition, Development, and the Brain," *The ASHA Leader* 14, no. 13 (2009): 10–13, https://doi.org/10.1044/leader.FTR2.14132009.10.

77 **perceptual and classification tasks:** Ellen Bialystok, "Coordination of Executive Functions in Monolingual and Bilingual Children," *Journal of Experimental Child Psychology* 110 (2011): 461–468, https://doi.org/10.1016/j.jecp.2011.05.005.

77 **increased cognitive flexibility:** Ágnes Melinda Kovács and Jacques Mehler, "Cognitive Gains in 7-Month-Old Bilingual Infants," *Proceedings of the National Academy of Sciences* 106, no. 16 (2009): 6556–6560, https://doi.org/10.1073/pnas.0811323106.

77 **metacognitive skills:** Sylvia Joseph Galambos and Kenji Hakuta, "Subject-Specific and Task-Specific Characteristics of Metalinguistic Awareness in Bilingual Children," *Applied Psycholinguistics* 9 (1988): 141–162, https://doi.org/10.1016/j.sbspro.2009.01.243.

77 **repeated word association task:** Li Sheng, Karla K. McGregor, and Viorica Marian, "Lexical-Semantic Organization in Bilingual Children: Evidence from a Repeated Word Association Task," *Journal of Speech, Language, and Hearing Research* 49, no. 3 (2006): 572–587, https://doi.org/10.1044/1092-4388(2006/041).

78 **focusing on what's important:** Michelle M. Martin-Rhee and Ellen Bialystok, "The Development of Two Types of Inhibitory Control in Monolingual and Bilingual Children," *Bilingualism: Language and Cognition* 11, no. 1 (2008): 81–93, https://doi.org/10.1017/S1366728907003227.

78 **version of the Flanker task:** Rosario Rueda Jin Fan, Bruce D. McCandliss, Jessica D. Halparin, Dana B. Gruber, Lisha Pappert Lercari, and Michael I. Posner, "Development of Attentional Networks

in Childhood," *Neuropsychologia* 42, no. 8 (2004): 1029–1040, https://
doi.org/10.1016/j.neuropsychologia.2003.12.012.

78 **takes only a second or two:** Sujin Yang, Hwajn Yang, and Barbara
Lust, "Early Childhood Bilingualism Leads to Advances in Executive
Attention: Dissociating Culture and Language," *Bilingualism:
Language and Cognition* 14, no. 3 (2011): 412–422, https://doi.org
/10.1017/S1366728910000611.

78 **Theory of mind:** Ester Navarro, Vincent DeLuca, and Eleonora Rossi,
"It Takes a Village: Using Network Science to Identify the Effect of
Individual Differences in Bilingual Experience for Theory of Mind,"
Brain Sciences 12 (2022): 487, https://doi.org/10.3390
/brainsci12040487.

78 **false-belief task:** Paula Rubio-Fernandez and Sam Glucksberg,
"Reasoning About Other People's Beliefs: Bilinguals Have an
Advantage," *Journal of Experimental Psychology: Learning, Memory,
and Cognition* 38 (2011): 211–217, https://doi.org/10.1037/a0025162.

80 **babies who were being raised with two languages:** Ágnes Melinda
Kovács and Jacques Mehler, "Cognitive Gains in 7-Month-Old
Bilingual Infants," *Proceedings of the National Academy of Sciences*
106, no. 16 (2009): 6556–6560, https://doi.org/10.1073/pnas
.0811323106.

80 **Jenny Saffran and colleagues:** Jenny R. Saffran, Richard N. Aslin, and
Elissa L. Newport, "Statistical Learning by 8-Month-Old Infants,"
Science 274, no. 5294 (1996): 1926–1928, https://doi.org/10.1126
/science.274.5294.1926.

81 **ability to learn a new language:** Margarita Kaushanskaya and Viorica
Marian, "The Bilingual Advantage in Novel Word Learning,"
Psychonomic Bulletin & Review 16, no. 4 (2009): 705–710, https://doi
.org/10.3758/PBR.16.4.705.

81 **musicians are often better language learners:** Julie Chobert and
Mireille Besson, "Musical Expertise and Second Language Learning,"
Brain Sciences 3, no. 2 (2013): 923–940, https://doi.org/10.3390
/brainsci3020923.

81 **perform better on certain music-related tasks:** Paula M. Roncaglia-
Denissen, Drikus A. Roor, Ao Chen, and Makiko Sadakata, "The
Enhanced Musical Rhythmic Perception in Second Language

Learners," *Frontiers in Human Neuroscience* 10 (2016): 288, https://doi
.org/10.3389/fnhum.2016.00288.

81 **nine-month-old bilingual babies:** Liquan Liu and Rene Kager,
"Enhanced Music Sensitivity in 9-Month-Old Bilingual Infants,"
Cognitive Processing 18 (2016): 55–65, https://doi.org/10.1007/s10339
-016-0780-7.

81 **executive function through experience-dependent plasticity:** Sylvain
Moreno, Zofia Wodniecka, William Tays, Claude Alain, and Ellen
Bialystok, "Inhibitory Control in Bilinguals and Musicians: Event
Related Potential (ERP) Evidence for Experience-Specific Effects," *PloS
ONE* 9, no. 4 (2014): e94169, https://doi.org/10.1371/journal.pone
.0094169.

82 **bilinguals, musicians, and bilingual musicians:** Scott R. Schroeder,
Viorica Marian, Anthony Shook, and James Bartolotti, "Bilingualism
and Musicianship Enhance Cognitive Control," *Neural Plasticity* 2016
(2016), https://doi.org/10.1155/2016/4058620.

82 **Two large-scale data sets:** Andree Hartanto, Hwajin Yang, and Sujin
Yang, "Bilingualism Positively Predicts Mathematical Competence:
Evidence from Two Large-Scale Studies," *Learning and Individual
Differences* 61 (2018): 216–227, https://doi.org/10.1016/j.lindif
.2017.12.007.

82 **bilingual two-way immersion (TWI) program:** Viorica Marian,
Anthony Shook, and Scott R. Schroeder, "Bilingual Two-Way
Immersion Programs Benefit Academic Achievement," *Bilingual
Research Journal* 36, no. 2 (2013): 167–186, https://doi.org/10.1080
/15235882.2013.818075.

83 **Other benefits of two-way immersion:** Nicholas Block, "The Impact
of Two-Way Dual-Immersion Programs on Initially English-
Dominant Latino Students' Attitudes," *Bilingual Research Journal* 34,
no. 2 (2011): 125–141, https://doi.org/10.1080/15235882.2011.598059.

83 **positive attitudes toward others:** Nicholas Block and Lorena Vidaurre,
"Comparing Attitudes of First-Grade Dual Language Immersion
Versus Mainstream English Students," *Bilingual Research Journal* 42,
no. 2 (2019): 129–149, https://doi.org/10.1080/15235882.2019.1604452.

83 **executive-function advantages:** Alena G. Esposito, "Executive
Functions in Two-Way Dual-Language Education: A Mechanism for

Academic Performance," *Bilingual Research Journal* 43, no. 4 (2020): 417–432, https://doi.org/10.1080/15235882.2021.1874570.

83 **often tested in one language:** Erika Hoff, Cynthia Core, Silvia Place, Rosario Rumiche, Melissa Señor, and Marisol Parra, "Dual Language Exposure and Early Bilingual Development," *Journal of Child Language* 39, no. 1 (2012): 1–7, https://doi.org/10.1017/S0305000910000759.

83 **When counted across both languages:** Lisa M. Bedore, Elizabeth D. Peña, Melissa García, and Celina Cortez, "Conceptual Versus Monolingual Scoring," *Language, Speech, and Hearing Services in Schools* 36, no. 3 (2005): 188–200, https://doi.org/10.1044/0161 -1461(2005/020).

83 **comparable combined number of words:** Annick De Houwer, Marc H. Bornstein, and Diane L. Putnick, "A Bilingual-Monolingual Comparison of Young Children's Vocabulary Size: Evidence from Comprehension and Production," *Applied Psycholinguistics* 35, no. 6 (2014): 1189–1211, https://doi.org/10.1017/S0142716412000744.

83 **no longer differ from monolingual children in vocabulary size:** Vivian M. Umbel and D. Kimbrough Oller, "Developmental Changes in Receptive Vocabulary in Hispanic Bilingual School Children," *Language Learning* 44, no. 2 (1994): 221–242, https://doi.org/10.1111 /j.1467-1770.1994.tb01101.x.

85 **brain when resolving linguistic competition:** Viorica Marian, Sarah Chabal, James Bartolotti, Kailyn Bradley, and Arturo E. Hernandez, "Differential Recruitment of Executive Control Regions During Phonological Competition in Monolinguals and Bilinguals," *Brain and Language* 139 (2014): 108–117, https://doi.org/10.1016/j.bandl .2014.10.005.

86 **brains of polyglots and hyperpolyglots:** Olessia Jouravlev, Zachary Mineroff, Idan A. Blank, and Evelina Fedorenko, "The Small and Efficient Language Network of Polyglots and Hyper-Polyglots," *Cerebral Cortex* 31, no. 1 (2021): 62–76, https://doi.org/10.1093/cercor /bhaa205.

87 **the brain stem of bilinguals encoded:** Jennifer Krizman, Viorica Marian, Anthony Shook, Erika Skoe, and Nina Kraus, "Subcortical Encoding of Sound Is Enhanced in Bilinguals and Relates to Executive

Function Advantages," *Proceedings of the National Academy of Sciences* 109, no. 20 (2012): 7877–7881, https://doi.org/10.1073 /pnas.1201575109.

Chapter 6: Another Language, Another Soul

90   **more than a thousand bilinguals were asked:** Jean-Marc Dewaele and Aneta Pavlenko, "Web Questionnaire on Bilingualism and Emotions," University of London, 2001–2003.

90   **higher on Extraversion, Agreeableness, and Conscientiousness:** Nairan Ramirez-Esparza, Samuel D. Gosling, Veronica Benet-Martinez, Jeffrey P. Potter, and James W. Pennebaker, "Do Bilinguals Have Two Personalities? A Special Case of Cultural Frame Switching," *Journal of Research in Personality* 40, no. 2 (2006): 99–120, https://doi .org/10.1016/j.jrp.2004.09.001.

90   **study with Chinese–English bilinguals:** Michael Ross, Elaine Xun, and Anne Wilson, "Language and the Bicultural Self," *Personality and Social Psychology Bulletin* 28 (2020): 1040–1050, https://doi.org /10.1177/01461672022811003.

90   **modifying one's behavior to different cultural norms:** Chi-Ying Cheng, Fiona Lee, and Verónica Benet-Martínez, "Assimilation and Contrast Effects in Cultural Frame Switching: Bicultural Identity Integration and Valence of Cultural Cues," *Journal of Cross-Cultural Psychology* 37, no. 6 (2006): 742–760, https://doi.org/10.1177 /0022022106292081.

91   **can already be observed during childhood:** Maykel Verkuyten and Katerina Pouliasi, "Biculturalism Among Older Children: Cultural Frame Switching, Attributions, Self-Identification, and Attitudes," *Journal of Cross-Cultural Psychology* 33, no. 6 (2002): 596–609, https:// doi.org/10.1177/0022022102238271.

92   **Economic behavior:** M. Keith Chen, "The Effect of Language on Economic Behavior: Evidence from Savings Rates, Health Behaviors, and Retirement Assets," *American Economic Review* 103, no. 2 (2013): 690–731, https://doi.org/10.1257/aer.103.2.690.

94   **A bilingual writer describes:** Eva Hoffman, *Lost in Translation: A Life in a New Language* (New York: Penguin, 1990).

94   shift how they feel across languages: Julie Sedivy, *Memory Speaks: On Losing and Reclaiming Language and Self* (Cambridge, MA: Belknap Press of Harvard University, 2021).

97   **the emotions *amae* in Japanese:** Yu Niiya, Phoebe C. Ellsworth, and Susumu Yamaguchi, "Amae in Japan and the United States: An Exploration of a 'Culturally Unique' Emotion," *Emotion* 6, no. 2 (2006): 279–295, https://doi.org/10.1037/1528-3542.6.2.279.

97   **presumed indulgent dependency:** Takeo Doi, *The Anatomy of Dependence* (Tokyo: Kodansha International, 1971).

97   *fago* **in Ifaluk:** Naomi Quinn, "Adult Attachment Cross-Culturally: A Reanalysis of the Ifaluk Emotion *Fago*," in *Attachment Reconsidered*, eds. Naomi Quinn and Jeannette Marie Mageo (New York: Palgrave Macmillan, 2013), 215–239, https://doi.org/10.1057/9781137386724_9.

97   **mix of love, compassion, and sadness:** Catherine Lutz, "Ethnopsychology Compared to What? Explaining Behavior and Consciousness Among the Ifaluk," in *Person, Self, and Experience: Exploring Pacific Ethnopsychologies*, eds. Geoffrey M. White and John Kirkpatrick (Berkeley: University of California Press, 1985), 35–79.

97   *lajja* **in Bengali:** Usha Menon and Richard A. Shweder, "Kali's Tongue: Cultural Psychology and the Power of Shame in Orissa, India," in *Emotion and Culture: Empirical Studies of Mutual Influence*, eds. Shinobu Kitayama and Hazel Rose Markus (Washington, DC: American Psychological Association, 1994), 241–282.

98   **article about childhood amnesia:** Jody Usher and Ulric Neisser, "Childhood Amnesia and the Beginnings of Memory for Four Early Life Events," *Journal of Experimental Psychology: General* 122 (1993): 155–165, https://doi.org /10.1037/0096-3445.122.2.155.

100   **recalling knowledge in subjects:** Viorica Marian and Caitlin M. Fausey, "Language-Dependent Memory in Bilingual Learning," *Applied Cognitive Psychology* 20, no. 8 (2006): 1025–1047, https://doi .org/10.1002/acp.1242.

103   **estimated certainty of a witness:** Luna Filipović, *Bilingualism in Action* (Cambridge: Cambridge University Press, 2019).

103 **language influences memory in legal settings:** Elizabeth F. Loftus, *Eyewitness Testimony* (Cambridge, MA: Harvard University Press, 1996).

103 **accepted the fabricated event as a true memory:** Elizabeth F. Loftus and Jacqueline E. Pickrell, "The Formation of False Memories," *Psychiatric Annals* 25, no. 12 (1995): 720–725, https://doi.org/10.3928 /0048-5713-19951201-07.

103 **a fabricated event about hitting a dog:** Viorica Marian, "Two Memory Paradigms: Genuine and False Memories in Word Lists and Autobiographical Recall," in *Trends in Experimental Psychology Research,* ed. Diane T. Rosen (New York: Nova Science Publishers, 2005), 129–142.

104 **"The Ones Who Walk Away from Omelas":** Ursula K. Le Guin, "The Ones Who Walk Away from Omelas" (Mankato, MN: Creative Education, 1993).

106 **can even suppress superstition:** Constantinos Hadjichristidis, Janet Geipel, and Luca Surian, "Breaking Magic: Foreign Language Suppresses Superstition," *Quarterly Journal of Experimental Psychology* 72, no. 1 (2019): 18–28, https://doi.org/10.1080/17470218.2017.1371780.

106 **foreign language can systematically alter:** Donnel A. Briley, Michael W. Morris, and Itamar Simonsson, "Cultural Chameleons: Biculturals, Conformity Motives, and Decision Making," *Journal of Consumer Psychology* 15, no. 4 (2005): 351–362, https://doi/abs/10.1207 /s15327663jcp1504_9.

106 **self-construal:** Viorica Marian and Margarita Kaushanskaya, "Self-Construal and Emotion in Bicultural Bilinguals," *Journal of Memory and Language* 51, no. 2 (2004): 190–201, https://doi.org /10.1016/j.jml.2004.04.003.

106 **non-native language elicited fewer gambles:** Shan Gao, Ondrej Zika, Robert D. Rogers, and Guillaume Thierry, "Second Language Feedback Abolishes the 'Hot Hand' Effect During Even-Probability Gambling," *Journal of Neuroscience* 35, no. 15 (2015): 5983–5989, https://doi.org /10.1523/JNEUROSCI.3622-14.2015.

106 **the 1979 "Disease Problem":** Daniel Kahneman and Amos Tversky, "Prospect Theory: An Analysis of Decision Under Risk," *Econometrica* 47, no. 2 (1979): 263–291, https://doi.org/10.2307/1914185.

106 **bias is reduced in a foreign language:** Boaz Keysar, Sayuri L. Hayakawa, and Sun Gyu An, "The Foreign-Language Effect: Thinking in a Foreign Tongue Reduces Decision Biases," *Psychological Science* 23, no. 6 (2012): 661–668, https://doi.org/10.1177/0956797611432178.

107 **nuclear power, pesticides, chemical fertilizers, and nanotechnology:** Constantinos Hadjichristidis, Janet Geipel, and Lucia Savadori, "The Effect of Foreign Language in Judgments of Risk and Benefit: The Role of Affect," *Journal of Experimental Psychology: Applied* 21, no. 2 (2015): 117–129, https://doi.org/10.1037/xap0000044.

107 **likely to drink certified-safe recycled water:** Janet Geipel, Constantinos Hadjichristidis, and Anne-Kathrin Klesse, "Barriers to Sustainable Consumption Attenuated by Foreign Language Use," *Nature Sustainability* 1, no. 1 (2018): 31–33, https://doi.org/10.1038 /s41893-017-0005-9.

107 **Even medical decisions:** Sayuri Hayakawa, Yue Pan, and Viorica Marian, "Language Changes Medical Judgments and Beliefs," *International Journal of Bilingualism* 26, no. 1 (2021): 104–121, https:// doi.org/10.1177/13670069211022851.

107 **accepting preventative care (like vaccinations):** Janet Geipel, Leigh H. Grant, and Boaz Keysar, "Use of a Language Intervention to Reduce Vaccine Hesitancy," *Scientific Reports* 12, no. 1 (2022): 1–6, https://doi .org/10.1038/s41598-021-04249-w.

107 **medical treatments (like surgeries):** Sayuri Hayakawa, Yue Pan, and Viorica Marian, "Using a Foreign Language Changes Medical Judgments of Preventative Care," *Brain Sciences* 11, no. 10 (2021): 1309, https://doi.org/10.3390/brainsci11101309.

Chapter 7: The Ultimate Influencer

114 **"The purpose of Newspeak":** George Orwell, *1984* (London: Secker & Warburg, 1949).

116 **"Political language . . . is designed":** George Orwell, "Politics and the English Language" (London: Horizon, 1946).

117 **President Barack Obama spoke differently:** Nicole Holliday, "'My Presiden(t) and Firs(t) Lady Were Black': Style, Context, and Coronal

Stop Deletion in the Speech of Barack and Michelle Obama," *American Speech: A Quarterly of Linguistic Usage* 92, no. 4 (2017): 459–486, https://doi.org/10.1215/00031283-6903954.

118 *hispandering*: Benjamin Zimmer and Charles E. Carson, "Among the New Words," *American Speech* 87, no. 4 (Winter 2012): 491–510, https://doi.org/10.1215/00031283-2077633.

118 **Spanish-targeted political campaigns:** Alejandro Flores and Alexander Coppock, "Do Bilinguals Respond More Favorably to Candidate Advertisements in English or in Spanish?" *Political Communication* 35, no. 4 (2018): 612–633, https://doi.org/10.1080/10584609.2018.1426663.

118 **survey of Republican voter attitudes:** Jessica Lavariega Monforti, Melissa Michelson, and Annie Franco, "Por Quién Votará? Experimental Evidence About Language, Ethnicity, and Vote Choice (Among Republicans)," *Politics, Groups, & Identities* 1, no. 4 (2013): 475–487, https://doi.org/10.1080/21565503.2013.842491.

118 **political articles had Spanish-language versions:** Joshua Darr, Brittany Perry, Johanna Dunaway, and Mingxiao Sui, "Seeing Spanish: The Effects of Language-Based Media Choices on Resentment and Belonging," *Political Communication* 37, no. 4 (2020): 488–511.

118 **marketing slogans:** Eric Yorkston and Geeta Menon, "A Sound Idea: Phonetic Effects of Brand Names on Consumer Judgments," *Journal of Consumer Research* 31, no. 1 (2004): 43–51, https://doi.org/10.1086/383422.

118 **more emotional in the native language:** Stefano Puntoni, Bart De Langhe, and Stijn Van Osselaer, "Bilingualism and the Emotional Intensity of Advertising Language," *Journal of Consumer Research* 35, no. 6 (2009): 1012–1025, https://doi.org/10.1086/595022.

118 **weaker feelings of ownership:** Mustafa Karataş, "Making Decisions in Foreign Languages: Weaker Senses of Ownership Attenuate the Endowment Effect," *Journal of Consumer Psychology* 30, no. 2 (2020): 296–303, https://doi.org/10.1002/jcpy.1138.

119 **Spanish versus English product ads:** Cecilia Alvarez, Paul Miniard, and James Jaccard, "How Hispanic Bilinguals' Cultural Stereotypes Shape Advertising Persuasiveness," *Journal of Business Research* 75 (2017): 29–36, https://doi.org/10.1016/j.jbusres.2017.02.003.

119 **ads related to the home:** Ryall Carroll and David Luna, "The Other Meaning of Fluency," *Journal of Advertising* 40, no. 3 (2011): 73–84, https://doi.org/10.2753/JOA0091-3367400306.

119 **ads for luxury goods:** Aradhna Krishna and Rohini Ahluwalia, "Language Choice in Advertising to Bilinguals: Asymmetric Effects for Multinationals Versus Local Firms," *Journal of Consumer Research* 35, no. 4 (2008): 692–705, https://doi.org/10.1086/592130.

119 **language of ads matters:** Camelia Micu and Robin A. Coulter, "Advertising in English in Nonnative English-Speaking Markets: The Effect of Language and Self-Referencing in Advertising in Romania on Ad Attitudes," *Journal of East-West Business* 16 (2010): 67–84, https://doi.org/10.1080/10669860903558433.

119 **Advertising of potato chips:** Joshua Freedman and Dan Jurafsky, "Authenticity in America: Class Distinctions in Potato Chip Advertising," *Gastronomica* 11, no. 4 (2011): 46–54, https://doi.org/10.1525/gfc.2012.11.4.46.

119 **language of food advertising:** Dan Jurafsky, *The Language of Food: A Linguist Reads the Menu* (New York: W. W. Norton & Company, 2014).

120 **detecting manipulative language:** Evelina Leivada, Natalia Mitrofanova, and Marit Westergaard, "Bilinguals Are Better Than Monolinguals in Detecting Manipulative Discourse," *PloS ONE* 16, no. 9 (2021): e0256173, https://doi.org/10.1371/journal.pone.0256173.

120 **political statements:** David Miller, Cecilia Solis-Barroso, and Rodrigo Delgado, "The Foreign Language Effect in Bilingualism: Examining Prosocial Sentiment After Offense Taking," *Applied Psycholinguistics* 42, no. 2 (2021): 395–416, https://doi.org/10.1017/S0142716420000806.

123 **George Bernard Shaw's *Pygmalion*:** George Bernard Shaw, *Pygmalion,* in *Four Plays by Bernard Shaw* (New York: Random House, 1953), 213–319.

124 **sociolinguistic experiments that examined language variation:** William Labov, *Sociolinguistic Patterns* (Philadelphia: University of Pennsylvania Press, 1972).

125 **Martha's Vineyard study:** William Labov, "The Social Motivation of a Sound Change," *Word* 19, no. 3 (1963): 273–309, https://doi.org/10.1080/00437956.1963.11659799.

133 **book about her ancestor Benjamin Banneker:** Rachel Webster, *Benjamin Banneker and Us: Eleven Generations of an American Family* (New York: Henry Holt, 2023).

134 **Other widely spoken languages:** "The Most Spoken Languages in America," WorldAtlas, https://www.worldatlas.com/articles/the-most -spoken-languages-in-america.html.

Chapter 8: Words of Change

135 **"You hear a blue jay":** Robin Kimmerer, "Speaking of Nature," *Orion,* June 12, 2017, https://orionmagazine.org/article/speaking-of-nature/.

136 **divide things into categories in interesting ways:** George Lakoff, *Women, Fire, and Dangerous Things* (Chicago: University of Chicago Press, 1987).

137 **German–English bilinguals described a key:** Lera Boroditsky, Lauren A. Schmidt, and Webb Phillips, "Sex, Syntax, and Semantics," in *Language in Mind: Advances in the Study of Language and Thought,* eds. Dedre Gentner and Susan Goldin-Meadow (Cambridge, MA: MIT Press, 2003), 61–79.

137 **experiment on grammatical gender:** Boroditsky, Schmidt, and Phillips, "Sex, Syntax, and Semantics," 61–79.

137 **gender effects emerged quickly:** Webb Phillips and Lera Boroditsky, "Can Quirks of Grammar Affect the Way You Think? Grammatical Gender and Object Concepts," *Proceedings of the Annual Meeting of the Cognitive Science Society* 25, no. 25 (2003): 928–933.

141 **assessment and intervention resources:** 2 Languages 2 Worlds, "2 Languages 2 Worlds," accessed February 18, 2022, http:// 2languages2worlds.wordpress.com.

146 **26 percent of school-age children:** United States Census Bureau, "Language Use," accessed February 18, 2022, https://www.census.gov /topics/population/language-use.html/.

147 **bilingual education continues:** National Association for Bilingual Education, "Welcome to the National Association for Bilingual Education," accessed February 18, 2022, https://nabe.org/.

147 **argue against bilingual education:** Richard Rodriguez, *Hunger of Memory: The Education of Richard Rodriguez* (New York: Bantam, 2004).

149 **Iceberg Model of bilingual education:** Jim Cummins, *Bilingualism and Special Education: Issues in Assessment and Pedagogy* (Clevedon, UK: Multilingual Matters, 1984).

150 **differences in the academic achievement:** John U. Ogbu, "Variability in Minority Responses to Schooling: Nonimmigrants vs. Immigrants," in *Interpretive Ethnography of Education: At Home and Abroad,* ed. Louise Spindler (Hillsdale, NJ: L. Erlbaum, 1987), 255–278.

Chapter 9: Found in Translation

153 **A 1933 study:** Shigeto Tsuru and Horace Fries, "A Problem in Meaning," *Journal of General Psychology* 8 (1933): 281–284, https://doi.org/10.1080/00221309.1933.9713186.

154 **match the meanings of forty-five antonym pairs:** Sayuri Hayakawa and Viorica Marian, "Sound Symbolism in Language and the Mind," submitted for peer review, 2022.

155 **Socrates described in Plato's dialogues:** Plato, *The Dialogues of Plato* (New York: Bantam Classics, 1986).

158 **sound-symbol judgments on the acoustic cues:** Klemens Knoeferle, Jixing Li, Emanuela Maggioni, and Charles Spence, "What Drives Sound Symbolism? Different Acoustic Cues Underlie Sound-Size and Sound-Shape Mappings," *Scientific Reports* 7, no. 1 (2017): 1–11, https://doi.org/10.1038/s41598-017-05965-y.

159 **"Those who dream by day":** Edgar Allan Poe, *The Fall of the House of Usher: And Other Tales* (New York: Signet Classics, 2006).

160 **four-legged version of the letter *m*:** "Fireflies—One Letter and One Word Poems," *Brief Poems,* accessed June 1, 2022, https://briefpoems.wordpress.com/2015/10/31/fireflies-one-letter-and-one-word-poems/.

160 **"closeup of a letter being born":** Bob Grumman, "MNMLST POETRY," *Light and Dust Mobile Anthology of Poetry,* 1997, https://www.thing.net/~grist/l&d/grumman/egrumn.htm.

160 **"The Shortest and Sweetest of Songs":** Joseph Johnson, *George MacDonald: A Biographical and Critical Appreciation* (London: Sir Isaac Pitman & Sons, Ltd., 1906).

160 **"All mimsy were the borogoves":** Lewis Carroll, *Through the Looking-Glass* (London: Macmillan, 1872).

160 **a four-line Chinese poem:** Eliot Weinberger, *Nineteen Ways of Looking at Wang Wei* (New York: New Directions, 2016).

161 **Nietzsche's Zarathustra:** Friedrich Wilhelm Nietzsche, *Thus Spoke Zarathustra: A Book for All and None,* trans. Walter Arnold Kaufmann (New York: Penguin Books, 1978).

166 **world's most extraordinary language learners:** Michael Erard, *Babel No More: The Search for the World's Most Extraordinary Language Learners* (New York: Simon & Schuster, 2012).

167 **the Gavagai thought experiment:** Willard van Orman Quine, "Two Dogmas of Empiricism," in *Challenges to Empiricism,* ed. Harold Morick (Indianapolis: Hackett Publishing, 1980), 46–69.

169 **affect and strategy interact:** Sayuri Hayakawa, James Bartolotti, and Viorica Marian, "Native Language Similarity During Foreign Language Learning: Effects of Cognitive Strategies and Affective States," *Applied Linguistics* 42, no. 3 (2021): 514–540, https://doi.org/10.1093/applin/amaa042.

169 **easier for bilinguals than monolinguals to learn:** James Bartolotti, Viorica Marian, Scott R. Schroeder, and Anthony Shook, "Bilingualism and Inhibitory Control Influence Statistical Learning of Novel Word Forms," *Frontiers in Psychology* 2 (2011), https://doi.org/10.3389/fpsyg.2011.00324.

169 **learn new languages faster and better:** Margarita Kaushanskaya and Viorica Marian, "The Bilingual Advantage in Novel Word Learning," *Psychonomic Bulletin & Review* 16, no. 4 (2009): 705–710, https://doi.org/10.3758/PBR.16.4.705.

169 **bilinguals' practice with inhibitory control:** Margarita Kaushanskaya and Viorica Marian, "Bilingualism Reduces Native-Language Interference During Novel-Word Learning," *Journal of Experimental Psychology: Learning, Memory, and Cognition* 35, no. 3 (2009): 829–835, https://doi.org/10.1037/a0015275.

169 **Using mouse tracking:** James Bartolotti and Viorica Marian, "Language Learning and Control in Monolinguals and Bilinguals," *Cognitive Science* 36, no. 6 (2012): 1129–1147, https://doi.org/10.1111/j.1551-6709.2012.01243.x.

170 **Venn diagram showing the uppercase letters:** Wikipedia, s.v. "Venn Diagram," last modified January 5, 2022, https://en.wikipedia.org/wiki/Venn_diagram/.

171 **increasingly more demanding to cognitively manage:** Narges Radman, Lea Jost, Setareh Dorood, Christian Mancini, and Jean-Marie Annoni, "Language Distance Modulates Cognitive Control in Bilinguals," *Scientific Reports* 11, no. 24131 (2021), https://doi.org/10.1038/s41598-021-02973-x.

Chapter 10: The Codes of Our Minds

174 **computers engage in conversations:** Nico Grant and Cade Metz, "Google Sidelines Engineer Who Claims Its A.I. Is Sentient," *New York Times*, June 12, 2022, https://www.nytimes.com/2022/06/12/technology/google-chatbot-ai-blake-lemoine.html.

176 **cuneiform wedge-shaped characters:** Saad D. Abulhab, "Cuneiform and the Rise of Early Alphabets in the Greater Arabian Peninsula: A Visual Investigation" (New York: CUNY Academic Works, 2018), https://academicworks.cuny.edu/cgi/viewcontent.cgi?article=1257&context=jj_pubs/.

178 **Leo Tolstoy wrote in 1936:** Leo N. Tolstoy, *Polnoe Sobranie Sochinenii* (Complete Collected Works), vol. 8 (Moscow: Jubilee, 1936), 70.

178 **children spontaneously inventing words:** Kornei Chukovsky, *From Two to Five* (Berkeley: University of California Press, 1963).

179 **"Hogwarts for Hackers":** Klint Finley, "Hogwarts for Hackers: Inside the Science and Tech School of Tomorrow," *WIRED*, May 31, 2013, https://www.wired.com/2013/05/hogwarts-for-hackers/.

182 **map Klingon sounds to symbols:** Csilla Kiss and Marianne Nikolov, "Developing, Piloting, and Validating an Instrument to Measure Young Learners' Aptitude," *Language Learning* 55, no. 1 (2005): 99–150, https://doi.org/10.1111/j.0023-8333.2005.00291.x.

183 **The Wug Test:** Jean Berko, "The Child's Learning of English Morphology," *Word* 14, no. 2–3 (1958): 150–177, https://doi.org /10.1080/00437956.1958.11659661.

183 **Morse code:** James Bartolotti, Viorica Marian, Scott R. Schroeder, and Anthony Shook, "Statistical Learning of a Morse Code Language Is Improved by Bilingualism and Inhibitory Ability," *Proceedings of the Annual Meeting of the Cognitive Science Society* 33 (2011): 885–890.

183 **mini artificial language called Colbertian:** James Bartolotti and Viorica Marian, "Language Learning and Control in Monolinguals and Bilinguals," *Cognitive Science* 36, no. 6 (2012): 1129–1147, https:// doi.org/10.1111/j.1551-6709.2012.01243.x.

188 **individual honeybees were trained to the numerical concepts:** Scarlett R. Howard, Aurore Avarguès-Weber, Jair E. Garcia, Andrew D. Greentree, and Adrian G. Dyer, "Numerical Ordering of Zero in Honey Bees," *Science* 360, no. 6393 (2018): 1124–1126, https://doi.org /10.1126/science.aar4975.

188 **abilities of bees:** Karl Von Frisch, *Bees: Their Vision, Chemical Senses, and Language* (Ithaca, NY: Cornell University Press, 2014).

188 **Nobel Prize in Physiology or Medicine:** Peter Marler and Donald Griffin, "The 1973 Nobel Prize for Physiology or Medicine," *Science* 182, no. 4111 (1973): 464–466, https://doi.org/10.1126/science.182.4111.464.

188 **mating competitions of túngara frogs:** Gary J. Rose, "The Numerical Abilities of Anurans and Their Neural Correlates: Insights from Neuroethological Studies of Acoustic Communication," *Philosophical Transactions of the Royal Society B: Biological Sciences* 373, no. 1740 (2018): 20160512, https://doi.org/10.1098/rstb.2016.0512.

188 **how many digits one can remember:** Stanislas Dehaene, *The Number Sense: How the Mind Creates Mathematics* (New York: Oxford University Press, 2011).

189 **longer words for numbers take longer:** Nick Ellis, "Linguistic Relativity Revisited: The Bilingual Word-Length Effect in Working Memory During Counting, Remembering Numbers, and Mental Calculation," in *Cognitive Processing in Bilinguals*, ed. R. J. Harris (Amsterdam: North-Holland, 1992), 137–155.

190 **math proves to be a special case:** Stanislas Dehaene, Elizabeth Spelke, Philippe Pinel, Ruxanda Stanescu, and Sanna Tsivkin, "Sources of

Mathematical Thinking: Behavioral and Brain-Imaging Evidence,"
Science 284, no. 5416 (1999): 970–974, https://doi.org/10.1126
/science.284.5416.970.

190 **math tasks like basic arithmetic:** Elena Salillas and Nicole Y. Y.
Wicha, "Early Learning Shapes the Memory Network for Arithmetic:
Evidence from Brain Potentials in Bilinguals," *Psychological Science*
23, no. 7 (2012): 745–755, https://doi.org/10.1177/0956797612446347.

190 **bilingual brains responded more to new math problems:** Andrea
Stocco and Chantel S. Prat, "Bilingualism Trains Specific Brain
Circuits Involved in Flexible Rule Selection and Application," *Brain
and Language* 137 (2014): 50–61, https://doi.org/10.1016/j.bandl
.2014.07.005.

190 **brain networks of expert mathematicians:** Marie Amalric and
Stanislas Dehaene, "Origins of the Brain Networks for Advanced
Mathematics in Expert Mathematicians," *Proceedings of the National
Academy of Sciences* 113, no. 18 (2016): 4909–4917, https://doi.org
/10.1073/pnas.1603205113.

191 **permutation problems:** Wikipedia, s.v. "Permutation," last modified
March 20, 2022, https://en.wikipedia.org/wiki/Permutation/.

Chapter 11: The Future of Science and Technology

195 **babbling of baby bats:** Ahana A. Fernandez, Lara S. Burchardt,
Martina Nagy, and Mirjam Knörnschild, "Babbling in a Vocal
Learning Bat Resembles Human Infant Babbling," *Science* 373, no.
6557 (2021): 923–926, https://www.science.org/doi/10.1126/science
.abf9279.

195 **Ants communicate with their guests:** Bert Hölldobler,
"Communication Between Ants and Their Guests," *Scientific American*
224 (1971): 86–95, https://doi.org/10.1038/scientificamerican0371-86.

195 **their language can be analyzed:** Zhanna Reznikova and Boris
Ryabko, "Analysis of the Language of Ants by Information-Theoretical
Methods," *Problemy Peredachi Informatsii* 22, no. 3 (1986): 103–108.

195 **Mushrooms can use up to fifty different:** Andrew Adamatzky,
"Language of Fungi Derived from Their Electrical Spiking Activity,"

Royal Society Open Science, April 6, 2022, https://doi.org/10.1098
/rsos.211926.

195 **"champignon" communicators:** Linda Geddes, "Mushrooms
Communicate with Each Other Using up to 50 'Words,' Scientist
Claims," *The Guardian,* April 6, 2022.

196 **dialects quickly became less stable:** Alison J. Barker, Grigorii
Veviurko, Nigel C. Bennett, Daniel W. Hart, Lina Mograby, and Gary
R. Lewin, "Cultural Transmission of Vocal Dialect in the Naked
Mole-Rat," *Science* 371, no. 6528 (2021): 503–507, https://doi.org
/10.1126/science.abc6588.

197 **Cutting-edge brain-computer interfaces:** Jihun Lee, Vincent
Leung, Ah-Hyoung Lee, Jiannan Huang, Peter Asbeck, Patrick P.
Mercier, Stephen Shellhammer, Lawrence Larson, Farah Laiwalla,
and Arto Nurmikko, "Neural Recording and Stimulation Using
Wireless Networks of Microimplants," *Nature Electronics* 4,
no. 8 (2021): 604–614, https://doi.org/10.1038/s41928-021
-00631-8.

197 **Neurograins are tiny microchips:** Emily Mullin, "'Neurograins'
Could Be the Next Brain-Computer Interfaces," *WIRED,* September
13, 2021, https://www.wired.com/story/neurograins-could-be-the
-next-brain-computer-interfaces/?mod=djemfoe/.

197 **garner one's neural activity and use technology:** Steven Gulie, "A
Shock to the System," *WIRED,* March 1, 2007, https://www.wired.com
/2007/03/brainsurgery.

198 **help people who have lost the ability to communicate:** Francis R.
Willett, Donald T. Avansino, Leigh R. Hochberg, Jaimie M.
Henderson, and Krishna V. Shenoy, "High-Performance Brain-to-Text
Communication Via Handwriting," *Nature* 593, no. 7858 (2021):
249–254, https://doi.org/10.1038/s41586-021-03506-2.

199 **proof-of-concept options already available:** Arielle Pardes, "Elon
Musk Is About to Show Off His Neuralink Brain Implant," *WIRED,*
August 28, 2020, https://www.wired.com/story/elon-musk
-neuralink-brain-implant-v2-demo.

200 **"The saddest aspect of life":** Isaac Asimov and Jason Shulman, eds.,
Isaac Asimov's Book of Science and Nature Quotations (London:
Weidenfeld & Nicolson, 1988).

200 **"Two things fill the mind":** Immanuel Kant, *Critique of Practical Reason*, trans. Lewis White Beck (London: Liberal Arts Press, 1985).

200 **"Science is not only":** Carl Sagan, *The Demon-Haunted World: Science as a Candle in the Dark* (New York: Random House, 2011).

201 **$20 in social benefits per $1:** Benjamin F. Jones and Lawrence H. Summers, "A Calculation of the Social Returns to Innovation," in *Innovation and Public Policy*, eds. Austan Goolsbee and Benjamin F. Jones (Chicago: University of Chicago Press, 2020).

201 **investment in research and development:** Benjamin F. Jones, "Science and Innovation: The Under-Fueled Engine of Prosperity," in *Rebuilding the Post-Pandemic Economy*, eds. Melissa S. Kearney and Amy Ganz (Washington, DC: Aspen Institute Press, 2021).

202 **Immigrant-founded firms employ more people:** Jones, "The Under-Fueled Engine of Prosperity."

202 **"Class Matters" interactive:** David Leonhardt, "A Closer Look at Income Mobility," *New York Times,* May 14, 2005, https://www.nytimes.com/2005/05/14/national/class/a-closer-look-at-income-mobility.html.

204 **"The history of research":** Umberto Eco, *Kant and the Platypus: Essays on Language and Cognition*, trans. Alastair McEwan (New York: Harcourt Brace, 2000).

204 **Imbalances in who gets cited:** Jordan D. Dworkin, Kristin A. Linn, Erin G. Teich, Perry Zurn, Russell T. Shinohara, and Danielle S. Bassett, "The Extent and Drivers of Gender Imbalance in Neuroscience Reference Lists," *Nature Neuroscience* 23, no. 8 (2020): 918–926, https://doi.org/10.1038/s41593-020-0658-y.

205 **one-tenth of Swiss GDP:** Simon Bradley, "Languages Generate One Tenth of Swiss GDP," Swissinfo.ch, November 20, 2008, https://www.swissinfo.ch/eng/languages-generate-one-tenth-of-swiss-gdp/7050488/.

205 **European Commission reported that 11 percent:** The European Commission, "ELAN: Effects on the European Economy of Shortages of Foreign Languages Skills in Enterprise," CILT, the National Centre for Languages (2006), https://ec.europa.eu/assets/eac/languages/policy/strategic-framework/documents/elan_en.pdf.

205 **U.K. economy is losing approximately £50 billion a year:** James
Foreman-Peck and Yi Wang, "The Costs to the UK of Language
Deficiencies as a Barrier to UK Engagement in Exporting," UK
Trade and Investment, May 9, 2014, https://www.gov.uk/government
/publications/the-costs-to-the-uk-of-language-deficiencies-as
-a-barrier-to-uk-engagement-in-exporting.

205 **Training a multilingual workforce:** Judith F. Kroll and Paola
E. Dussias, "The Benefits of Multilingualism to the Personal and
Professional Development of Residents of the US," *Foreign
Language Annals* 50, no. 2 (2017): 248–259, https://doi.org/10.1111
/flan.12271.

205 **study of otoacoustic emissions:** Viorica Marian, Tuan Q. Lam, Sayuri
Hayakawa, and Sumitrajit Dhar, "Spontaneous Otoacoustic Emissions
Reveal an Efficient Auditory Efferent Network," *Journal of Speech,
Language, and Hearing Research* 61, no. 11 (2018): 2827–2832, https://
doi.org/10.1044/2018_JSLHR-H-18-0025.

206 **bilingual experience had larger changes:** Viorica Marian, Tuan Q.
Lam, Sayuri Hayakawa, and Sumitrajit Dhar, "Top-Down Cognitive
and Linguistic Influences on the Suppression of Spontaneous
Otoacoustic Emissions," *Frontiers in Neuroscience* 12, no. 378 (2018),
https://doi.org/10.3389/fnins.2018.00378.

206 **hidden moderator driving findings:** Krista Byers-Heinlein, Alena G.
Esposito, Adam Winsler, Viorica Marian, Dina C. Castro, Gigi Luk,
Benjamin Brown, and Jasmine DeJesus, "The Case for Measuring and
Reporting Bilingualism in Developmental Research," *Collabra:
Psychology* 5, no. 1 (2019), http://doi.org/10.1525/collabra.233.

207 **hierarchical structure, generativeness, recursion:** Marc D. Hauser,
Noam Chomsky, and W. Tecumseh Fitch, "The Faculty of Language:
What Is It, Who Has It, and How Did It Evolve?" *Science* 298, no. 5598
(2002): 1569–1579, https://doi.org/10.1126/science.298.5598.1569.

Conclusion

209 **language not spoken for decades:** Ludmila Isurin and Christy Seidel,
"Traces of Memory for a Lost Childhood Language: The Savings

Paradigm Expanded," *Language Learning* 65, no. 4 (2015): 761–790, https://doi.org/10.1111/lang.12133.

210 **Seven types of intelligence:** Howard Gardner, *Frames of Mind: The Theory of Multiple Intelligences* (New York: Basic Books, 1983).

211 **Later, naturalistic intelligence:** Howard Gardner, *Intelligence Reframed: Multiple Intelligences for the 21st Century* (New York: Basic Books, 1999).

211 **interpret intelligence as one's worth:** Richard J. Herrnstein and Charles Murray, *The Bell Curve* (New York: Free Press, 1994).

212 **$7,000 more per year:** Christopher Davis, "In Florida, It Pays to Be Bilingual, University of Florida Study Finds," University of Florida, January 31, 2000, https://news.ufl.edu/archive/2000/01/in-florida-it -pays-to-be-bilingual-university-of-florida-study-finds.html/.

212 **large-scale analysis of 669,498 people:** Joshua K. Hartshorne, Joshua B. Tenenbaum, and Steven Pinker, "A Critical Period for Second Language Acquisition: Evidence from ⅔ Million English Speakers," *Cognition* 177 (2018): 263–277, https://doi.org/10.1016/j.cognition .2018.04.007.

212 **no evidence for a critical age:** Frans van der Slik, Job Schepens, Theo Bongaerts, and Roeland van Hout, "Critical Period Claim Revisited: Reanalysis of Hartshorne, Tenenbaum, and Pinker (2018) Suggests Steady Decline and Learner-Type Differences," *Language Learning* 72, no. 1 (2021): 87–112, https://doi.org/10.1111/lang.12470.

213 **data from the U.S. Department of State:** U.S. Department of State, "Foreign Language Training," accessed June 22, 2022, https://www .state.gov/foreign-language-training/.

214 **a few months of experience immersed:** Andrea Takahesu Tabori, Dennis Wu, and Judith F. Kroll, "Second Language Immersion Suppresses the Native Language: Evidence from Learners Studying Abroad," *Proceedings of the International Symposium on Bilingualism* (2019): 90.

214 **six months of taking an Introduction to Spanish:** Margot D. Sullivan, Monika Janus, Sylvain Moreno, Lori Astheimer, and Ellen Bialystok, "Early Stage Second-Language Learning Improves Executive Control: Evidence from ERP," *Brain and Language* 139 (2014): 84–98, https://doi.org/10.1016/j.bandl.2014.10.004.

215 **intensive one-week Gaelic course:** Thomas H. Bak, Madeleine R. Long, Mariana Vega-Mendoza, and Antonella Sorace, "Novelty, Challenge, and Practice: The Impact of Intensive Language Learning on Attentional Functions," *PloS ONE* 11, no. 4 (2016): e0153485, https://doi.org/10.1371/journal.pone.0153485.

215 **Interpreter Academy recruits:** Johan Mårtensson, Johan Eriksson, Nils Christian Bodammer, Magnus Lindgren, Mikael Johansson, Lars Nyberg, and Martin Lövdén, "Growth of Language-Related Brain Areas After Foreign Language Learning," *NeuroImage* 63, no. 1 (2012): 240–244, https://doi.org/10.1016/j.neuroimage.2012.06.043.

215 **language learning through smartphone apps:** Jed A. Meltzer, Mira Kates Rose, Anna Y. Le, Kiah A. Spencer, Leora Goldstein, Alina Gubanova, Abbie C. Lai, Maryam Yossofzai, Sabrina E. M. Armstrong, and Ellen Bialystok, "Improvement in Executive Function for Older Adults Through Smartphone Apps: A Randomized Clinical Trial Comparing Language Learning and Brain Training," *Aging, Neuropsychology, and Cognition* (2021): 1–22, https://doi.org/10.1080/13825585.2021.1991262.

220 **ability to speak two or more languages:** Viorica Marian and Anthony Shook, "The Cognitive Benefits of Being Bilingual," *Cerebrum,* October 31, 2012, https://dana.org/article/the-cognitive-benefits-of-being-bilingual.

220 **cognitive and social benefits that come with it:** Samantha P. Fan, Zoe Liberman, Boaz Keysar, and Katherine D. Kinzler, "The Exposure Advantage: Early Exposure to a Multilingual Environment Promotes Effective Communication," *Psychological Science* 26, no. 7 (2015): 1090–1097, https://doi.org/10.1177/0956797615574699.

LIST OF ILLUSTRATIONS

INDEX

ABOUT THE AUTHOR

Dr. Viorica Marian is the Ralph and Jean Sundin Endowed Professor of Communication Sciences and Disorders and professor of psychology at Northwestern University. Since 2000, Marian has directed the university's Bilingualism and Psycholinguistics Research Lab. Marian is a native speaker of Romanian, a native-like speaker of Russian, and a fluent speaker of English, and has studied or conducted research with a variety of other languages, including American Sign Language, Cantonese, Dutch, French, German, Japanese, Mandarin, Polish, Spanish, Thai, and Ukrainian. Her research on the architecture of bilingual language processing and the consequences of multilingualism for cognition, development, and the brain is supported by the National Institutes of Health, the National Science Foundation, Northwestern University, and private foundations.